CAVALCADE of Journalists

BY THE AUTHOR

Twentieth-Century Journalists: America's Opinionmakers

Mencken Revisited: Author, Editor & Newspaperman

The Editorial Art of Edmund Duffy

Florida's Editorial Cartoonists

CONTRIBUTING AUTHOR

Graphic Opinions: Editorial Cartoonists and Their Art

Broadcast Advertising and Promotion

CAVALCADE of Journalists

1900-2000

Chroniclers of an American Century

S. L. Harrison

WOLF DEN BOOKS
2002

ISBN 0-9708035-1-6
First Edition

Wolf Den Books
Miami, Florida 33155
www.wolfdenbooks.com

PRINTED AND BOUND IN THE UNITED STATES OF AMERICA

for

Frances June
Larry, Carroll, Linda and Vernon

together we witnessed a century

Contents

Introduction ix

Acknowledgments xi

Chroniclers of an
American Century, 1900-2000 1

Notable Newspaper Comics
and their Creators 97

Selected Bibliography 109

Index 130

Introduction

JOURNALISM LEAVES A LEGACY worth remembering. Where once newspapers were the nation's main source of news and information, most Americans today, the polls tell us, receive their news from television. Much "news" today is a mixture of public relations fluff and feel-good features calculated to be non-controversial. Television news itself has undergone change. Newton Minow and Edward R. Murrow early warned of that danger. Trivialization of television is a menace that has come to pass. Network news has fallen from its once-high standards, and the effects are markedly noticeable in local news programming. This is a situation unlikely to change for the better.

People today read fewer books and newspapers than people did a generation or two ago. Many reasons are advanced: people are in a hurry, with too many more things to do; work is more demanding; and new means of technology offer information faster and more conveniently. All of these explanations may contribute, but the cause is more direct. Reading is in decline generally. Newspapers–and television–are not as good as they once were. One thing is clear; the people–many of them–who populate communication media lack a sense of history.

Schools of journalism are charged with training future journalists. These students will become the future experts in communication, opinion-makers and information gate-keepers. President John F. Kennedy, in his last prepared address, asked, "who will watch the watchers?" H.L. Mencken observed that American schools of journalism were mostly third-rate operations, presided over by charlatans, staffed by failed journalists, and populated by students too dull to qualify for more-demanding academic disciplines. This was more than a half-century ago. Have things really improved? Are their products better at their jobs? Do they write well? Do they know relevant background? Read and listen; you decide. The technology is surely vastly improved. Technology is only as good as the human minds guiding the mechanism.

We have made progress, but progress and innovation are not necessarily improvements. One element surely lacking in many students is a sense of history, an awareness of the past. Need exists for that sense of history; remembrance of what was once good–and an awareness of those things perhaps not so good–can stimulate a demand for the best. A small beginning can be made through an introduction to those men and women who contributed to the opinion-making process that underlies our American culture.

Included here are other individuals who are not, strictly speaking, journalists, but each of whom has played a significant role in our nation's newspapers. Cartoonists, with comic strips and panels, have been an integral part of our newspapers for more than one hundred years; their influence spans the past century and a number of them continue well into their sixth decade. It is fitting that a representative number of these cartoons and their creators be mentioned. They have influenced our thought, our interests, our language and our culture.

The individuals identified on the following pages are some of the people who played a distinct role in our nation's journalism through the past century–encompassing three generations of Americans. Their comments–through newspapers, magazines, television, and radio–played a considerable role in shaping the ideas, thoughts, and opinion of the American people. In the descriptions, brief identification is presented of their main topics of thought and where their words appeared. Each description is accompanied with a brief listing of their major published works. A selective but comprehensive bibliography provides a significant list of books by and about a number of these people.

No claim is made that the information contained here is inclusive–a number of individuals absent may deserve mention–but this book provides a useful beginning to arouse an awareness and appreciation of past contributions–which grow more distant and dimmer each dawn as time hurtles us into the future.

Acknowledgments

AN UNDERTAKING OF THIS MAGNITUDE is not presented without a great deal of thought. More than two hundred journalists are identified and arguably as many more could be included; for any omissions, I can only offer abject apologies with the expectation that future editions of this book will rectify the omission of worthy individuals neglected through oversight or ignorance A stopping point must be made, however, else the compilation continues endlessly.

An earlier and more limited book–*Twentieth Century Journalists*–served as the nucleus for this collection and a good deal of research and investigation went into selecting those twenty-odd people who were deemed the most significant. A host of others not discussed in that book are identified here with a recognition that their journalistic work is worthy of remembrance, for good or ill.

Tracking down information concerning people of the past–even in the arena of journalism with its propensity for self-publicity–is an onerous task. The news media, especially newspapers, and more especially the *New York Times Index* and past issues have been most helpful. Obituaries are not as good as they perhaps might be, it seems. This writer is overly sensitive on the subject, perhaps; it is where an early apprenticeship in newspaper work acquainted him with an appreciation for getting all the facts, sometimes omitting distasteful truths that might be objectionable to the bereaved family. What you have here is the author's opinion of what should be told–"with the bark on," as John Nance Garner put it. Many newspapers fail this basic objective.

Gratitude must be expressed to Gail Shivel, without whom this book would not have seen the light of day, and to Frances June, who shared many months with phantoms from the past.

The opinions are the author's: any errors of fact or interpretation rest with him alone and he accepts full responsibility for what is written here.

S.L. HARRISON

Chroniclers of an American Century, 1900-2000

The following listing identifies more than two hundred and thirty individuals who played a significant journalistic role in the century past: 1900 through 2000. Brief descriptions provide pertinent identification of the personal and professional work relating to their influence on twentieth-century American thought and opinion.

Robert S. Abbott (1870-1940) founded in 1905 the weekly Chicago *Defender,* which became the nation's largest-circulation African-American newspaper. Abbott, a graduate of Clafin College (S.C.) and Kent Law School, unable to gain admittance to the Illinois bar, opted for publishing. The *Defender* became a significant voice of protest against United States foreign policy in Haiti in 1915, an organ of job opportunities for blacks in the South, and a major force in persuading blacks to join the Democratic Party to back the New Deal. Under Abbott, the *Defender,* with a national circulation of 100,000, played a major role in counseling and instructing blacks on the means–social and economic–by which they could enter into the mainstream of American life.

Franklin P(ierce) Adams [FPA] (1881-1960) won fame as FPA, writer of "The Conning Tower" column for the New York *World,* a genuinely literate and humorous gem in an era when columns were a major feature of most metropolitan newspapers. During his early years, family financial troubles limited him to one year at the University of Michigan. Adams self-published a volume of verse, *In Cupid's Court,* and took a job selling insurance; he sold a policy to George Ade, the newspaper columnist, and that led to Adams' landing a job writing a weather column for the Chicago *Tribune* in 1904. He moved to the New York *Evening Mail* to write a column, "Always in Good Humor." Adams switched to the New York *Tribune* in 1914 and began "The Conning Tower." After an interruption to serve with the A.E.F. in Europe during World War I and work with *Stars and Stripes,* Adams rejoined the *Tribune.* His popularity attracted the attention of Herbert Bayard Swope, editor of the *World,* and Adams joined that newspaper in 1922. Adams was an early contributor to Harold Ross' *New Yorker* and a founding member of the Algonquin Round Table. When the *World* folded in 1931, Adams refused a reduced salary from the *Herald Tribune,* and found himself without a job. Ross gave Adams work writing a tennis column. Adams returned to newspaper work briefly in 1938 with a column for the New York *Evening Post,* and began a radio career with the witty quiz program "Information, Please." Adams' career ended in 1948 with the onset of Alzheimer's disease and he spent his last years doing make-work for the *New Yorker.* In his prime, Adams was one of the most-quoted figures in New York newspaper circles and his column was a sought-for place for celebrities, literary and otherwise. His many books include: *The Melancholy Lute, Innocent Merriment, The Diary of Our Own Samuel Pepys, By and Large, The Conning Tower Book.*

George Ade (1866-1944), a newspaper columnist of exceptional merit, began with the Lafayette (Ind.) *Call,* then joined the Chicago *Morning News,* and later the *Record.* His column, "Stories of the Streets and of the Town," illustrated by cartoonist John T. McCutcheon, earned wide popularity—essays of the commonplace with witty, flippant, and racy prose. His *Fables in Slang* (1904) was a popular success; later Ade gained recognition as a Broadway playwright with "The County Chairman" (later a film starring Will Rogers) and "The College Widow." His plays, like his column, reflected the humor and common sense of ordinary people. Critic H.L. Mencken lamented Ade's neglect as a writer of unusual merit. Books include *Ade's Fables, Forty Modern Fables.*

Robert S. Allen (1900-81) worked for Hearst's International News Service, the United Press, and the Washington *Herald.* He was co-author, with Drew Pearson, of the "Washington Merry-Go-Round," a column that took its title from his book (which began as an article in the *American Mercury*). Allen was Washington bureau chief for the *Christian Science Monitor.* At the outbreak of World War II, he sold his interest in the column to Pearson for a pittance. Allen saw action with Gen. George S. Patton's Third Army in Europe and lost his right arm in combat. Books include *The Nine Old Men, Why Hoover Faces Rejection, Washington Merry-Go-Round, Lucky Forward.*

Joseph Alsop (1911-89) wrote a nationally syndicated column, "Matter of Fact," with his brother Stewart, originally for the New York *Herald Tribune* and later for the *Washington Post* (1946-58). Well-connected, a distant relation of Theodore Roosevelt, Alsop was an unrelenting anti-Communist and an influential Washington journalist during the "Cold War" era. Books include: *I've Seen the Best of It, FDR: A Century Remembrance.*

Jack Anderson (1922-), a self-proclaimed modern muckraker–an aggressive newspaperman who seeks out the inside story–won a Pulitzer prize in 1972 for investigative reporting. He began as a war correspondent for the Salt Lake City *Deseret News* (to avoid combat during World War II), and later served as a reporter in Shanghai with *Stars and Stripes.* He went to Washington and was hired by Drew Pearson to assist with the "Merry-Go-Round" and inherited the column after Pearson's death. Anderson parlayed his career into an industry, including radio and television, lectures, and pieces in *Parade* magazine; his column was syndicated by United Features. Books include *Confessions of a Muckraker, The Anderson Papers, Alice in Blunderland, Inside the NRA,* and (with Drew Pearson) *The Case Against Congress.*

Louis Azrael (1904-81) was a prominent columnist for more than fifty years with Hearst's Baltimore *News-Post.* His "Day by Day" column discussed local people, politics, and events with rare insight. He was a Hearst favorite—his column helped the *News-Post* beat the powerful *Sunpapers* in street sales. As a war correspondent, Azrael covered the Maryland-Virginia 29th Division and its D-Day landing in Normandy; he was the sole reporter present when Allied war criminal Alfried Krupp, the German steel baron, was apprehended by U.S. forces.

"Bugs" (Arthur) Baer (1886-1969), a genuinely humorous writer, conducted his daily "One Word Led to Another" column for more than thirty years; it was syndicated by King Features and read by an estimated fifteen million readers. Baer left school at age twelve to go to work, attended art school and became a lace designer at age fourteen. He joined the Philadelphia *Public Ledger* as an artist, then joined the Washington *Times* as a sports columnist. He illustrated his column with baseball-shaped insects and earned the name "Bugs." He later joined the New York *World* as a columnist. William Randolph Hearst lured Baer to the New York *American* when one of Baer's column quips amused him: "His heart was full of larceny, but his feet were too honest," describing a would-be New York Yankee base-stealer. Baer continued his column until shortly before his death.

Russell Baker (1925-) conducted "The Observer" column for the *New York Times* from 1962 until 1999, and was awarded two Pulitzer prizes. He began in 1947 as a police reporter for the Baltimore *Sun* and by 1952 was London bureau chief. His work caught the attention of James Reston of the *Times,* and he joined the *Times* in 1954. After covering the absurdities of the Senate, Baker began the column that earned him a reputation as a humorist. His splendid little essays–not knee slappers, but sophisticated surreal satire–were always well-written. His column was syndicated to 500 newspapers and he earned a reputation as the best columnist in America.

After leaving the *Times,* Baker contributed essays to the *New York Review of Books* and other publications. Baker ventured into television, succeeding Alistair Cooke as host of PBS' "Masterpiece Theatre." Books include his Pulitzer-winner *Growing Up, The Good Times, Poor Russell's Almanac, The Next President.*

Hanson Baldwin (1903-91), writing for the *New York Times,* was considered one of the leading authorities on military and naval affairs during World War II. As an oracle, he was more often wrong than correct, but he brought insightful analysis to the general reader. Baldwin often cited the aphorisms of Admiral Alfred T. Mahan, the apostle of seapower. Baldwin, a 1924 graduate of the U.S. Naval Academy, resigned his commission in 1927 and joined the Baltimore *Sun,* He joined the *Times* a year later and was named military editor in 1942; he won a Pulitzer prize for his reporting of the Pacific war in 1943. Baldwin was author of more than a dozen books on military strategy and policy, including: *United We Stand, The Great Arms Race, Battles Lost and Won, The New Navy.*

L(yman) Frank Baum (1856-1919), as a Chicago newspaperman seeking money through free-lance work, wrote *The Wonderful Wizard of Oz,* a book that made his name immortal. Born in prosperous circumstances, Baum managed through family connections to get a job with the New York *World* by age seventeen. Two years later he founded the Bradford (Penn.) *New Era* newspaper. Twenty-four months later, Baum was a salesman for his father's oil business, toured as an actor, and eventually became editor of the Aberdeen (S.D.) *Saturday Pioneer.* After the newspaper failed, Baum continued his career with the Chicago *Post.* He wrote books on chicken farming, store window decorations and a children's book, *Mother Goose in Prose.* He self-published the Oz book in 1900, and it was a success; more than 90,000 copies were sold the first year. Baum described his work as "simple fairy tale," but amidst his puns and jokes was a serious theme; the conflict between agrarian interests, labor, and the ruling class. Baum worked other subtle themes into later books, but readers welcomed the fun and fantasy. In later works Baum included themes of social moment: women's suffrage and other feminist ideas. He opposed them. A Broadway production followed the Oz book and ran for ten years. Baum tried other works before returning to the Oz theme; four years elapsed before Baum wrote a sequel. He wearied of the Oz books, but wrote eighteen before his death. Meanwhile, under a number of pseudonyms, Baum continued to seek his fortune with less-successful book ventures. Oz made Baum a wealthy man and his story–a metaphor for America's industrial age–continues to enchant readers. The 1939 Metro-Goldwyn-Mayer motion picture helped continue Baum's classic for a century. Books include: *The Road to Oz, The Emerald City, The Scarecrow of Oz.*

Lucius Morris Beebe (1902-66) chronicled the doings of New York's cafe society for a quarter-century; his Saturday morning column in the *Herald Tribune* was a major feature. He loved high society and went to personal extremes–he once covered a fire in morning clothes and regularly attended theater openings in a flowing cloak. Characters like Beebe were rare in that era and unknown today. In 1950, he left New York and went West to purchase and publish Mark Twain's former newspaper, the Virginia City (Nev.) *Territorial Enterprise.* His twenty books include: *People on Parade, Fallen Stars, High Iron: A Book of Trains, The Trains We Rode.*

Robert C. Benchley (1889-1945) is known as a notable humorist, but generally unknown are his contributions as a perceptive newspaper critic; these were written under a pseudonym for the *New Yorker* magazine. Even as a Harvard College undergraduate Benchley demonstrated his humorous bent; he was editor of the *Lampoon.* He turned down a job offer as a humor columnist from the Boston *Journal* after he left college. His early professional career included advertising work for the Curtis Publishing Co. before F.P. Adams hired him for the New York *Tribune* in 1916. Fired from that job, Benchley tried theatrical public relations, advertising copywriting (Dr. Lyon's tooth powder), then served with the federal Aircraft Board in Washington, and Liberty Loan drives. In 1920, Benchley served as managing editor for *Vanity Fair* and contributed a column to the New York *World,* "Books and Other Things" (1920-29). Benchley wrote a column as theater critic–his college desire–for *Life,* the humor magazine. He also wrote a syndicated column for David Lawrence, "Of All Things." Meanwhile, Benchley produced several books, appeared in the Irving Berlin production, "Music Box Review," and was writing movie subtitles for Paramount Pictures studios in New York. In 1929, Benchley left *Life* to become drama critic for the *New Yorker;* he had begun free-lance pieces to the *New Yorker* in 1927. He originated the "Wayward Press" department and wrote as "Guy Fawkes;" and he continued that feature, along with his drama reviews, until 1939-40. Other activities included a syndicated column for King Features, a radio program, and acting and writing in a series of motion picture short subjects. Benchley won an Academy Award in 1935 for this work. In all, he made some forty-eight shorts and appeared in a number of feature roles. Much of his motion picture work and his more than a dozen books are generally known, but Benchley's press criticism has been neglected; it was humorous, witty, and dead on the mark pointing out faults and errors of the New York press. Benchley had no peer as a humorist and his press criticism can be read to advantage by contemporary media people. His books include: *Of All Things!, Love Conquers All, Pluck and Luck, Inside Benchley, Benchley Beside Himself, The Benchley Roundup.*

Meyer Berger (1898-1959) began his career as an office boy in 1911 for the New York *Morning Herald* and later served as an infantryman with the A.E.F. (American Expeditionary Force) in 1917-18. He was a reporter with the *Herald* (1919-22) then joined the Standard News Association until 1927, when he left for the *New York Times* in 1948. He later became a staff writer for the *New Yorker* and wrote a number of "Profiles." Books include: *The Eight Million, The Story of the New York Times, Men of Maryknoll, City on Many Waters.*

Clifford K. Berryman (1869-1949) was the senior member of the only father-son team to win a Pulitzer prize for editorial cartooning; the elder in 1944 and son James in 1950. Berryman joined the Washington *Evening Star* in 1907 and forty years later was described as a great cartoonist "without malice" by President Harry Truman. His greatest distinction, however, came early in his career as editorial cartoonist for the *Washington Post,* when in 1902 he depicted President Theodore Roosevelt sparing the life of a bear cub during a Mississippi hunt. The "Teddy Bear" was an instant success and became a symbol in Berryman's cartoons through his long career. The "Teddy Bear" vogue swept the nation; the artist never capitalized on his creation, but toy manufacturers made millions. Berryman died at his desk November 11, 1949.

Ambrose Bierce (1842-1914) a journalist and author whose misanthropic and pessimistic views influenced H.L. Mencken and Ring Lardner. Bierce viewed mankind as essentially reprobate and his work reflects that view. With little education, when he was seventeen Bierce spent a year at the Kentucky Military Institute, then enlisted in the Union Army and saw action in the field with the 9th Indiana Infantry and was promoted to lieutenant. After the war, he spent a a brief period as a night watchman, then turned to journalism. From 1866-72, he wrote for the San Francisco *Argonaut* and then for the *News Leader,* where he became editor. From 1872-76, he practiced his trade in London, where he became known as "Bitter Bierce." He returned to San Francisco to write again for the *Argonaut* and the *Wasp.* From 1887-96 he wrote a column for Hearst's San Francisco *Examiner,* and from this source derived many of his books. Following the *Examiner* period, Bierce served as Washington correspondent for the New York *American* and later *Cosmopolitan,* both Hearst enterprises. In 1913 Bierce set off for Mexico to interview Pancho Villa and was never heard from again. Bierce's work, dark and depressing, goes against the optimistic American grain. His books include: *The Devil's Dictionary [The Cynic's Word Book]; Can Such Things Be?, In the Midst of Life, Fantastic Fable, The Parenticide Club.*

Homer Bigart (1907-91) was described by *Newsweek* as "the best war correspondent of an embattled generation," meaning the generation following World War II that experienced Vietnam as an epiphany. Bigart began as a copyboy with the New York *Herald Tribune,* while attending New York University and began full time in 1929 after dropping out of school. He became a reporter in 1932, and performed distinguished work as a war correspondent; he won Pulitzer prizes in 1946 and again in 1950 for his coverage of the Korean War. He joined the New York *Times* in 1956 and covered conflicts in Cyprus, Yemen, and Vietnam. Bigart was a reporter who always asked the right questions. His one book is a collection of his dispatches: *Forward Positions.*

Herbert L(awrence) Block [Herblock] (1909-2001) for more than fifty years commanded the editorial page of the *Washington Post* with his perceptive cartoons that influenced politicians and politics across the nation. His work was syndicated to more than 300 newspapers. Block, under the pen name "Herblock," won three Pulitzer prizes (after Rollin Kirby and Edmund Duffy) for editorial cartooning that was forthright and distinctive. He won an art scholarship at the Chicago Art Institute and attended college for two years. He began his professional career in 1929 with the Chicago *Daily News;* in 1933 he joined the NEA (Newspaper Enterprise Association) syndicate and won his first Pulitzer prize in 1942. Block joined the Army in 1943 and worked as an artist with the Information and Education Division. He began with the *Post* in 1946. Herblock was one of the few cartoonists free to present his own views; his work was not reviewed or approved by an editor before it appeared in print. When the cartoonist's view disagreed with the *Post's* editorial stance, the newspaper dropped the cartoon. Herblock presented his art work in a traditional vertical format (most cartoonists today follow a horizontal block), eschewed gags and thought balloons that dominate editorial cartoons today, His art made a forthright statement for itself, and there was no misunderstanding his message. Herblock is credited with coinage of the term "McCarthyism" that described the hysteria of the Communist-fear of the 1950s. His dozen books include: *Herblock's Here and Now, Herblock's At Large, Herblock's State of the Union, Herblock: A Cartoonist's Life.*

Nellie Bly [Elizabeth Cochran Seaman] (1864-1922) made her early reputation in the nineteenth century as a journalist, notably for Joseph Pulitzer's *World.* Her around-the-world feat and her expose of social conditions affecting women were extraordinary news events. After Bly retired from journalism, financial drawbacks prompted her return to the New York *Journal.* In 1914, she was the first woman to file dispatches from the Austrian front. In 1920, Bly was one of the first female reporters to cover an execution. She ended her career writing an advice column for the

Journal. Time passed her by, but Bly was eulogized by the *New York Times* as "the greatest journalist in America." With her pioneering work, Bly helped pave the way for female journalists, who were no longer "journalistic freaks" by the time of her death. Books include: *Six Months in Mexico, Ten Days in a Mad-House, Nellie Bly's Book: Around the World in Seventy-Two Days.*

Edward W. Bok (1863-1930), a crusading and innovative magazine editor brought about significant change to American middle-class life. Through advertising, promotion, and innovative editing, Bok made the *Ladies' Home Journal* into an influential and successful magazine. Brought to the United States from Holland, as a child of seven, Bok left school at thirteen to work as an office boy for Western Union. He cultivated his contacts and joined Henry Holt, publishers, as a stenographer in 1884. He worked on advertising and promotion, then joined Charles Scribner's Sons doing more of the same. Bok pursued a self-education program and followed a program of writing to the famous and well-known, he cultivated those who responded (and most did). His initiative helped him become editor of the *Brooklyn Magazine* in 1884. Two years later, he created the Bok Syndicate, selling features and book promotions that had previously been submitted gratis. His innovative use of type and white space for his ad promotions drew the attention of Cyrus H.K. Curtis and Bok was appointed editor of the *Ladies' Home Journal.* Bok built circulation through scholarships, hiring popular writers, and hiring women to write on women's topics. Bok, through his magazine, instructed readers how to dress, decorate their homes, clean up their cities, and generally strove to elevate American taste and culture. Bok's stand against suffrage for women, and his dictates on fashion, for example, angered some women readers but his campaigns against patent medicine fraud and stand for conservation won him plaudits. Bok's formula for success was simple: hard work and dedication (but it helped to marry the boss's daughter as he did). In the modern politically correct era, Bok's paternalism and unilateral control would fail, but his contribution can not be ignored. His reign as editor of the *Journal* (1889-1919) was notable for its sociological contributions. Bok was awarded a Pulitzer prize for his 1920 autobiography. Books include: *The Americanization of Edward Bok, The Edward Bok Book of Knowledge*

Erma Bombeck (1927-96), whose columns converted the humdrum into humor, commanded the attention of millions of readers and proved that people still read newspapers even in the electronic age. She wrote of cooking, cleaning, teenagers, and husbands—with a wry humor that every housewife understood. Bombeck's twice-a-week column reached more than 600 newspapers through Universal Press Syndicate. Although she started as a reporter, Bombeck's columns made her a national celebrity. From 1975 through 1986, she appeared on ABC's "Good Morning

America," wrote a dozen books, and signed a $12 million book contract. Bombeck's success spawned dozens of imitators, but there was only one Erma. Her dozen books include: *At Wit's End; The Grass is Always Greener Over the Septic Tank, Forever, Erma.*

Margaret Bourke-White (1904-71) exemplified the best of modern photojournalism and was instrumental in establishing the powerful images of picture magazines, *Fortune* and *Life.* As an undergraduate, White (Bourke was added during college years, the hyphen later) conducted a lucrative business in photography. After graduating from Cornell in 1927, White landed a job with a Cleveland architectural firm and worked for trade publications and advertising. Her striking photographs of buildings attracted the attention of Henry Luce, who sought that kind of "excitement" for his new publication, *Fortune.* This was a magazine to glorify business and Luce hired White as the first (and only) photographer for the new enterprise. She asked for and received a credit line for her work, making an impression in a man's world. Bourke-White became famous for her magazine and advertising photographs. In the mid-thirties, with Erskine Caldwell, she teamed to produce a social documentary, *You Have Seen Their Faces,* that became a best-seller. In 1936, she became one of the original staff photographers for Luce's new venture, *Life.* In 1939, Bourke-White was in Europe and captured startling images of the Nazi blitz. Discontent with her salary prompted a brief tenure with New York newspaper *PM,* but she shortly returned to *Life* as a contract photographer; she was on hand when the Nazis warred on Russia in 1941. The next year she was covering the USAAF air war and her photographs helped publicize the daylight bombing raids of the B-17 Flying Fortress. With the reputation as a prima donna, Bourke-White was unable to win accreditation in Europe and accepted an assignment to document the lesser-known Italian campaign. Her book, *They Called it Purple Heart Valley,* was another best-seller that helped draw attention to that neglected war zone. After the war, Bourke-White photographed a ravaged Germany and this resulted in another book that displayed her sorrow over that nation's destruction. In the 1950s Bourke-White was attacked unjustly as a fellow-traveler by columnist Westbrook Pegler for her past "crimes" of glamorizing share-croppers and the sympathy elicited by her photographs of post-war Germany. One way to "clear her name," Bourke-White reasoned, was to cover the United Nations action in Korea. By 1955 Parkinson's disease prevented her from further work and, as she observed in her unfinished reminiscence, "in the end it is only the work that counts." The record is clear that Bourke-White, a consumate professional, resorted to any means, whatever the moral or ethics involved, to get her pictures. That work endures as a legacy to her dedication to get the story. Books include: *Dear Fatherland, Rest Quietly; Eyes on Russia; Halfway to Freedom; The Taste of War; Say, is This the U.S.A.*

Ben (Benjamin Crowninshield) Bradlee (1921-) served as executive editor of the *Washington Post* (1968-99) and led that newspaper to become one of the best; during his tenure the *Post* won eighteen Pulitzer prizes for distinguished reporting. The *Post* was the third-best newspaper in a four-paper town when Bradlee began his program and he left it one of the nation's most influential and respected publications when he retired in 1991. Bradlee was born into a line of privileged Brahmins, not rich but wealthy enough to visit Europe in the summers (returning on the *S.S. Normandie* tourist-class). Education was at St. Mark's, a private prep school; Harvard was taken for granted–Bradlee's had attended Harvard since 1795. When he left Harvard in August 1942 (a few credits short), Bradlee acquired an ROTC ensign's commission, a wife (a Saltonstall), and a $100,000 trust fund. He saw action in a destroyer squadron in the South Pacific. In October 1945, with no more experience than a summer job with the *Beverly* (Mass.) *Evening Times,* Bradlee and some friends started the *New Hampshire Sunday Times* (a portion of Bradlee's financial share came from his uncle, Frank Crowninshield). The venture lasted for twenty-five months before it was purchased by William Loeb–who fired Bradlee. Radio news announcing for WKBR, Manchester, N.H., and stringing for *Time-Life* and *Newsweek,* helped during this time. In December 1948, armed with a letter of introduction from former Massachusetts governor Christian Herter, Bradlee landed a job with the *Washington Post.* In 1951, he left to become a press attache in Paris for the State Department; that post lasted until 1954, when Bradlee became European correspondent for *Newsweek*– along with free-lance broadcasts for CBS and articles (as Ben Lenox or Anthony Lenox for the Washington *Evening Star*). In 1957 *Newsweek* assigned Bradlee to Washington, where in 1959 he met a new Georgetown neighbor, Senator John F. Kennedy–that friendship helped make Bradlee a celebrity and provided an avenue of journalistic advancement. Bradlee's fortunes soared when in 1961, the *Washington Post* (he had urged Philip Graham to do so) purchased *Newsweek* from the Astor Foundation. Bradlee was made Washington bureau chief and earned *Post* stock as a finder's fee. Publisher Katharine Graham, following Walter Lippmann's advice, invited Bradlee to return to the *Post* (she assumed control when her husband Philip L. Graham committed suicide). Two years later, Bradlee became executive editor. His leadership bought the *Post* to the first rank of American newspapers. Books: *That Special Grace; Conversations with Kennedy; A Good Life: Newspapering and Other Adventures.*

Berton Braley (1882-1966), a newspaper poet, was described by the *Brooklyn Eagle* in 1925 as "the most prolific verse-writer in America today." Little of his work is remembered, but his poem "The Thinker" remains a favorite of Ayn Rand zealots. Braley's major brush with fame came in 1920 with publication of his satiric "Three–Minus One," a lampoon of H.L. Mencken and George Jean Nathan, editors of the *Smart Set* magazine and the literary style-setters of the era. Braley's poem appeared in Don Marquis's New York *Sun* column, the "Sun Dial" and its refrain "Mencken, Nathan and God" amused millions of readers. Braley advocated individualism, free enterprise, and staunch opposition to the New Deal. He began his newspaper career in 1901, became a war correspondent for *Collier's Weekly* in 1917 and upon his return began to write verse for many popular magazines. His syndicated column of verse continued until the late 1930s. Braley ended his career as an advertising copywriter in 1952. His books include *New Deal Ditties, Virtues in Verse.*

David (McClure) Brinkley (1920-) often called himself "the other side of the hyphen," referring to his fame as a member of NBC's "Huntley-Brinkley Report." Beginning as a newspaperman, with no degree, in Wilmington, N.C., with the *Star-News,* Brinkley joined the Army in 1940. After his discharge, he went to Washington, joined NBC and became White House correspondent in 1943. His big break came in 1956 with the "Huntley-Brinkley Report" and his sardonic commentary and dry wit was a pleasing contrast to Chet Huntley. Brinkley left NBC after thirty-eight years and joined ABC for a Sunday program, "This Week with David Brinkley," and retired in 1996. His television career yielded ten Emmys and two George Foster Peabody Awards. Brinkley is a writer with the knack of a straight-forward, no-nonsense delivery. His books include: *Washington Goes to War, David Brinkley: A Memoir, Everybody's Entitled to My Opinion.*

Arthur Brisbane (1864-1936) was a respected newspaperman in the late 1880s–he joined the New York *Sun* in 1883 and became managing editor of the *Evening Sun* in 1887; Sunday editor of Joseph Pulitzer's New York *World* in 1890; and by 1897, managing editor of its arch-rival the New York *Journal.* Brisbane was an influential journalist by the early 1900s. He managed the campaigns of William Randolph Hearst for Congress, for Mayor of New York, and for Governor. By 1910, he was the highest-paid newspaper editor in America. His many innovations–he was the architect of "yellow journalism"–influence the makeup and content of newspapers to this day. In 1917 he began his column, "Today," which by 1923 was syndicated and read by millions. Brisbane's prose was florid and orotund, but readers–and Hearst–loved it. Books include: *Editorials from the Hearst Newspapers, The Book of Today, Today and the Future Day.*

David S. Broder (1929-), political correspondent for the *Washington Post,* writes a twice-weekly column syndicated to 300 newspapers. Arguably one of the most respected and knowledgeable observers of contemporary politics, he was awarded a Pulitzer prize in 1973. After a B.A. and M.A. from the University of Chicago and two years' Army service, Broder began his career with the Bloomington (Indiana) *Pantograph.* In 1955, he joined *Congressional Quarterly,* and then the Washington *Evening Star (*1960-65); he was with the *New York Times* briefly in 1966 and left for the *Post.* He is a frequent television guest on "Meet the Press," (NBC); "Inside Politics" (CNN), and "Washington Week in Review" (PBS). Books include: *Behind the Front Page, The Man Who Would be President, The System, The Changing of the Guard: Power and Leadership in America.*

Heywood (Campbell) Broun (1888-1939) said of himself, "I was really a newspaperman, not merely a columnist." Broun was better than most mere columnists; his "It Seems to Me," for the New York *World,* was an influential voice in American opinion-making for two decades. It was said of Broun that "he launched a crusade every hour." He was one of the founders of the Newspaper Guild. Broun failed to be elected to the Harvard *Crimson* for three years, but in a class that included Walter Lippmann, John Reed, and Stuart Chase, Broun proved to be one of the best newspapermen who ever attended Harvard. Broun worked summers at the New York *Sun* and the *Morning Telegraph.* Academic deficiencies forced him to drop college in 1910 and Broun went to work for the *Telegraph,* and then, in 1912, the New York *Tribune.* He became its drama critic in 1917, then went to Europe with the A.E.F. (he published a book castigating Army ineptness with supplies), and became the *Tribune's* literary critic. His lively column, "Books and Things," was more often about things than books. In 1921, Broun joined the *World* and began his column, "It Seems to Me." His passionate defense of Sacco and Vanzetti resulted in his exile from the *World* in 1927, and Broun wrote for the *Nation,* His exile was brief, but the next year the *World* management fired Broun for his attacks on the Roman Catholic birth-control issue, and he joined the *Telegram.* During the economic crises of the Great Depression, Broun helped organize the Newspaper Guild and was elected national president. In 1938, Broun purchased and ran a weekly "celebrity" newspaper, the Broun *Nutmeg* (ironically, a non-Guild enterprise). When his contract was not renewed by the *World-Telegram* in 1939 (ostensibly for economic reasons–publisher Roy Howard was tired of Broun's liberal tone), Broun signed with the New York *Post* at a greatly-reduced salary; he wrote one column before his death. Broun was a successful, well-to-do celebrity newspaperman–he was an active and continuing participant in the Algonquin Round Table–who never forgot the problems of the average worker and embraced liberal causes and the New Deal. Broun's lasting monument is the Newspaper Guild. His books include: *Our Army at the Front, Seeing Things at Night, Sitting on the World, Christians Only, It Seems to Me.*

Heywood Hale Broun (1918-2001), the son of Heywood Broun and Ruth Hale, managed to have a distinguished career of his own mainly as a sportswriter and television commentator. Broun was noted for his wry and sometimes droll delivery. As a child, he was a precocious observer to the Algonquin Round Table antics and after graduation from Swarthmore College in 1940, went to work for the New York newspaper *PM.* During World War II he served as an enlisted man in the field artillery. Upon his return, he resumed with *PM* as a sports columnist and later its successor the New York *Star.* When the *Star* folded in 1949, Broun turned to acting, including roles on Broadway and in Hollywood. He accepted an offer from CBS to be a television sports commentator in 1965 and covered all sports, particularly horse racing. Books: *Whose Little Boy Are You?, A Studied Madness, Tumultuous Merriment*

Herb (Herbert E.) Caen (1916-96) conducted one of the nation's longest-running columns, "Baghdad-By-The-Bay," later identified simply as "Herb Caen." A regional writer who made San Francisco his base, Caen started in 1932 as a sportswriter for the Sacramento *Bee;* in 1936 he moved to the San Francisco *Chronicle* with a radio column. Caen began his long-running (fifty years) general column in 1938, a source of news, tips, city gossip, and comment. In 1950 Caen moved to the San Francisco *Examiner,* but returned to the *Chronicle* in 1958. He was awarded a Pulitzer prize in 1996. Immensely popular, Caen's books include: *Baghdad-By-The-Bay, Don't Call It Frisco, The Cable Car and the Dragon.*

Abraham Cahan (1860-1951) edited and wrote for the Jewish *Daily Forward,* one of the most influential newspapers for Jewish immigrants that reached its flood in New York City in 1907. Under his stewardship, the *Forward* fostered a sense of pride, understanding, and community. Cahan came to America in 1882, a refugee from revolutionary Russia. In 1886 he started a short-lived Yiddish-language newspaper, the *New Era.* By 1897 he had mastered English sufficiently to work for the *Forward* and then the *Commercial Advertiser,* under the tutelage of Lincoln Steffens. He returned to the *Forward* as editor and changed it from a Marxist advocate to a Yiddish newspaper that aimed to assist newly-arrived Jews. A column he began, the "Bintel Brief" (bundle of letters) answered questions and gave advice. It was the first its kind and established a format that continues to this day. His enterprise was successful, and was published with twelve editions in various cities. His books met with critical success; William Dean Howells described Cahan as "a new star of realism." Unlike other journalists who made a success in literary enterprises, Cahan continued with his newspaper career for more than a half-century. Cahan served as managing editor of the *Forward* until his death in 1951, and is remembered, as he wished, as "the best foreign language editor in America." Books include: *The Education of Abraham Cahan, The Rise of David Levinsky, From the Ghetto, Yekl: A Tale of the New York Ghetto, The Imported Bridegroom and Other Stories of the New York Ghetto.*

James M. Cain (1892-1977) described himself as "a newspaperman who writes yarns on the side." After graduating from Washington College (Md.) he taught English for several years, and after wartime service editing his company newspaper Cain began his professional newspaper career with the Baltimore *American,* later joining the Baltimore *Sun.* He became acquainted with H.L. Mencken, who recommended Cain to Arthur Krock and he became one of Walter Lippmann's editorial writers for the New York *World.* Cain was also an early and frequent contributor to Mencken's *Smart Set* and *American Mercury.* Cain began writing novels after the *World* folded. Later, after a stint as managing editor of the *New Yorker,* he returned briefly to teaching at St. Johns College (Md.). He became a master of the "hard-boiled" thriller and relocated to Hollywood as a screenwriter for the next seventeen years. In 1934-35, Cain produced a column for the Hearst newspapers. His books include *Our Government, The Postman Always Rings Twice, Double Indemnity, Mildred Pierce, The Enchanted Isle.*

Vincent Canby (1924-2000) for more than thirty-five years was film critic for the *New York Times,* whose elegant reviews were frequently more entertaining than the motion pictures themselves. Canby joined the *Times* in 1965 as film critic and was named theater critic in 1993. His early background included service in World War II as a Navy officer in the Pacific. After a brief period in Paris after the war, he earned a degree from Dartmouth in 1947. Canby began his journalism career in 1948 with the *Chicago Journal of Commerce,* and turned to public relations in 1950 in New York. For the next eight years Canby worked for the *Motion Picture Herald* (1958-65), He was a staff member for *Variety* until he joined the *Times.* Canby's writing for the *Times* provided lively wit with literate opinion. Books include*: Living Quarters, Unnatural Scenery.*

Jimmy (James) Cannon (1910-73) gained fame as a sportswriter, and was described by the *New York Times* as "an artisan of the language." After a year of high school, he joined the New York *Daily News* in 1926 as a copyboy. He became a sportswriter in 1934 for the New York *World-Telegram* and later for the *Journal-American* and *PM.* During the war he was a combat correspondent for the *Stars and Stripes* then joined the New York *Post.* It was Cannon who described boxing champion Joe Louis as "a credit to his race–the human race." Cannon played a significant role in publicizing the "Yankee

Clipper," New York Yankee outfielder Joe DiMaggio. In 1959, Cannon rejoined the *Journal-American* and wrote a syndicated column for King Features. Books include: *It Seems to Me; It Seems to Me, But...*

Robert Capa [Andre Friedman] (1913-54), was correctly described by John Hersey as "the man who invented himself." Capa began as an unknown Hungarian who made up his name (as "the well-known American photographer") to sell his pictures to French newspapers. Capa specialized in the shot-and-shell school of photography and covered most major wars: Spain, China, Sicily, Italy, Normandy, Germany, and Vietnam. He was killed by a land mine in Vietnam on assignment for *Life* magazine. Arguably one of the best photographers of men at war, Capa however never was awarded a Pulitzer prize. He helped form the Magnum agency and was its president in 1950. His one book is *Images of War.*

Willa [Wilella] Cather (1873-1947) built her distinguished literary career on a firm foundation of twenty years as a journalist. During her lifetime Cather veiled her journalism background, but it colored her career. For the most part, her novels draw portrayals of real people and autobiographical incidents from her newspaper background that played a significant role in her life. As an undergraduate at the University of Nebraska, Cather wrote for the school yearbook, newspaper, and literary magazine. As an undergraduate, she wrote a column, "One Way of Putting It," for the Lincoln (Neb.) *State Observer,* After graduation, she worked briefly for the Lincoln *Courier,* with a new column, "The Passing Show," before returning to the *Observer.* Both columns contained book reviews, drama criticism, and music commentary–subjects and characters that were to appear in later books. In 1896 Cather accepted a post as editor of a homemaking magazine, the *Home Monthly,* in Pittsburgh. She continued her column with the *Journal,* however. The next year Cather joined the Pittsburgh *Leader,* first as telegraph editor and then as drama critic; she continued her *Observer* column along with free-lance writing for the *Saturday Evening Post* and other magazines. Cather taught English from 1900-03 at Central High School and published her first book, *April Twilights* in 1903, the same year she became an editor for *McClure's.* Much of the editorial and writing burdens of the magazine occupied Cather. She became *de facto* managing editor of *McClure's* in 1906. The success of her earlier works and her first novel, *Alexander's Bridge,* prompted her resignation from *McClure's* in 1912 to concentrate on free-lance and her books. She continued to work, off and on, for McClure, and when he was ousted from the magazine, was the ghostwriter for his *Autobiography.* Cather was awarded a Pulitzer prize in 1922 for *One of Ours.* Other books include: *O Pioneers!, The Song of the Lark, My Antonia, A Lost Lady, The Professor's House.*

Turner Catledge (1901-83) for many years the chief news executive for the *New York Times* who was responsible for the rise of A.M. Rosenthal and his reign of power. In Catledge's time the newspaper was a series of independent fiefdoms–the Sunday edition under Max Frankel, the Washington bureau under Arthur Krock, and foreign reporting under Punch Sulzberger–that Catledge tried to pull together. His era saw the last of the gentleman's club that was the *Times,* where few were ever fired and one waited patiently for years to advance in station. During his reign, Catledge help rid the *Times* of its stodgy image, but it was still known as "the gray lady." Catledge graduated from Mississippi A&M (now Mississippi State University) in 1922 and went to work for his father's friend's paper, the Neshoba *Democrat* and then the Memphis *Press.* Fired after three weeks, he was hired by the Memphis *Commercial Appeal.* He met Herbert Hoover during a flood crisis and Hoover, unbeknownst to Catledge sent a letter of recommendation to the *Times*–it was unacknowledged. Catledge joined the Baltimore *Sun* in 1927 and was assigned to the Washington bureau. Hoover asked the *Times* publisher about his letter and Catledge joined the *Times* in 1929. Bureau chief Krock promised Catledge that job in "ten or fifteen years." Catledge got on well, professionally and with people; Joseph Alsop invited him to write a column, but Catledge declined. Wendell Willkie orchestrated a job offer from the New York *Herald Tribune,* which Catledge declined after a hefty raise. He did not refuse a $25,000 offer from Marshall Field to join the Chicago *Sun.* His job as editor for that chaotic enterprise lasted nineteen months. Catledge returned to the *Times'* Washington bureau as chief news correspondent–a newly-minted title, but at a reduction to $14,000. Catledge managed overseas service to cover the Red Cross activities in Africa, Italy, and Burma; later he and publisher Arthur Hays Sulzberger jointly visited the Pacific theater of operations for the same purpose. That was a test Catledge passed; in 1945, he was promoted to assistant managing editor. He was made executive managing editor in January 1951. Catledge rejected offers to become publisher of the Houston *Chronicle* and later, editor of the Cleveland *Plain Dealer;* his loyalty to the *Times* was rewarded when he was named executive editor in 1964. He served until 1968, when he was asked to step down by Arthur Ochs Sulzberger in 1968, His final two years with the *Times,* Catledge served as a vice president and advisor to the publisher. Catledge was the architect who brought the many elements of the *Times* together into a unified newspaper–a not insignificant task. Books: *The 168 Days* (with Joseph Alsop), *My Life and the Times.*

John Chancellor (1927-96) was a commentator for television's "NBC Nightly News" from 1970-82 and for a time served as host of NBC's morning show, "Today," 1961-62. A college drop-out, Chancellor was hired as an advertising copy runner for the Chicago *Daily News,* then he moved to the

Chicago *Sun-Times* as a copyboy in 1947 and he rose to be a rewrite man, copy editor and feature writer. He joined NBC's WNBQ-TV as a street reporter.in 1950, and rose to become in 1957 NBC's Midwest correspondent, based in Chicago. He covered the Little Rock, Ark., school desegregation crisis. Chancellor was promoted to NBC's Vienna bureau; he was named "Today" host in 1961. He returned to Europe in 1962 to cover the Common Market. Other assignments included the White House, and he won some measure of fame when he was arrested covering the 1964 Republican National Convention. He became an anchor for "NBC Nightly News" with David Brinkley, by himself, and again with Brinkley. In 1982 he became the program's news analyst with a thrice-weekly comment from 1982 until he retired in 1993. The Overseas Press Club honored Chancellor in 1993 for his refusal to turn television news into theatrical entertainment. Chancellor left NBC News in 1994 to serve two years as director of the Voice of America. Books include: *Peril and Promise, The News Business* (with Walter Mears).

Harry Chandler (1864-1944) became the publisher of the *Los Angeles Times* when he married the owner's daughter. Chandler, an astute businessman with vast holdings in cotton and real estate, amassed the Times-Mirror Company as well. After college at Dartmouth, he went West for his health and became a clerk in the circulation department of the *Times* After his fortuitous marriage, he took title as publisher. Shortly after he purchased the largest cotton plantation on the continent in Southern California and created the Suburban Home Company, a tract of 47,000 acres adjoining Los Angeles. Two years later his purchase of the Tejon Ranch, 281,000 acres in Los Angeles County brought more wealth. He assumed editorial control of the *Times* in 1912; the newspaper prospered as the region grew. Chandler was president of the American Newspaper Publishers Association in 1930 and 1931.

Richard Clurman (1924-96) had a distinguished career in journalism and wrote a number of perceptive books about the industry. After his graduation from the University of Chicago in 1946, following service during World War II with the Army, he joined the magazine *Commentary*. He joined *Time* magazine in 1949 and for six years served as a press officer, and during his twenty-three years with *Time,* served as chief of correspondents and head of Time-Life News Service. In 1958 he joined the ambitious Long Island tabloid *Newsday* and contributed a major role toward making that newspaper respectable. In the 1980s he went into consulting work and from 1981 until 1990 was chairman of Columbia University's Seminars on Media. Clurman was active in New York cultural circles associated with Lincoln Center, the Citizens Committee for New York, and in 1973 served as Administrator of Parks, Recreation and Cultural Affairs during Mayor

John Lindsay's administration. Clurman's books dealing with media and the press are perceptive and useful guides. Books include: *Who's In Charge, To the End of Time: The Seduction and Conquest of a Media Empire, Beyond Malice: The Media's Year of Reckoning.*

Frank Irvin Cobb (1869-1923) succeeded Joseph Pulitzer as editor of the New York *World.* His early career included reporting for the Grand Rapid (S. D.) *Eagle* and the Detroit *Evening News.* He was the leading editorial writer for the Detroit *Free Press* until he joined the *World* in 1904. He became editor-in-chief in 1911. Cobb, a dedicated and courageous ideologue, maintained Pulitzer's course for the *World's* liberal views and selected Walter Lippmann to be his successor when he learned he was dying of cancer.

Irvin S[hrewsbury] Cobb (1876-1944) wrote a column for the New York *World* and won fame as a humorist; his work appeared in magazines such as the *Saturday Evening Post* and *Collier's Weekly.* His "Judge Priest" stories, featuring a folksy, shrewd Kentucky magistrate were made into a number of successful films. Cobb became a Hollywood screenwriter and acted in several motion pictures himself. His books include *Speaking of Operations, Back Home, Judge Priest, Exit Laughing.*

Bob (Robert Bernard) Considine (1906-75), a consumate professional, was a sportswriter, columnist, war correspondent, radio commentator, Hollywood scriptwriter and author of more than twenty-five books Known for sometimes manning two typewriters, his newspaper work for Hearst was outstanding and timely. Considine wrote in his last "On the Line" column–syndicated to 140 newspapers–"I'll croak in the newspaper business." He did. Considine dropped out of high school, but continued his education with night classes at George Washington University. His start in journalism was unique. As a State Department messenger at a tennis tournament, the Washington *Herald* misspelled his name. He complained that he could do a better job and was hired as a sportswriter. Considine began his "On the Line" column in 1933, and his work attracted the attention of William Randolph Hearst, who offered Considine a position with the New York *American* in 1936. He was linked to Hearst publications for the next four decades, including the New York *Mirror, Journal American, World Journal Tribune,* the International News Service, King Features and Hearst Headline Service. During World War II, he served as a correspondent in Asia, Africa, and Europe. Considine had, for a brief time, a fifteen-minute NBC radio program and was a regular on the television news show, "America After Dark." His Hollywood credits include "The Babe Ruth Story," "The Beginning of the End," and "The Church of the Good Thief." Considine wrote biographies of Jack Dempsey, Babe Ruth, and Toots Shor.

Considine was co-author (with Capt. Ted Lawson) of *Thirty Seconds Over Tokyo,* a great wartime success. His other books include: *MacArthur, the Magnificent, General Wainwright's Story, It's the Irish, Panama Canal, It's All News to Me: A Reporter's Deposition.*

Alistair Cooke (1908-), an English newspaperman, came to America and became a pioneer in electronic broadcasting–radio and television. Cooke came to the United States in 1930 as a correspondent and began a series of broadcasts for the BBC in 1934 as a film critic. In 1936 he was London correspondent for NBC, American correspondent for the *Times* of London (1938-40), and American correspondent for the (London) *Daily Herald (*he became an American citizen in 1940), then for the Manchester *Guardian* (1948-72). Cooke was host of the innovative television series "Omnibus" (1952-61). He served as the literate master of ceremonies for PBS' "Masterpiece Theatre" for two decades (1971-92), a program that uplifted middle-class minds. Cooke won four television Emmys and a George Foster Peabody award. Books include: *Six Men, Around the World in Fifty Years, America 1973, America Observed,* (ed.) *The Vintage Mencken, Memories of the Great & The Good.*

Ashely Cooper [Frank Gilbreth Jr.] (1912-2001) wrote one of the longest-running columns in America, "Doing the Charleston," (1947-83) for the Charleston (S.C.) *Post and Courier,* but gained fame under his own name with his 1949 bestselling book, and later motion picture, *Cheaper by the Dozen.* After graduating from the University of Michigan in 1933, he worked as a reporter for the New York *Herald Tribune,* the Buenos Aires *Herald,* and the Associated Press. After service with the Navy in the Pacific during World War II, he joined the *Post and Courier* in 1947, began his column and eventually rose to assistant publisher and vice president of the newspaper. Gilbreth wrote his novel based on his parents, pioneers in management efficiency and motion study, and his eleven siblings. Gilbreth wrote a number of other works, including a successor to his first book, *Belles on Their Toes* (with his sister). Other works include: *Held's Angels, I'm a Lucky Guy, Of Whales and Women, How to be a Father, Time Out for Happiness, He's My Boy.*

Gardner Cowles (1903-1985) is remembered as the founder of *Look* magazine, a picture magazine that proceeded *Life* in concept and at its peak exceeded *Life's* circulation. Cowles initially worked for his family-owned newspaper, the Des Moines *Register and Tribune.* Cowles tried other magazine ventures–*Quick, Flair,* and *Venture*–none lasted more than a year. He founded Puerto Rico's first English-language newspaper, the San Juan *Sun* and purchased a number of other newspapers and the magazine *Family Circle.* Cowles served as deputy director of the OWI (Office of War

Information) during World War II. His one book: *Mike Looks Back.*

James M. Cox (1870-1957), an Ohio newspaperman, was in 1920 the Democratic presidential candidate, with Franklin D. Roosevelt as the nominee for vice-president. (His opponent was Senator Warren G. Harding, another Ohio editor, of the Marion *Star,* who won with Calvin Coolidge as his running-mate.) Cox had only a public school education and served as a school teacher and paper-route operator for the Middletown (Ohio) *Weekly Signal.* He joined the Cincinnati *Enquirer* as a reporter in 1892, a contact that led to his becoming a Congressional aide from 1894-98. His former boss helped him purchase the Dayton *Evening News* and Cox demonstrated a knack for attracting advertisers and subscribers. Cox next served three terms in the House of Representatives and continued as an editorial writer for his newspapers–he added newspapers in Springfield. In 1913 Cox began the first of his three terms as governor of Ohio. In 1920, the Democratic Party tapped him to be its candidate. Known as a liberal reformer and anti-Prohibitionist, Cox dithered on his stance nationally and lost to Harding, one of the worst Presidents in American history. Cox attributed his loss to "racism" by Irish, Italian, and German voters who could not abide Woodrow Wilson. Cox, a better business man than political analyst, returned to his newspaper work and prospered. Cox was no paragon as a newsman: he, his staff and his newspaper totally ignored the hometown experiments of Orville and Wilbur Wright, thus missing one of the century's biggest stories. Cox conceded that he was "negligent." But when Wall Street crashed in 1929, editor and publisher Cox ruled the news off his front pages lest it "harm business." Cox added newspapers to his chain that he termed a "league," from Atlanta and Miami to Texas and beyond. Cox never sought public office again and devoted the rest of his days to his newspapers. His legacy is the modern billion-dollar enterprise Cox Communication with some two dozen newspapers, interactive media, and CoxNet. Cox wrote an autobiography: *Journey Through My Years.*

George Creel (1876-1953) earned the title of "Uncle Sam's Press Agent" when he headed the U.S. Committee on Public Information during World War I. Creel was a cheerleader for Woodrow Wilson, originating the "Four Minute Man" lunch-hour talks pep-talks to boost the war effort. His censorship affected news coverage in the United States as well as South America and Asia. Creel, through his committee, was an effective censor of any criticism of the war effort; the First Amendment eroded in this era. Press criticism was suppressed, as were stories such as Heywood Broun's reports of military logistic failures and the questions concerning U.S. aims printed in the *Masses.* Creel's committee "suggested" editorials and cartoon topics suitable for America's war aims and America's newspapers knuckled under. Creel was an active newspaperman—he worked for the

Kansas City *World,* published the Kansas City *Independent* (1899-1909), then worked for the Denver *Post* and the *Rocky Mountain News.* Creel was a political animal, however, and after his wartime service, he ran unsuccessfully for governor in California and held a number of political appointments. Creel was especially close to the California politician William Gibbs McAdoo. In the late 1940s, Creel became an advisor to the United Mine Workers. His more than fifteen books include: *The German-Bolshevik Conspiracy, Wilson and the Issues, How We Advertised America, Rebel at Large.*

Gib (Gibson) Crockett (1913-) succeeded Cliff Berryman as editorial cartoonist for the Washington *Evening Star,* when it was the preeminent voice in the nation's capital, and remained with that newspaper until his retirement in 1975. Crockett's cartoons, which regularly appeared on the front page, were distinguished by the fact that each figure's face was a distinct miniature portrait. Crockett was self-taught and drew cartoons in high school in Kingsport, Tennessee. When he journeyed to Washington in the 1930s, he found work illustrating grocery store windows, and later with the Treasury Department. A family friend introduced him to Berryman at the *Evening Star,* and he began as an apprentice (no pay). did well and was hired by Cliff Berryman in 1933 (at ten dollars weekly). Crockett did spot art and sports cartoons, modeled after Willard Mullin. Berryman's failing health gave Crockett opportunity; he filled-in part-time beginning in 1947 and full-time in 1949 after Berryman's death. A conservative, Crockett followed the *Evening Star's* old-school credo: don't cause a "ruckus," never embarrass a woman, and avoid vicious stereotypes. Nevertheless, Crockett's sly humor earned him the wrath of presidents Eisenhower, Nixon, and Truman. Crockett's art graced the program covers of the classic Army-Navy football games for forty-one years and his work covers the dining room wall of Washington's Burning tree Country Club–"they run the country from that place." Crockett was awarded the Overseas Press Club's Headliner Award, a Treasury Department Citation for wartime work, and the Freedom Foundation Medal.

Walter Cronkite (1916-), publicly avuncular and at ease before the television cameras, was known as "Uncle Walter" to millions of Americans who watched "CBS News with Walter Cronkite" for nineteen years (1962-81). A genuine newsman, his beginnings were in print: the Houston *Post,* United Press International, the wartime *Stars and Stripes,* and later radio as a sometime sports announcer. In 1950 he became a CBS radio-TV news commentator in Washington, D.C., and a CBS television news anchor in 1962. After he retired, Cronkite spoke openly about the decline in quality of television news; significantly, CBS never invited him back to comment on news. Cronkite sought impartiality and fairness, despite his undisguised enthusiasm for NASA and America's space program. Books include: *The*

Challenge of Change, A Reporter's Life.

Frank (Francis Welch) Crowninshield [Arthur Loring Bruce] (1872-1947), a one-time editor of *Vanity Fair* and an advisor to Conde Nast, brought America's attention to the French modernists through his magazine. As editor of *Vanity Fair* for twenty-two years, he was an influential member of New York's artistic and literary circles. Born in Paris, he was educated in private schools and began his career with George Putnam publishers; four years later, in 1895, he became publisher of the *Bookman* for Dodd, Mead & Co., and wrote under his pen-name, Arthur Loring Bruce. In 1900, he became assistant editor of *Munsey's Magazine,* and from 1907-10 was a literary agent in London. When he was appointed art editor of the *Century Magazine,* he became more closely associated with art. The Armory Show hastened his interest in acquiring an American collection. In 1913, Nast invited Crowninshield to become editor of *Vanity Fair,* a magazine heavily weighted toward the arts and theater. The magazine merged with *Vogue* in 1936, and Crowninshield became an advisor for all Conde Nast publications. Crowninshield is remembered as the man who fired Dorothy Parker (because her theater review irked Florenz Ziegfeld) and lost two staff members, Robert Benchley and Robert Sherwood, who resigned in protest. The magazine attracted a stable of outstanding writers, however, and set a standard for excellence. Books, written as Arthur Loring Bruce, include: *Manners for the Metropolis, The Bridge Fiend.*

Arthur Daley (1904-74) wrote the column, "Sports of the Times" for thirty-two years and was awarded a Pulitzer prize in 1956 for that work.He joined the *Times* in 1936. Directly after graduating from Fordham University, where he served as sports editor for the college newspaper, the *Ram.* Daley covered all sports, but his speciality was baseball and most of his columns reflected that interest. Daley's writing was, as the Pulizer citation noted, "distinguished." Books: *The Story of the Olympic Games* (with John Kieran).

"Ding" (Jay Norwood) Darling (1876-1949) was for more than fifty years one of America's popular editorial page cartoonists. His cheery outlook, with strong rural themes, helped recall an America that had all but disappeared by the first half of the century. He began with the Sioux City (Iowa) *Journal* in 1900, but most of his career was with the Des Moines (Iowa) *Register* (1909-1949). Beginning in 1917, he also contributed cartoons to the New York *Tribune,* later syndicated by the *Herald Tribune* to more than 200 newspapers. For a time he was the editorial page cartoonist for *Collier's* magazine. Awarded two Pulitzer prizes (1924 and 1943), Darling was active in wildlife conservation, and a conservative politically; his cartoons portrayed a benign view of America with light humor. He was leader in the passage of the Duck Stamp Act in 1934 and he founded the National Wildlife Federation in 1936; Darling served for twenty months as Chief of the Biological Survey, under the department of Agriculture, but worked closely with Harold L. Ickes. Secretary of the Interior. Darling's enemy, Franklin Roosevelt, proved to be more helpful as a President effecting conservation than had his good friend, Herbert Hoover. A 6,700 acre wildlife refuge, named in Darling's honor, encompasses a portion of his summer retreat on Sanibel Island, Florida. Darling was a constant battler for conservation–often profane and eloquent in personal denunciation–produced art, absent of bitterness, that appealed to the better instincts of American life. Books include: *Ding's Half Century, As Ding Saw Hoover.*

Elmer Holmes Davis (1890-1958), a plain-spoken, honest, sometimes blunt reporter and broadcaster, served as director of the Office of War Information during World War II. Davis began as a printer's devil for his hometown Aurora (Ind.) *Bulletin,* then went on to Franklin College and work with the Indianapolis *Star.* He won a Rhodes scholarship and returned to work for *Adventure* magazine in 1913. The next year he joined the *New York Times,* where he reported on national affairs until 1923, when he left to pursue writing novels. In 1939 CBS invited him to fill in briefly as a broadcaster; he was successful with his factual, incisive reporting. In a 1942 broadcast, Davis suggested a government organization for news. President Franklin Roosevelt heeded that advice and named Davis to head the OWI (Office of War Information) and Davis succeeded in his fights against the military and the bureaucrats to bring facts, not propaganda, to the American public. With the close of OWI, Davis joined ABC in 1945; he was an outspoken critic of Sen. Joseph McCarthy and the Cold War hysteria. Upon his death, the *New York Times* described Davis as "the Mount Everest of commentators." Books include: *But We Were Born Free, Giant Killer, History of the New York Times: 1851-1921, I'll Show You the Town.*

Richard Harding Davis (1864-1916) made his newspaper fame in the 1800s, primarily as a war correspondent, but he was a major influence until the early 1900s, especially as an inspiration on young writers–Booth Tarkington and H.L. Mencken, for example. Davis was a newspaperman with dash and distinction who brought an air of chivalry to newspapering. Davis is best remembered for his role as Hearst's special correspondent for the New York *Journal* who helped instigate the Spanish-American war. Davis was born into a writing background; his mother, Rebecca Harding, was a popular writer and his father was editor of the Philadelphia *Public Ledger.* After he was suspended from Lehigh University, Davis began his career with the Philadelphia *Record.* then moved to the Philadelphia *Press* and later the New York *Evening Sun.* He began writing short stories, one series featured "Gallegher," a newspaper messenger boy. Davis was editor of *Harper's Weekly* (1891-93) but temperamentally unsuited as editor, he continued as a roving correspondent until his death. Davis wrote travel pieces of the American West and England. He covered wars in Asia, Europe, and the Boar War in Africa. Months prior to his death, Davis was writing of the European action in Serbia during World War I. His many novels are largely unread, as dated as the newspaper accounts they were based on. His early death at fifty-two before the participation of the United States in the Great War helped eclipse his career. Books include: *Cuba in War Time, A Year from a Reporter's Note-Book, Real Soldiers of Fortune, With the Allies, Notes of a War Correspondent.*

Samuel H. Day Jr. (1926-2001) led a life-long fight for First Amendment rights and won a landmark court decision to publish an article that explained how to make a hydrogen bomb. After schooling at Exeter Academy and Swarthmore College, Day began his journalism career as a copyboy for the Washington *Evening Star* in 1949. During the Korean War, he served with the Army in Europe as a writer for *Stars and Stripes* and after Army service joined the Associated Press in San Francisco. From 1956 until 1974, he worked for several Idaho newspapers, including the *Intermountain Observer,* known as a muckraking, crusading paper. After the paper folded in 1973, Day located in Chicago as managing editor of the *Bulletin of Atomic Scientists.* He became editor of the *Progressive,* a monthly magazine. In 1979, publication of an article, "The H-Bomb Secret,"was enjoined by the Justice Department to not publish (the information was known scientific fact); the U.S. Court of Appeals lifted the injunction and the article was published in November 1979. The next year, Day left as editor but continued as a member of the magazine's Editorial Advisory Board until his death. For the next several decades, Day pursued a career as a peaceful but active demonstrator against nuclear weapons, and served two terms in federal prisons for his efforts.

Dorothy Dix [Elizabeth Meriwether Gilmore] (1861-1951) was a pioneer of the newspaper advice column. She began work for the New Orleans *Picayune* in 1894, writing an advice column, "Sunday Salad." That success led to an offer from the New York *Journal* in 1901, and she earned some fame as a "sob sister" covering trials and other sensational events. She began a six-day-a-week column in 1917, "Dorothy Dix Talks." For the next fifty-five years her widely-syndicated column continued to give advice to the lovelorn and earned her fame and wealth; her salary in 1927 was $75,000 (more than million dollars in today's purchasing power). Dix helped pave the way for modern advice columns that continue to be useful aids to newspaper circulation. Books include collections of her columns and *Fables for the Elite, Hearts a la Mode, My Joy Ride Around the World.*

Carrie (Carolyn Gertrude Amelia) Donovan (1928-2001), an innovative and creative fashion editor for the *New York Times, Vogue* and *Harper's Bazaar,* was otherwise unfamiliar with other facets of journalism; she never mastered the mysteries of a typewriter. Nevertheless, she became a major media celebrity in the world of fashion After graduating from the Parsons School of Design in 1950, she joined the *Times* in 1953 as a reporter. She was outclassed by more-experienced colleagues, but an interview with Diana Vreeland led to a job with *Vogue* in 1963. In 1971, after Vreeland was fired, Donovan joined *Harper's Bazaar* as a fashion editor. She left that post for a brief stint as public relations expert for Bloomingdales before rejoining the *Times'* magazine as style editor. In 1997, Donovan launched a new career with the Old Navy retail clothing store and a series of ads brought her wide celebrity. She was one of few newspaper people to be caricatured by Al Hirschfeld. In her final year Donovan returned to the *Times* and fashion writing.

W(illiam) E(dward) B(urghardt) DuBois (1868-1963) was the founder and editor of the *Crisis,* an influential publication for the National Association for the Advancement of Colored People (NAACP). DuBois made a major contribution to studies of black sociology and black culture and he was a leading intellectual force. The first black to earn a Ph.D. in history from Harvard, he served with distinction at Atlanta University. DuBois helped organize the NAACP in 1909 and served until 1934 when an internal controversy caused his ouster. The *Crisis* reached a circulation of 100,000 and was a major social force in American race relations under DuBois' direction. Books include: *The Quest of the Silver Fleece, The Negro, The Gift of Black Folk, Black Reconstruction.*

Edmund Duffy (1899-1962) won three Pulitzer prizes for editorial cartooning in the space of nine years–in 1931, 1934, and 1940. Duffy, independent and a man of integrity, expressed his personal opinion for the editorial page and would not compromise. If his publisher supported an opposition candidate, Duffy took a vacation. Duffy was unique in that he, not the editor or publisher, decided the topic of his cartoon; not many cartoonist then or now enjoy that privilege. Duffy left high school to study at the Art Students' League under John Sloan and Boardman Robinson. Robert Benchley bought his first illustrations for the New York *Tribune* in 1918. By 1922, he was illustrating sports events and theatrical pages for the Brooklyn *Eagle.* Duffy became editorial cartoonist for the worker-owned New York *Leader* in 1923. When that newspaper died six months later, he returned to the *Eagle.* The next year, H.L. Mencken arranged a ninety-day tryout for the cartoonist with the Baltimore *Sun.* Duffy remained for the next quarter-century and earned the newspaper its first Pulitzer prizes.

Duffy then joined the large-circulation *Saturday Evening Post* magazine as its exclusive editorial cartoonist. When the conservative *Post* policy clashed with liberal Duffy's views, his cartoon did not appear that week. He resigned from the the *Post* in 1956, and he joined the Long Island tabloid *Newsday.* Duffy's independence clashed with the wishes of the publisher, who wanted a cartoonist to draw what was directed. Duffy was not fired, nor did he quit; he simply never came back one day in 1956. Duffy worked again briefly for the *Washington Post,* in 1959-60, filling in for the ailing Herblock. Duffy usually dealt with somber topics in a sober era and his stark cartoons devoid of humor mark an era when editorial cartoons were confrontational and expressed conviction that aroused reader reaction.

Finley Peter Dunne (1867-1936), an extraordinary columnist and newspaperman, was a political sage and wit. Dunne created "Mr. Dooley," an Irish-American figure who commented in the Chicago *Post* on politics, people, and events. Immensely popular, Dooley employed broad humor, satire and sardonic ridicule in a brogue dialect that attacked the high and mighty or the commonplace. In 1900 Dunne moved to New York City, and national syndication. He was editor of the New York *Telegraph* in 1902. By 1906 he was an editor with the *American Magazine* and in 1919 he succeeded Mark Sullivan as editor of *Collier's Weekly.* Mr. Dooley was one of President John F. Kennedy's favorite characters and the Irish-Catholic president was known to produce an apt quotation from that source on more than one occasion. Books include: *Mr. Dooley in Peace and War, Mr. Dooley's Philosophy, Mr. Dooley Says.*

Max Eastman (1883-1969) was a passionate advocate of his beliefs in controversial and often unpopular causes, including women's suffrage and the Socialist movement. After graduate study at Columbia and Harvard, he became editor of the Socialist magazine the *Masses* in 1913. His opposition to World War I led to the closing of the *Masses* and he became editor of the *Liberator* (1918-24). In 1918, Eastman and his *Masses* colleagues were tried and acquitted under the wartime Sedition Act for published material considered detrimental to the war effort. Eastman spent considerable time writing and translating, focusing on Leon Trotsky and Communism. In later years he was an editor (1941-69) with the *Reader's Digest* and with the *National Review* (1955). His more than fifty books include: *Journalism versus Art, The Sense of Humor, Since Lenin Died, Seven Kinds of Goodness, Enjoyment of Living.*

Rowland Evans (1921-2001), a conservative columnist, teamed with Robert Novak to write one of the most influential columns–"Inside Report"–during the 1960s, and helped to make the transition from print to television influence. Their television show, "Evans and Novak," was often dominated by the flamboyant Novak (known as the "dark prince" or "Robert No-facts") among the press corps, but Evans was a quiet champion of conservative causes. Evans left Yale College after 1941 to serve as a combat Marine and saw service in the South Pacific. After the war, he went to work for the Philadelphia *Bulletin* and in 1945 joined the Associated Press in Washington. In 1958, he joined the New York *Herald Tribune* and was directed by editor James Bellows to write an off-beat Washington column. "Inside Report" began in 1963 and continued until 1993. Evans was a relentless reporter, who knew how to get the facts and report an accurate story.

Beatrice Fairfax [Marie Manning Gasch] (1873-1945) became one of the first and well-known "advice to the lovelorn" columnists. From a good family, she was educated in New York and London, but had a desire to be a journalist. A chance dinner conversation with Arthur Brisbane led to an offer to work for him on the New York *World*. She was a successful reporter, covering mostly women's issues, but when she joined Brisbane and others who bolted to Hearst's rival *Journal,* Manning turned that opportunity into a column written as Miss Beatrice Fairfax. Her advice was typified by "Dry your eyes, roll up your sleeves and dig for a practical solution." Through King Features her column was syndicated to more than 200 newspapers. She wrote extensive free-lance pieces and a number of books. After a brief retirement for marriage in 1905, she returned to work in 1929 after the Wall Street crash. She continued her column until the mid-forties. Manning covered Washington news for the INS (International News Service) as well. Unlike the modern advice columnists–Ann Landers or Abigail Van Horn, for example–Fairfax was a reporter with solid journalistic credentials. Books include: *Judith of the Plains, Personal Reply, Ladies Now and Then.*

Eugene Field (1850-1895) established the column format of comment and poetry that held sway in American newspapers for the first half of the twentieth century. Field is the author of beloved poems, such as "Wynken, Blinken, and Nod," and "Little Boy Blue." In the early years of the century, schools across America would annually observe a "Eugene Field Day" to honor his poems of childhood. Field did not graduate from college; he joined the St.Louis *Evening Journal* in 1873 as a reporter and then city editor. In 1875, he moved to the St. Joseph (Mo.) *Gazette* as city editor, then two years later, back to the St. Louis *Times-Journal* as city editor. His poetry gained national attention with "Little Peach" in 1879. Field moved to several newspapers–the Kansas City *Times* in 1880, as managing editor; the Denver *Tribune,* as managing editor in 1881; and later that year to the Chicago *Daily News,* as managing editor. There he began his column "Sharps and Flats" where many of his poems would appear. Field wrote on polities, baseball, and theatrical events, but his poetry made his name a household word. With his verse based on the classics (Horace was his guide), Field's reputation as a lover of children and childhood might suffer if the public knew of his scatological verse, prepared for newspaper cronies. Nonetheless, Field left a legacy rarely matched by newspaper poets, and his work established the pattern that was followed for more than fifty years. A monument commemorating Field's work stands in Chicago's Lincoln Park. Books include *Poems of Childhood, The Tribune Primer, The Eugene Field Book.*

Daniel R. Fitzpatrick (1891-1964) produced powerful editorial cartoons for forty-five years for the St. Louis *Post-Dispatch.* After training at the Chicago Art Institute, he joined the Chicago *Daily News* and moved to the *Post-Dispatch* in 1913, remaining there until he retired in 1958. He was awarded two Pulitzer prizes (1926 and 1955), and his work was known for its distinctive, powerful portrayals with a usually liberal tone–his depictions of the Depression-era victims were particularly moving. His work was influential nationally, but Fitzpatrick's art never neglected local issues or local politics–he was an early admirer of Missouri Senator Harry Truman. Fitzpatrick during the war years portrayed the Nazi military as a massive, destructive swastika-machine of death and devastation that received national attention through frequent appearances in *Collier's* magazine. Books include *As I Saw It.*

Doris Fleeson (1901-70), an ardent feminist and New Deal advocate, was a newspaper reporter and columnist for forty years. Even though she considered herself a liberal, Fleeson pulled no punches and attacked Republicans and Democrats alike when she felt they deserved it. After graduating from the University of Kansas in 1923, her first newspaper job was with the Pittsburgh (Kansas) *Sun.* Later with the Evanston (Ill.) *News-Index,* she attempted with no success to break into the Chicago newspaper world. She came East in 1927 to work for the Great Neck (L.I.) *News* and eventually won a job with the New York *Daily News.* After she was assigned to the Albany bureau, she became acquainted with Governor Franklin Roosevelt, whom she covered when he became president. in 1933. During her time with the Washington bureau, she started her column, "Capitol Stuff" which ran in the *Daily News* for the next thirty years. In 1933 she worked with Heywood Broun in the formation of the Newspaper Guild and was elected to the national executive committee. In 1943 she left the *Daily News* to become a war correspondent for the *Woman's Home Companion.* After the war, she returned to Washington to write a political column for the *Evening Star,* that was syndicated to ninety newspapers. Fleeson was awarded the Raymond Clapper award in 1954 by the ASNE (American Society of Newspaper Editors).

Gene Fowler (1890-1960), called "the last of the troubadours" by Lucius Beebe, was one of the colorful newspapermen who chronicled Americana in the 1920s and beyond. From Denver, he was a boyhood friend of boxing champion Jack Dempsey. He began his career with the Denver *Post* and with the help of his fellow-Westerner Damon Runyon, won a spot with William Randolph Hearst's New York *American.* Fowler reported the kidnappings, murders, executions and other news with that rare quality that makes a true story teller. He rose to be a managing editor at the *American,* and continued writing for Hearst. Fowler spent a good deal of his time in Hollywood as a successful screenwriter and collaborated with Ben Hecht and others on a number of motion pictures. (he was an uncredited contributor to the dialogue for "The Front Page"). His chronicles of those years provide an intimate view of Hollywood and its denizens. Fowler's fame will rest on his many excellent books. A trilogy recounts his newspaper days: *Timberline, A Solo in Tom-Toms,* and *Skyline: A Reporter's Reminiscence of the 1920s.* Other books include: *Trumpet in the Dust; Shoe the Wild Mare; Beau James; Schnozzola; Good Night, Sweet Prince; Minutes of the Last Meeting.*

Pauline Frederick (1908-90), a true pioneer, opened the doors to broadcast journalism for women. Frederick was once billed by ABC as "the only female correspondent on radio or television." Later, she was NBC's United Nations correspondent for twenty-one years. Her roots were in print journalism. After graduating from American University (D.C.), she wrote for the Washington *Evening Star* and later for the *United States Daily,* a predecessor of *U.S. News & World Report,* then for NANA (North American Newspaper Alliance). She made several radio broadcasts before becoming a war correspondent in 1943. She broadcast from China in 1943. Frederick in 1948 reported by radio the three national presidential nominating conventions in Philadelphia. She joined NBC in 1953 and the next year was awarded an Alfred I. DuPont award, and a Peabody award the following year. Her weekday radio show, "Pauline Frederick Reports," ran from 1949 until her retirement in 1980. She contributed a number of chapters to *America Prepares for Tomorrow: The Story of Our Total Defense Effort.*

Clayton W. Fritchey (1904-2001), a newsman and syndicated columnist, had a long career in government as well. He began his newspaper career in Baltimore as a reporter for the *American* and moved to the Baltimore *Post* as city editor in 1931. After a brief time with the Pittsburgh *Press,* Fritchey returned to the *Post* as managing editor. Later, he performed notable work for the Cleveland *Press,* as an investigative reporter covering the work of Eliot Ness in cleaning up the corruption in the Cleveland Police Department. Fritchey then moved to the New Orleans *Item,* where his work led the Louisiana state senate to consider censoring him for "disrespect." Fritchey joined the Pentagon as its spokesman in 1950 at the invitation of Gen. George C. Marshall and served until 1952. President Harry Truman called on Fritchey to become a White House assistant and he later served as deputy chairman of the Democratic National Committee until 1956. He returned to newspaper work, as publisher of the *Northern Virginia Sun* until 1960. In 1961 he joined the United Nations as director of public affairs for the United States Mission and served until 1965. Fritchey returned to newspaper work to begin a syndicated column for *Newsday* that continued until his retirement in 1984.

Hugh S. Fullerton (1873-1945) was the first to expose the 1919 "Black Sox" World Series scandal. He began his career after high school in 1889 with the Cincinnati *Enquirer,* and then enrolled in Ohio State University, where most of his activity was with the baseball team. He resumed his newspaper career in 1893 with the Chicago *Record* and four years later moved to the leading Chicago newspaper, the *Tribune.* He won fame by predicting the exact score for every game of the White Sox win over the Cubs in the 1906 World Series. From 1908 to 1912, he worked for the Chicago *Herald,* and later, the Chicago *Examiner* before returning to the *Tribune* in 1912. In 1920 he became editor of the New York *Mail* until 1928, when he returned to Ohio to join the Columbus *Dispatch.* Fullerton's articles reporting organized gambling and criminal activities by several players helped bring about the movement to clean up baseball. He was one of the first sportswriters to advance beyond statistical reporting and write about players on and off the field. Books include *Baseball in the Big Leagues, Tales of the Turf, Racing Yarns.*

William B. Furlong (1927-2000) had a serendipitous name for a sportswriter, and he was one of the most widely read columnists in the last third of the century. After graduating from the Illinois Institute of Technology, he began writing for the Southtown (Chicago) *Economist.* Later, he worked for the Chicago *Daily News* and the *New York Times Magazine.* From 1974-79, he was a sports columnist for the *Washington Post.* Furlong, who was known for his intriguing leads, also wrote for *Sports Illustrated, Newsweek* and the *Saturday Evening Post.* He left journalism to become a management consultant in Washington D.C. His books include: *Go For Broke* (with Arnold Palmer), *Season with Solti, More Than Two Aspirin.*

Paul Gallico (1897-1976) earned his fame as a short-story writer, but his beginnings were in journalism. He served as a seaman gunner in the U.S. Navy in 1918; after graduating from Columbia, then became a movie critic for the New York *Daily News* (1922-23). He eventually became a sportswriter, editor, and columnist, and served as a war correspondent for *Cosmopolitan* magazine during World War II. After the war, he contributed his popular short stories to a number of magazines such as *Good Housekeeping,* the *New Yorker,* the *Saturday Evening Post,* and *Esquire.* He won fame primarily through his books which include *The Snow Goose, Mrs. 'Arris Goes to Paris, Lou Gehrig: Pride of the Yankees.*

Frank E(arnest) Gannett (1876-1957) from humble beginnings as a newsboy, built a communications empire that included twenty-two newspapers, four radio and four television station at the time of his death. He was an anti-New Dealer, an ardent Republican, and an aspirant for the presidency in 1940. After graduating from Cornell University in 1898, he served with the Philippine Commission and declined an offer to serve in the Islands and took a job as editor of the Ithaca (N.Y.) *News.* Within a few years he owned the paper; in 1906, he purchased the Elmira (N.Y.) *Gazette.* Moving to Rochester in 1918, Gannett bought the Rochester *Union and Advertiser* and the *Times,* and merged them into the *Times-Union.* Between 1919 and 1929, he concentrated on building his newspaper chain, which he preferred to call a "group." He formed the Gannett Foundation to hold his stock. Gannett fought FDR's court-packing scheme and most other New Deal measures, as well as Harry Truman's Fair Deal legislation.

Howard Garis (1873-1962) wrote the popular newspaper feature, "Uncle Wiggily," and was author of the long-running "Tom Swift" books. After an early career as a railroad baggage handler, Garis, in 1896, joined the Newark (N.J.) *Evening News* as a reporter. After several failed efforts at writing adult novels, Garis joined the Stratemeyer Syndicate in 1908, to write as Clarence Jones, producing a series of juvenile adventure series–"The Motor Boys," and the "The Racer Boys." He began the "Uncle Wiggily" column in 1910 for the *Evening News* and began "The Tom Swift" series writing as Victor Appleton. His column was widely syndicated and his book, *Uncle Wiggily's Adventures,* became a best-seller, but Garis continued his syndicate work. Garis wrote hundreds of books as Victor Appleton and Clarence Jones–he was also Marion Davidson, author of the "The Camp Fire Girls." Garis continued his "Uncle Wiggily" column six days a week for more than fifty years, along with several dozen books, and a popular "Uncle Wiggily" game. Garis wrote for and entertained millions of readers and his newspaper feature sold many newspapers. A sample of his books include: *Larry Dexter, Reporter; The Motor Boys Across the Plains* (as Clarence Jones)*; Tom Swift and His Airship* (as Victor Appleton); *Uncle Wiggily Stories.*

Jack W. Germond (1928-), a political reporter, and one of the best—for more than four decades, for Gannett, the Washington *Evening Star,* and the Baltimore *Sun*–and known to millions of television viewers of talk shows including "Meet the Press," "The McLaughlin Group," and "Inside Washington." Born in Boston, he grew up in Louisiana and attended Louisiana State University. After one semester in college, he served in the Army Air Corps in Greenland (1945-48). He returned to LSU and after graduation, went to work in 1951 as a sports editor for the *Jefferson City* (La.) *Post-Tribune.* After three months, he moved on to the Monroe (Mich.) *Evening News* as a general assignment reporter. After that two-year "learning experience," Germond joined the staff of the Rochester (N.Y.) *Times-Union,* a Gannett newspaper. He went on to cover politics in Albany (Governor Nelson Rockefeller offered him a staff position, which was refused), and later Washington and became bureau chief in 1969. After new management came into Gannett, Germond joined the Washington *Evening Star* in 1974 and stayed until the paper folded in 1981 He and Jules Witcover had jointly written a political column which they shifted to the Baltimore *Sun,* and later for the *National Journal.* Germond had also appeared on national television–visibility that enhanced his stature: on NBC's "Meet the Press" in 1972, a continuing appearance on NBC's "Today" show (1988-92), and Cable News Network (CNN) from 1988 to 1992. Germond's real celebrity came with the "The McLaughlin Group" (1981- 96), a political talk show that defies description. Germond was the "liberal" amidst a howling group of mainly right-wing fanatics. In later years, Germond dropped his collaboration with Witcover and column for the *Sun* and appears regularly on "Inside Washington"–he's the "fat man" in the middle and the panelist with the most political savvy. Books include: *Fat Man in a Middle Seat* and (with Jules Witcover) *Blue Smoke and Mirrors: How Reagan Won and Why Carter Lost the Election of 1980; Mad as Hell: Revolt at the Ballot Box, 1992.*

Floyd Gibbons (1887-1939), an adventuresome reporter, was wounded in action during World War I, who later became a pioneer in radio broadcasting. Dismissed from Georgetown University for pranks, Gibbons began his newspaper work in Minneapolis with the *Daily News* and with the rival *Tribune,* and later with the Milwaukee *Free Press.* After a brief stint with the Chicago *World,* he joined the Chicago *Tribune* in 1914. He covered America's war with Mexico and became friends with General John J. Pershing. Gibbons was promoted to the *Tribune's* Washington bureau and by 1918 joined the A.E.F. in Europe, Gibbons was wounded in action at Belleau Wood and thereafter a dashing eyepatch became his distinctive trademark. Following the war, he headed the *Tribune's* European foreign news bureau and was conspicuous at every newsworthy event. Back in Chicago in 1925, he broadcast for the *Tribune's* radio station WGN (World's Greatest Newspaper). A year later he left to devote time to writing, but in 1929 began a radio news program, "The Headline Hunter." By 1932, Gibbons was starring in a series of motion picture shorts–with settings of news-adventure. His last major assignment was the Spanish Civil War, where Gibbons was suspected of being a spy because he covered both the insurgents and the loyalists. Gibbons was the prototypical foreign correspondent. Books include: *Floyd Gibbons: Your Headline Hunter, The Red*

Knight of Germany, The Red Napoleon, And They Thought We Wouldn't Fight.

Mike Gold [Irwin Granich] (1893-1967) was a crusading liberal, who was once described by writer John Fanti as "a platitude carrying a cross." Born in poverty, Gold managed to attend New York University and later Harvard, he never forgot his impoverished beginnings, however, and that heritage drove Gold to write with passion and become a major contributor to proletarian literature. After a stint on the Socialist, worker-owned New York *Call,* he joined the radical *Masses* from 1911 to 1917. Gold fled to Mexico to avoid the draft in World War I, and returned in 1920 as editor of the *Liberator,* successor to the *Masses,* which had been suppressed by the wartime Wilson Administration. Gold served as editor of the *New Masses* from 1926 until 1935. From 1933 through 1967, Gold wrote a column for the Communist Party newspaper, the *Daily Worker.* In the 1950s Gold moved to San Francisco and wrote also for the *People's World.* Books include his classic *Jews Without Money, The Hollow Men, Money,* and *The Mike Gold Reader.*

Katharine Graham (1917-2001), a leading publisher in twentieth-century journalism, took a middling metropolitan newspaper and established the *Washington Post* into the base for a media empire. Graham was responsible for publishing the "Pentagon Papers" in 1971, a secret government account of the war in Vietnam. The next year, the *Post,* under her direction, led the Watergate investigation that brought down a president and won a Pulitzer prize. Graham is credited with the personal decision to publish these sensitive stories–courage that recognized her newspaper was at risk, but established First Amendment rights that were upheld by the Supreme Court. A child of privilege and wealth (her father Eugene Meyer, governor of the Federal Reserve Board, bought the bankrupt *Post* in 1933), Graham worked briefly following college–Vassar and the University of Chicago–for the San Francisco *News* and the *Post's* circulation department. She married Philip L. Graham in 1940 and he was named publisher in 1946, and began to improve the *Post.* After his suicide in 1961, she assumed full control as president of the newspaper. Graham followed advice from James Reston of the *New York Times* and Walter Lippmann of the *Herald Tribune,* two knowledgeable newsmen. Graham hired Benjamin C. Bradlee, and under his direction and with an able staff, the *Post* began to gain stature. Graham was an astute manager and the patrician won the undying gratitude of newspaper owners when she successfully broke the power of the trade unions and the Newspaper Guild in a prolonged and acrimonious strike in 1971. Son Donald E. Graham took over as publisher in 1979, and Mrs. Graham was overseer of a media empire that includes newspapers, six television stations, and Cable One with holdings in nineteen states, *Newsweek* magazine and joint ownership (with the *New York Times*) of the *International Herald Tribune,* published in Paris. Graham won a Pulitzer prize for her 1998 autobiography *Personal History.*

John Gunther (1901-70), a newspaperman who turned journalism into history, became famous (and wealthy) through his series of popular "Inside" books, from the 1930s through the 1950s. If journalism is the first draft of history, Gunther capitalized on that fact in an era when people were hungry for news about events happening in arcane and exotic places. Gunther came out of the University of Chicago, and as a student, wrote a literary feature for the school paper and managed to sell two articles to H.L. Mencken's *Smart Set.* After graduation, he went to work for the Chicago *Daily News* in 1922 and by 1924 was in its London bureau. After hours, Gunther worked on novels, largely autobiographical. As a newspaperman, Gunther was assigned to cover the hot-spots in Europe and Africa for the *Daily News.* When his novels attracted Hollywood, Gunther succumbed briefly, but screenwriting proved unrewarding. He returned to Europe when the *Daily News* offered him the post of Vienna bureau chief in 1930, a good position to observe Europe's unrest and the rise of Nazism. Gunther, went on to be bureau chief in London, and kept meticulous notes of European events and interviewed anyone who could give him inside information. His 1936 book, *Inside Europe,* was an instant best-seller; Gunther resigned from his newspaper job to devote his time to books. The next year, Gunther was writing a series of articles (suitable for his next book) for NANA (North American Newspaper Alliance) and the *Reader's Digest.* His next books examined Asia and Latin America, both became best-sellers. The American public was eager for news of the possible future battle fronts. During the war, Gunther worked briefly writing films for the Office of War Information, then in 1943, was a war correspondent for NANA and the NBC Blue Network. After the war, Gunther produced his monumental *Inside USA.* He continued to write for popular magazines such as *Collier's* and *Reader's Digest,* and during 1959 had a weekly television program broadcast by the ABC network. He continued with his books and a review of South America was unfinished at the time of his death in 1970. The timeliness of Gunther's topics has dated most of his work, but his *Death Be Not Proud,* a portrait of his son's illness and death, is likely to endure. His other books include: *Red Pavillion, Golden Fleece, Inside Asia, Inside Latin America, Inside Africa, D-Day, Inside Russia Today, Eisenhower: The Man and the Symbol.*

Percy Hammond (1873-1936) in the 1920s and 1930s was one of New York's most influential drama critics. After graduating from Franklin College, he was a reporter, correspondent, editorial writer and drama critic for the Chicago *Evening Post* (1908-1921). He then moved on to a more influential post, the New York *Herald Tribune,* as drama critic and served there until his death. Hammond was one of the legendary "Three Fat Fates of Broadway" (with Alexander Woollcott and Heywood Broun) because of his size and the weight of his criticism. His passing closed the era when critics dressed in formal evening wear for opening nights. Books include *But is it Art?*

Teenie (Charles H.) Harris (1908-98), a photojournalist, for more than sixty years, captured the life of African-Americans as a photographer for the Pittsburgh *Courier.* His archive of more than 84,000 negatives and prints was exhibited in the Westmoreland Museum of American Art. Harris centered his work in the inner city. The *Courier,* one of America's major minority newspapers, featured Harris' work in various editions that reached several cities in the United States, the Caribbean the Philippines, and Africa. Harris was known for snapping only one shot of the thousands of photographs he took. His incomparable collection constitutes one of the finest records known to exist of black life in America.

Joel Chandler Harris (Uncle Remus) (1848-1908), a folklorist and editor, was the creator of the wily and wise Br'er Rabbit. President Theodore Roosevelt commented: "Presidents may come, Presidents may go, but Uncle Remus stays put." Harris managed to capture the dialect of the black South and through his stories became a great interpreter of the Reconstruction Era. Before the Civil War, Harris began his apprenticeship on the weekly Georgia *Countryman,* owned by a slave holder. Harris heard firsthand stories of a trickster rabbit, told to him by two elderly slaves. After the war, Harris worked for the Macon (Ga.) *Telegraph* and later moved to the New Orleans *Crescent Monthly,* and the magazine published a number of his early writings. In 1876, Harris returned to Georgia with the Macon *Monroe Advertiser,* where he worked as a paragrapher (editorial writer) and his work led to a position on the Savannah *Morning News,* the leading daily in Georgia. He joined the Atlanta *Constitution* in 1876 and two years later began the column that continued for the next thirty years, containing his "Uncle Remus" stories. His stories captured the dialect and preserved the slave culture, topics widely popular then, but eschewed by today's politically correct. Nevertheless, Harris made a significant contribution to America's history and national culture that should be recognized. The richness of the black culture imported into and adopted in American lore, was captured by Harris as no other writer has. In 1907, Harris created *Uncle Remus's Home Magazine,* the "sweet, clean and wholesome" monthly attracted readers and advertisers and was widely popular and clearly followed the ideas of Harris; it failed to outlast him, however. The magazine folded in 1909, a year after Harris' death, an example of a magazine belonging to its editor. Books include: *Gabriel Tolliver, On the Plantation, Stories of Georgia, Uncle Remus's Songs, Sayings, and Fables.*

William Randolph Hearst (1863-1952) played a major role in American twentieth-century journalism. He battled Joseph Pulitzer for New York City newspaper domination and created "yellow journalism," a pejorative term attached to Hearst for the rest of his career. His newspapers set a tone for poor taste and sensationalism, but Hearst was also a constructive muckraker who should receive credit for his many crusading causes. The Hearst newspapers, for example, were one of the major forces responsible for passage of the G.I. Bill of Rights, the legislation that enabled millions of service veterans to attend college. Hearst began with one newspaper. From his base, anchored in the San Francisco *Examiner* in the west, to his New York *Journal* in the east, Hearst built a newspaper empire of twenty-three dailies and fifteen Sunday newspapers. Magazines, book publishing, motion pictures, news and feature syndicates, radio and television stations also constituted Hearst's vast communication holdings. By 1925, one in four Americans were consumers of Hearst news and information. He was reputed to be the prototype of Charles Foster Kane in the motion picture "Citizen Kane," which depicted a power-hungry megalomaniac (Orson Welles maintained it was Col. Robert McCormick). The Great Depression and loss of newspaper circulation helped erode Hearst's empire, but significant elements of his communication colossus remain. Hearst, except for two terms in Congress, never managed to use his newspapers' influence to gain the high political offices he sought, including the presidency.

Gabriel Heatter (1890-1972) was a radio commentator known for his invariable optimistic greeting to his audience, "Ah, there's good news tonight," even when the news was not especially good. Heatter found school difficult growing up in Brooklyn; he was much better as an orator, campaigning in 1906 for William Randolph Hearst's mayoral race. He began neighborhood reporting for Brooklyn newspapers, then joined the New York *Journal*. His 1932 article in the *Nation* led to an offer from radio station WMCA and later from WOR, a Mutual station. Heatter's big break came with the radio coverage of the Lindbergh baby kidnapping trial. During the war years his catch-phrase was born and Heatter's reputation for emotional, cheery commentary was established. In 1941 he originated a popular radio show, "We, the People." Heatter's news commentary was supplemented by his regular program, "A Brighter Tomorrow," which continued on radio and television until 1965. Heatter continued to write a six-times-a-week column for the Miami Beach (Fla.) *Sun* until his death. Heatter wrote an autobiography, *Ah, There's Good News Tonight.*

Ben Hecht (1894-1964), a man of many talents, established America's mythic stereotype of the raffish, rough-and-tumble newspaperman with his 1930 play "The Front Page" (with Charles MacArthur). The main characters–Walter Burns, the flinty city editor, was drawn from Walter Hovey, of the Chicago *Tribune* and *Herald-Examiner,* and Hildy Johnson (a real person) was an amalgam of the two playwrights–reflected the riotous journalism of Hecht's Chicago newspaper apprenticeship. (Some of the play's uncredited script was contributed by George S. Kaufman and Gene Fowler.) Hecht began his career in 1909 with the Chicago *Journal* (as a picture-chaser, charged with getting a photo whatever the risk or circumstance) and then moved to the Chicago *Daily News* in 1914. His reporting skills earned him an overseas assignment and he covered post-war Germany in 1919. His work was syndicated to more than seventy-five newspapers. Back in Chicago, he established and edited the Chicago *Literary Times* in 1923. Early in his career he was a frequent contributor to H.L. Mencken's *Smart Set.* Mencken would dictate plots and Hecht supplied the dialogue for two-dozen Hecht stories. Two years later he went to Hollywood, already author of three books and three plays. Hecht received an Academy Award for his first screen play and another "Oscar" several years later. His success with "The Front Page" was followed by "20th Century" and set the format for Hollywood's "screwball" comedies. Hecht and MacArthur formed their own company and their motion pictures, filmed in New York, won critical acclaim, but were box office failures. In all, Hecht was responsible for sixty-five credited motion pictures, some forty others that were non-credited, but which paid well (the major goal for Hecht), nineteen books, and thirteen plays. He never abandoned journalism; in 1939-40, he was writing for New York's *PM,* primarily propaganda messages attacking the Nazi's treatment of the Jews. Hecht supported the Irgun and other active Zionists fighting for a Jewish homeland with his writing and with his personal funds (for such items as full-page newspaper ads and a ship for Jewish refugees). In the late 1960s he published a portion of his memoirs (much like his biography, imaginative and unreliable as to fact) in *Playboy.* Most of his memoirs are fanciful, elaborated stories, as were many of his slice-of-life newspaper columns. Practically all of Hecht's books are really little more than hidden autobiography. Unquestionably, Hecht was inventive and one of the best screenwriters in Hollywood. Much of his material was drawn from his newspaper experience, especially the gangster era in Chicago. His screenplay for "Scarface" was a portrait of Al Capone, with factual incidents that read like fiction and was the forerunner of the gangster-saga motion picture. Hecht's many books include: *A Child of the Century; A Jew in Love; 1001 Afternoons in Chicago; Miracle in the Rain; A Book of Miracles; Gaily, Gaily.*

Mark Hellinger (1903-47) became the first newspaperman to make it big in Hollywood; he was a screenwriter for more than forty motion pictures, including such classics as "Broadway Bill," "They Drive by Night," "The Roaring Twenties," and "The Naked City." Hellinger began his career in 1921, reviewing plays and motion pictures for *Zit's Weekly,* then moved to the New York *Daily News,* then to the *Journal* and a contract with King Features Syndicate. In 1937 Hellinger moved to Hollywood and continued his screenwriting and column. At the time of his death, Hellinger's column, that followed an O. Henry format, was estimated to have had eighteen million readers. Hellinger is one of the few newspapermen to have a Broadway theater named for him. Books include *Moon Over Broadway, The Ten Million.*

Ernest Hemingway (1899-1956), well-known for extravagant personal hyperbole, perpetuated a self-made myth of his newspaper background. Hemingway was not a good reporter; he was a novelist and superb. His beginnings after high school (where he emulated his hero, Ring Lardner) were with the Kansas City *Star,* where he was hired through family connections and the wartime manpower shortage. After only a short apprenticeship of six months, Hemingway was off to wartime service as a volunteer ambulance driver. Upon his return, Hemingway went to Canada, where he wrote advertising copy, worked for a magazine, the *Cooperative Commonwealth,* and freelanced for the Toronto *Star.* After his first book, *Three Stories,* was published, he was hired full-time by the *Star* doing feature stories. He regaled his colleagues with his exploits (mostly contrived) at Kansas City and produced features modeled after Lardner. An overseas assignment for the *Star* resulted in his being fired for poor reporting. Hemingway found success with his books: *The Sun Also Rises, In Our Time,* and *Farewell to Arms.* During this era Ben Hecht reported that Hemingway talked unconvincingly in Chicago of his newspaper days, but had little time for "real" reporters. Hemingway took an assignment for ready money from the *New Masses* to report on the 1935 Labor Day hurricane in the Florida Keys. The result was a propaganda piece, lax with factual accuracy and heavily larded with accusations against the New Deal. When Hemingway was hired by NANA to report the Spanish Civil war, he was fired for lifting stories from the *New York Times.* In 1941 he was engaged by the New York newspaper *PM* to report on developments in the Far East; he saw no threat for the United States from the Japanese. The Chinese, he reported, could control the militant aggression of the Japanese. In 1944, Hemingway became a war correspondent with his headquarters in Paris, and knew nothing of the political decision to allow the French forces to occupy the capital. His journalism work continued until his death, for *Look* magazine (1951-56) with a series of articles. His books, not newspaper reporting, are Hemingway's monument. He persisted in the myth of Hemingway, intrepid reporter, legend that lives on in newsrooms and journalism schools. See: *By-Line Ernest Hemingway: Selected Articles and Dispatches of Four Decades* and *Ernest Hemingway: Cub Reporter.*

O. Henry [William Sidney Porter] (1862-1910) wrote masterful newspaper stories that conclude with a twist–the O. Henry surprise attempted by many, mastered by few. He was one of America's most prolific and entertaining writers. From 1901 until his death in 1910, he turned out a weekly short story for the New York *World.* He began his newspaper career as a columnist and cartoonist for the Houston (Texas) *Post.* Earlier, as a bank teller, Porter was convicted of embezzlement; in prison he assumed the pen name O. Henry and wrote fiction for magazines. In New York after 1901, he produced popular books and stories, but drink led to poverty by the time of his death. Books include *Heart of the West, The Four Million, The Voice of the City, Whirligigs.*

Josephine Herbst (1897-1969) was typical of the writers of the left–Marxist-driven, who wrote of the plight of the workers, farmers, and the poor. Her work appeared regularly in the *New Masses* and the *New Republic* but also in *Scribners* and the *American Mercury.* Herbst attended several colleges–Morningside, University of Iowa, University of Washington–before graduating from the University of California at Berkeley. She initially went to work as an editorial staff member for the *Smart Set,* but in 1922-23 she went to Germany and, the next year, to Paris with her husband, writer John Herrmann. After 1926 in New York City writing free-lance pieces for a number of magazines, they spent much of 1928 in Key West with Ernest Hemingway. Herbst was in Russia in 1929, writing of the problems and progress of the Soviet state–she was one of those writers who saw hope in socialism and communism. In the 1930s her writing dwelt on the problems of the Great Depression, lynchings in the American South, and the threat of the Nazi rise to power. In the 1940s she turned her attention to the rise of Latin American fascists. During the war, she was fired from the federal Office of War Information for her Communist ties. She turned to book reviews for the Chicago *Sun* and public relations work for Chicago's Board of Health. Her books failed to earn much, her liberal causes were lost in wartime interests, and her circle of friends vanished. She died in poverty. Books include: *The Dark Blue Sky of Spain and Other Memoirs, Nothing Is Sacred, Money for Love, New Green World, Satan's Sergeants.*

John Hersey (1914-98), with a panoramic overview of events in World War II, converted contemporary journalism into history through his timely books. Born in China, son of a missionary, Hersey acquired a solid education–Hotchkiss School, Yale, and Cambridge. He served briefly as a secretary to Sinclair Lewis in 1937. Through his connections–his family knew Henry Luce in China–he joined Time Inc. in 1937 and became a correspondent for *Time* (1939-45) and *Life* (1942-45). His first book, *Men on Bataan,* was adulatory of General Douglas MacArthur. Hersey served as a correspondent in China, the South Pacific theater (he reported the PTboat heroics of John F. Kennedy that first appeared in the *New Yorker* and abridged for the *Reader's Digest*), the Mediterranean–Sicily and Italy–and in Moscow. For his wartime novel, *A Bell for Adano,* Hersey won a Pulitzer prize in 1945. In 1945-46, he was on assignment in Japan for the *New Yorker* and *Life;* his story about six survivors of the nuclear bombing of Hiroshima appeared in a precedent-setting single topic issue of the *New Yorker* and his account of the horrors of nuclear war created a sensation. (Hersey and the *New Yorker* never addressed the quarter-million American casualties expected from a land invasion of the Japanese homeland that the bomb negated.) His books addressed a number of issues of social significance–his fictive journalism may or may not be literature–but his writing was notable for its timeliness and passionate, even evangelic themes. After 1965, Hersey was associated with Yale University. His twenty books include: *Hiroshima, Men of Bataan, A Bell for Adano, The War Lover, The Wall, A Single Pebble, The Child Buyer.*

Marguerite (Maggie) Higgins (1920-66) earned the first Pulitzer prize awarded to a woman. In an era when women were rare in a newsroom, she was energetic and persistent–qualities that irritated colleagues. Fresh out of the graduate journalism program at Columbia, she landed a job with the New York *Herald Tribune.* Higgins managed to get an assignment overseas in 1945 by appealing to Helen Reid, wife of the publisher–a ploy that annoyed her colleagues. She covered the closing days of the European war with the Third Army's drive across France into Germany. She was appointed Berlin bureau chief and reported the crisis of the Russian blockade in 1948 and the drama of the Berlin airlift. In 1950 she was transferred to head the *Herald Tribune's* Tokyo bureau in time to cover the Korean War. Her reporting won her a Pulitzer prize in 1951. Later, Higgins visited Vietnam ten times between 1953 and 1965 and reported facts that editors did not wish to hear. Her twenty-two year association with the *Herald Tribune* ended in a petty quarrel over travel expenses and she continued her career with New York *Newsday* and the Washington *Evening Star.* On her last trip to Vietnam, Higgins contracted the disease that killed her. No prima donna, "Maggie" Higgins was a first-rate correspondent who reported the facts and was never led astray by military PIO flacks, nor filed copy that suited the desires of desk-bound editors. Books include: *News is a Singular Thing, War in Korea, Our Vietnam Nightmare.*

Eric Hodgins (1899-1971), wrote a book that touched all Americans in the housing shortage that followed World War II. After M.I.T. and Harvard (1924), Hodgins became managing editor of *Technical Review* and editor of *Youth's Companion* until 1929, when he joined *Redbook* as associate editor. He joined Time Inc. and was managing editor of *Fortune* until 1937; then he became publisher until 1946. Hodgins' notable fame came with his humorous book (later a motion picture) *Mr. Blandings Builds His Dream House,* which recounted the perils of home-building. This was in the era when a $10,000-a-year salary was the epitome of success, and a house cost little more. Other books include: *Blandings' Way, Episode.*

Richard Holman (1933-2000) founded the *Wall Street Transcript.* After graduation from Cornell University, Holman served in the Army during World War II, then pursued investment banking. He began the *Transcript* in 1963 (he sold his interest in 1998). This specialized business publication, highly priced, furnished stock exchange quotations and other information. The tabloid won an important case from the Securities and Exchange Commission in the federal courts to make the point that this financial information was legitimate news and not simply a tout sheet. Holman steadfastly resisted government subpoena for the paper's records, including reporter's notes. Holman's court victory should be remembered as a notable First Amendment achievement for journalism.

Roy W. Howard (1883-1964), remembered as the owner of the powerful Scripps-Howard newspaper chain, was notorious as the reporter who "scooped" the world with the bogus premature news of the November 1918 armistice. Howard was also the man who fired columnist Heywood Broun for his liberal views and promoted reactionary Westbrook Pegler. Howard's beginnings were modest; he began as a newsboy and went on to become a reporter for the Indianapolis *News.* Then he became a telegraph editor for the St. Louis *Post-Dispatch.* Denied a promotion, he joined the Cincinnati *Post* and began an association with owner E.W. Scripps. In 1906, Howard became a correspondent for the Scripps-McRae League and New York manager of the United Press by the next year. Howard improved and expanded foreign outlets for United Press, but it never gained the stature of its prime competitor, the Associated Press. Howard developed close ties with Scripps. By 1922, Howard was expanding the syndicate, now renamed Scripps-Howard, to include newspapers. He acquired the New York *World* and merged it with the *Telegram* and later with the *Sun*–the result in the 1950s was the *World-Telegram-Sun,* a conglomerate with little resemblance to its heritage.

E(dgar) W(atson) Howe (1853-1937) was editor of the Atchison (Kansas) *Daily Globe* (and columnist, "Globe Sights"), until 1911. He was editor and publisher of *E.W. Howe's Monthly* until 1933, which was praised by H.L. Mencken. Howe's major contribution to American letters is his masterpiece, *The Story of Country Town* (1882), a narrative by a mid-western county newspaper editor that reveals a less-than-idylic life that questioned the American Dream. Howe paved the way for American realists. Books: *Another Country Town, Adventures in Common Sense.*

Marjorie (Maggie) Hunter (1922-2001) was a pioneering correspondent. and a competent newspaper professional who helped women win equal rights with males. Hunter served as president of the Women's National Press Club until the National Press Club admitted women and the two organizations merged in 1985. A graduate of Elon College (N.C.), she was editor of the school newspaper and the local Burlington *Times-News*. After graduation, Hunter worked for the Raleigh *News and Observer*, the Houston (Texas) *Press*, and the Winston-Salem *Journal*. Hunter joined the *New York Times* to cover Eleanor Roosevelt in the era when the first lady allowed only female reporters to attend her press conferences. Hunter soon tired of this limited duty and requested the bureau chief to assign her to cover Congress, where she performed admirably. Hunter was a firm advocate of the watchdog role of the press and her work demonstrated that belief.

Chet (Chester Robert) Huntley (1911-74) teamed for fifteen years with David Brinkley and made NBC the nation's most popular television news network. Millions of viewers watched "Huntley-Brinkley" every week-day evening, even if perhaps they were not quite sure which was which (Huntley had the deeper voice). Huntley began to acquire a broadcast background before he finished college at the University of Washington. He worked at KPCB, then joined the NBC affiliate in Los Angeles. In 1939 he began a twelve-year association with CBS and won a George Foster Peabody award. In 1951, Huntley moved to ABC and a daily news program over KABC. In 1955 he moved to NBC and the East Coast, where he had a daily news broadcast and a Sunday show, "Outlook." He teamed with Brinkley in 1956 after the two scored a success over rival CBS during the presidential conventions broadcasts. Huntley's books include: *Generous Years: A Frontier Boyhood, Chet Huntley's News Analysis, Chet Huntley Reporting.*

Ralph Ingersoll (1900-85) devoted his considerable talents to a wide range of journalism. He began with the New York *American* in 1924 and became managing editor of the *New Yorker* in 1925. He moved to *Fortune* magazine in 1930 as managing editor. With the Henry Luce empire Ingersoll became general manager of Time Inc. (1935), helped launch *Life* magazine (1936), and later became publisher of *Time*. In 1939 Ingersoll founded the New York tabloid *PM* and except for wartime service, held that post until he resigned in 1946. He owned a number of newspapers, as Ingersoll Publications, but his lasting claim to fame is the experimental, innovative *PM*, a newspaper distinguished for its unrelenting liberalism. Books include *Report on England, America is Worth Fighting For, Top Secret, Wine of Violence, Point of Departure.*

Will (William Henry) Irwin (1873-1948) was a reporter, a newsman from the "old school" who was versatile, prolific, and wide-ranging in his scope of activities. Two major contributions, among many, mark his fame: the chronicle of the San Francisco earthquake of 1906, and his extensive multi-part series in *Collier's* magazine of "the American newspaper." After he finally obtained his degree from Stanford, Irwin worked for the San Francisco *Wave,* where he replaced Frank Norris, then he moved to the *Chronicle.* After 1904 he joined the New York *Sun,* the goal of every newspaperman of that era, where he produced his monumental series "the City that Was." Based in New York, and drawing on his past residence and his recollections, Irwin wrote a series of articles about San Francisco's devastation that proved to be startlingly accurate. In 1906, Irwin joined *McClure's* as a "writing editor" but left after a year. Irwin, like many others, failed to get along with McClure. Irwin turned to free-lance and produced his magazine series on the American newspaper during this time. He also wrote a number of books. With the outbreak of the war in 1914, Irwin became a correspondent in Europe for *Collier's* and the *American* magazine. He took time out to serve with Herbert Hoover's Commission on Relief, but in 1915 returned to work as a war correspondent for the New York *Herald Tribune.* His excellent reporting and thwarting of censorship earned him plaudits as a first-rate correspondent, but had him barred from the front. Now reporting for the *Saturday Evening Post,* Irwin championed the League of Nations following the war, and his work was syndicated through NANA (North American Newspaper Alliance). He continued his magazine work and books. His deadline obituary of Herbert Hoover for the United Press led to one his best books, *Herbert Hoover: A Reminiscent Biography.* Irwin produced more than forty books, mostly factual and much of his fiction was based on the solid facts he gathered as a newsman. Books include: *The Next War, Propaganda and the News, The Making of a Reporter, The American Newspaper, Confessions of a Con Man.*

Marquis James (1891-1955) won two Pulitzer prizes after he gave up full-time journalism to write biographies. After a brief stay at Oklahoma Christian University James decided that newspaper experience would be a better education; he worked for the Enid (Ok.) *Eagle,* the Kansas City *Journal,* the St. Louis *Globe-Democrat,* and the New Orleans *Item.* In Chicago he held editorial positions with the *Tribune* and the *Daily Journal.* By 1916, James was a rewrite man with the New York *Tribune.* He saw service in France as a captain and after the war founded the *American Legion Monthly;* he was one of the original staff for the *New Yorker.* He gave up full-time journalism to write–biographies, for the most part, and for two of these he was awarded Pulitzer prizes, in 1930 and 1938. His dozen books include: *A History of the American Legion, The Raven, Andrew Jackson: Portrait of a President, Mr. Garner of Texas.*

Earl J. Johnson (1900-74) for thirty years directed the editorial operations of United Press International with 265 bureaus to 6,000 newspapers. He retired from U.P.I. (successor to United Press) in 1965. He quit high school at seventeen to take his first newspaper job with the Winfield (Kan.) *Courier.* Later, he attended the University of Kansas and served as a part-time correspondent for United Press and two Kansas City papers, the *Journal* and the *Post.* He joined United Press full-time in 1921 in its Chicago office and over the next ten years served there and in Cleveland and New York. In 1933 he took over UP's European office in Berlin; by 1935 he was made director of UP in New York. According to Johnson, "UP ran rings around the Associated Press" covering the coming of war in Europe.

Alva Johnston (1888-1950), with only a high school education, joined the Sacramento (Cal.) *Bee* and in 1912 moved to the *New York Times* until 1928. He won a Pulitzer prize for reporting in 1923. Johnston later joined the New York *Herald Tribune,* but left in 1932 to devote his time to magazine work. His major effort was with the *New Yorker,* where he produced more than seventy "Profiles," specializing in Hollywood figures. Books include *The Great Goldwyn, Wilson Mizner: The Legend of a Sport.*

Pauline Kael (1919-2001), one of the most-influential film critics of her time, won wide fame through her reviews for the *New Yorker,* from 1968-91. Motion pictures were her primary interest from an early age and her opinions were provocative and often passionate. Kael enrolled in the philosophy program at the University of California at Berkeley, planning to continue with law school. After school, for a time she wrote advertising copy and worked as a textbook writer. She never wrote criticism until she was thirty-five; her first review appeared in a local magazine, *City Lights,* and she later was in *Sight and Sound* and the *Partisan Review.* Her reviews were aired locally on KPFA and her program reviews for an art theater she managed led to magazine assignments. She was film critic for *Life* (1966). *McCall's* (1965-66) and the *New Republic* (1966-67). The *New Yorker* invited her to be a film critic with no restriction on topic and ample space (1968-79), and she joined the magazine after a brief interlude working in the film industry, from 1980-91. Her reviews, outspoken and opinionated, would infuriate or enchant readers–Kael was never dull. It was said of Kael when she retired in 1991 that she influenced a generation of imitators. Her books include: *I Lost it at the Movies, Kiss Kiss Bang Bang, Going Steady, Deeper Into Movies, When the Lights Go Down, Hooked, For Keeps.*

H(ans) V(on) Kaltenborn (1878-1963) was known to a generation as the broadcaster who was mimicked by President Harry S Truman for his on-air die-hard refusal to acknowledge the 1948 election results. Republican favorite Thomas E. Dewey was upset (according to opinion polls and experts) by Truman. Kaltenborn was one of broadcasting's pioneers and was known to million of listeners. His distinctive delivery, "the suave voice of doom," informed the public of his views–and he always had views, sometimes controversial–on the meaning of the news. His beginning was in print journalism; he started with the Merrill (Wis.) *Advocate* and joined the Brooklyn *Eagle* in 1902. He left to get an education at Harvard and returned to the *Eagle* in 1910. He made his first radio broadcast in 1922 for WEAF, New York, and left newspapering for full-time radio in 1930, Kaltenborn covered the Spanish Civil War and made a notable contribution covering the Munich crisis. He joined NBC in 1940 and continued until 1953. Books include: *We Look at the World, Kaltenborn Edits the News, Fifty Fabulous Years.*

George S. Kaufman (1887-1961), one of America's outstanding playwrights–he won two Pulitzer prizes for drama–began his career with a solid newspaper background. A dour eccentric, Kaufman excelled at humor and satire. From 1921 through 1941, he had a yearly hit on Broadway, a number of which are classics of theater: "Of Thee I Sing," "The Man Who Came to Dinner," and "You Can't Take It With You." After public schools in Pittsburgh and Paterson, N.J., he studied law for three months, but quit to become a ribbon salesman. He was a contributor of humorous quips to F.P.A.'s column in the New York *Mail* and Adams helped him get his first job in 1912 as a humor columnist on the Washington *Times.* Fired after a year, Adams arranged for Kaufman to take over his column when FPA moved to the *Tribune.* When Kaufman lost that post in 1915, FPA secured a job for him as an assistant drama critic on the *Tribune,* where he was an assistant to Heywood Broun. Kaufman joined the *New York Times* as a drama reporter; he eventually became drama editor, succeeding Alexander Woollcott and remained with the *Times* until 1930. He began writing for the Broadway stage in 1921 and collaborated with a number of people, including Edna Ferber, Marc Connelly, and Moss Hart. Kaufman's well-known work includes the Marx Brothers' "Coconuts," "Merton of the Movies," "Dinner at Eight," and "Once in a Lifetime." Kaufman also directed a number of productions.

[James] Murray Kempton (1917-97), an even-handed ideologue, was one of the best writers to appear in American newspapers in the later twentieth-century–with ornate, even baroque, but always enlightening prose. His 1985 Pulitzer prize citation described him as "witty and insightful." After college he became a labor organizer and publisher for the *American Labor Party.* He joined the New York *Post* in 1941, interrupted by wartime military service, and became the *Post's* labor editor in 1949. Kempton was a columnist for the *New Republic* and the New York *World-Telegram* (1964-66), rejoined the *Post* (1966-69), and finally was with New York *Newsday* from

1961 until his death. Books include: *Part of Our Time; Some Ruins and Monuments of the Thirties; America Comes of Middle Age; Columns, Rebellions, Perversities and Main Events.*

Frank R. Kent (1877-1958) for more than fifty years reported American politics honestly and with outspoken candor. Practically his entire career was with the Baltimore *Sunpapers.* After a brief apprenticeship in 1889 with the Columbus (Ga.) *Enquirer-Sun,* he joined the Baltimore *Sun* in 1900, and for the next fifty-eight years was an astute political reporter. Kent helped make the *Sun* become a newspaper of national stature. Kent was one of the first to regularly write reviews and comments that dealt exclusively with politics. In 1910 he became Washington bureau chief; by 1911 he was managing editor of the *Sun* and the *Evening Sun,* a post he held until 1921. In 1922 Kent began his political column, "The Great Game of Politics," which was syndicated to 200 newspapers and continued until his death. He was a reporter who knew how politics worked, from the precinct clubhouse to the White House in an era when the party organization meant something. Kent was a writer of conservative opinion (for years, however, he wrote anonymously as T.R.B. for the liberal *New Republic*), and a man of unquestioned integrity. His books include *The Great Game of Politics; The Democratic Party, A History; Without Gloves; The Sunpapers of Baltimore; Without Grease.*

James J. Kilpatrick (1920-) is a respected conservative columnist, and one of the most literate. He began as a reporter for the Richmond (Va.) *News-Leader* in 1941 and in 1949 succeeded Douglas Southall Freeman as editorial page editor. He originated his column, "A Conservative View," in 1964, and began "The Writer's Art" in 1981. His book of the same name is used by students to advantage. (combined with Strunk and White's *The Elements of Style,* and a brain, promising students can skip college writing courses). Another column, "Covering the Courts," began in 1992, and is syndicated to more than 200 newspapers. Kilpatrick appeared regularly on CBS's "Sixty Minutes" and NBC's "Meet the Press." His dozen books include: *Fine Print, The Foxes Union, The Smut Peddlers, Conversations on Virginia, The Writer's Art, The Ear is Human.*

Rollin Kirby (1875-1952) was the first cartoonist to win three Pulitzer prizes (in 1922, 1925 amd 1929) and the only individual to do so in a span of seven years. Kirby was America's preeminent editorial cartoonist in the 1920s. At the outset of his career, in 1901 his work had appeared in several national magazines. He joined the New York *Mail* in 1911 and a year later moved to the New York *Sun.* His work flourished in the New York *World* from 1913 until its demise in 1931. He created "Mr. Dry," the universal symbol of prohibition, and was a relentless foe of the Ku Klux Klan and Tammany Hall. When the *World* folded, Kirby moved to the *World-*

Telegram until 1939, when he joined the New York *Post,* a more liberal newspaper, until 1942. He continued cartoon work for *Look* magazine and the *New York Times* magazine until his death in 1952. Walter Lippmann wrote the introduction to his book, *A Cartoon History of the Nineteen Twenties.*

Arthur Krock (1886-1974) for thirty-one years served as Washington bureau chief for the *New York Times* and wrote the politically influential column "In the Nation." His early years were spent with Louisville (Ky.) newspapers and later with the New York *World* until 1927, when Walter Lippmann banished Krock for his free-lance public relations "counseling" work conducted on the premises. The two men harbored a mutual dislike thereafter. Krock was awarded two Pulitzer prizes for outstanding reporting and the use of sources. Books include: *In the Nation 1932-1966, Memoirs: Sixty Years in the Firing Line.*

Ring (Ringgold Wilmer) Lardner (1885-1933), newspaper columnist and author–a writer of uncommon merit–is virtually ignored by serious critics, as H.L. Mencken predicted seventy years ago. Lardner managed to capture the buffoonery of sports and with savage wit the ordinariness of society's boors. After a variety of odd jobs, Lardner became a reporter for the South Bend (Ind.) *Times.* His ability to report baseball games beyond the score card earned him a job with the Chicago *Inter-Ocean* in 1907. Later that year, he joined the Chicago *Examiner.* He moved again, to the *Tribune,* from 1908-10. The next year, he held a series of jobs: with the *Sporting News* as managing editor; with the Boston *Herald;* and finally, back to Chicago with the *Examiner.* He rejoined the *Tribune* to write a column, "In the Wake of the News," for the next six years. Meanwhile, Lardner had been submitting baseball stories to the *Saturday Evening Post* and these proved to be widely popular; his earnings jumped from $250 to $1,500 for each story. A number of books drawn from these stories followed, and he left the *Tribune* to write a syndicated column for the Bell Syndicate. During the war years, Lardner served as a war correspondent for *Collier's.* The baseball "Black Sox" scandal turned Lardner against the game, no longer humorous with lovable louts. For the next years Lardner wrote for the Ziegfeld Follies, the *Saturday Evening Post* and other magazines, and wrote a failed play, "Elmer, the Great" (with George M. Cohan) that became a successful motion picture. In 1930, Lardner signed to write a column for the New York *Telegraph* and another column for the Bell Syndicate. During his last illness, Lardner wrote a column of radio criticism for the *New Yorker* that was concerned with the off-color content of programs; he suggested radio censorship. First and last, Lardner saw himself as a newspaperman, and so he was–with a literary legacy that should not be forgotten. Books include: *You Know Me, Al; Shut Up, He Explained; The Love Nest and Other Stories; The Big Town; Lose With a Smile.*

David Lawrence (1888-1973) was a reporter, columnist, and most notably, founder of the weekly news magazine *U.S. News & World Report.* He began his career in high school selling photographs to the Buffalo *Express,* went on to Princeton and earned his way working for the Associated Press. He scored a beat with the first report of President Grover Cleveland's death. After graduation he was assigned to the Washington bureau of AP, where he covered the Mexican War; then his link to his former college president enabled him access to President Woodrow Wilson. In 1915 he joined the Washington bureau of the New York *Evening Post.* In 1919, Lawrence organized his own syndicate, the Consolidated Press Association. In 1926 he launched a newspaper, the *United States Daily News,* that reached a peak circulation of 40,000 by 1930. Lawrence also conducted a Sunday morning radio program, "Our Government," for NBC from 1929-33. With a strong commercial bent, Lawrence sold off his features, reorganized his newspaper into a weekly and established a Bureau of National Affairs to sell features to news outlets. Lawrence was a strong anti-New Deal proponent, as his books and column made clear. In 1940, he changed the *News* format into a weekly magazine; founded in 1945 a new magazine, *World Report,* focusing on international affairs. He merged the two publications in 1947. Weekly circulation at the time of his death was 1.4 million, and his column, with his conservative view, appeared regularly until his death. Lawrence was awarded the Medal of Freedom in 1970. Books include: *The True Story of Woodrow Wilson, Beyond the New Deal, Nine Honest Men, Diary of a Washington Correspondent.*

A(bbott) J(oseph) Liebling (1904-63) was a preeminent critic of the press. His newspaper career began with the *New York Times* after he was expelled from Dartmouth College. Fired by the *Times* for adding fictional names to his sports stories, Liebling joined the New York *World* and when it folded, joined the *World-Telegram.* He left in 1935 for the *New Yorker* until his death in 1963. Liebling wrote a number of "Profiles" and covered the European theater of war as an able correspondent. After the war, he convinced editor Harold Ross to revive Robert Benchley's "Wayward Press" series. Liebling's press criticism was acerbic, accurate, and angry–absent the whimsy and humor of Benchley–distinguished by factual documentation, and written with meticulous attention. Books include: *The Road Back to Paris, Normandy Revisited, The Wayward Pressman, The Press, The Sweet Science, Back Where I Come From.*

Walter Lippmann (1889-1976), an intellectual titan among American newspapermen during two-thirds of the twentieth century, distinguished himself in other fields as well. No one is likely to play a similar role in American journalism. A number of his books are classics and his influence affected nations and their leaders. Lippmann's was a distinguished class at

Harvard: classmates included Robert Benchley, John Reed, T.S. Eliot, and Heywood Broun. None was more distinguished than Lippmann; he was founder and president of the Harvard Socialist Club and his writing for the *Harvard Illustrated Review* brought him to the attention of William James. Lippmann was offered a post as assistant to George Santayana after graduation, but an academic career held little interest for him. He served a short while with the *Boston Common* before joining Lincoln Steffens' *Everybody's* magazine. In 1910, he joined the administration of Socialist George Lunn, mayor of Schenectady, briefly before he took time out to produce two books: *A Preface to Politics* and *Drift and Mastery*. This work led to an invitation in 1913 from Herbert Croly to be an editor for the *New Republic,* a new magazine that was one of the early supporters of Woodrow Wilson. Lippmann took a leave of absence during the war years to serve in Wilson's administration. First, he was an assistant to Secretary of War Newton D. Baker, then was invited to serve as secretary to the Inquiry, a top-secret planning group for post-war peace efforts. Lippmann became a captain in the U.S.Army in 1918, and worked on propaganda missions to help promote President Wilson's "Fourteen Points" peace plan. After his wartime service, Lippmann returned to the *New Republic* and also served as a correspondent for the *Manchester Guardian*. He left the *New Republic* in 1921, to devote time to books, but found a writing outlet with *Vanity Fair*. By 1922, Lippmann accepted an offer from Herbert Bayard Swope to become editor of the New York *World,* the same year his classic *Public Opinion* was published. During his time with the *World,* Lippmann continued to publish a series of intellectually challenging books that questioned American values and its system of government. Lippmann's outlook was unquestionably elitist and he was no academic; for those reasons his work sometimes is devalued today. When the *World* ended, Lippmann accepted an offer from the New York *Herald Tribune* and began his column, "Today and Tomorrow." It ran for the next forty years. Lippmann joined the *Washington Post* in 1962, and continued when he wrote for *Newsweek* the next year. His last column appeared in January 1971. Lippmann, a felicitous writer who could penetrate the thickets of the complexities of a changing world in terms understatable, crafted his thoughts in a superb literary style. His books and newspaper commentary influenced the leaders of nations and the common reader. Lippmann exemplified the search for truth and persistently sought that vision. Other books include: *Essays in the Public Philosophy, Men of Destiny, The Good Society, The Phantom Public, Liberty and the News.*

Andy (Isabel Ann) Logan (1920-2000) was one of the first women to write for the *New Yorker's* "Talk of the Town" department. Logan made her reputation as a knowledgeable reporter covering the "About City Hall,"department for the magazine, beginning in 1969 and continuing until her death. Logan's perceptive political reporting and analysis contained irony and wit, and often portrayed the comic side of municipal events and its political people. She joined the *New Yorker* in 1942 after graduating from Swarthmore (she adopted her name in honor of E.B. White). As an undergraduate, Logan won an O. Henry Award in 1941 for her first short story. Logan's reporting often made her unpopular with city officials, a badge of honor for any respectable journalist. Books include: *Against the Evidence, The Man Who Robbed the Robber Barons.*

Henry R. Luce (1898-1967), with Briton Hadden, created in 1923, *Time, the Weekly News-Magazine.* In the early years, Luce was in charge of the business side; Hadden gave *Time* its unique voice, later called "Timespeak." Hadden's early death left Luce with total ownership and complete control, and he built a media empire, Time Inc. Luce, born in China, the son of a missionary, received an excellent education: Hotchkiss School, Yale College, and Oxford University. While preparing plans for his magazine, Luce worked for a year as a newspaperman for the Baltimore *News* in 1922, then with financing largely from his colleagues at Yale, he launched his magazine in 1923. Its distinctive style won readers and it soon made money. Luce added to his growing empire: *Literary Review* in 1924; in 1929, his magazine about business for businessmen, *Fortune;* in 1931, he began "The March of Time" radio programs to boost the sales of his magazine–the motion picture short subjects began in 1935. Luce established the first picture magazine. *Life* was a weekly journal of photojournalism that depicted events in America and abroad. It became a major element in creating Time Inc. as a lucrative media empire that influenced readers, national decision-makers, and world leaders. In 1954 *Sports Illustrated,* another Luce enterprise, was created to take advantage of the public's leisure time and Luce nursed it through five lean years before it turned a profit. After Luce's death, Time Inc. created *People* and *Money,* both profitable, popular magazines aimed at the middle-class market. Henry Luce exercised a tight and continuing editorial control over the content of his magazines. The "news" in *Time* and later *Life* was truth, as interpreted by Luce; fact seldom interfered with the reportage as Luce wanted it published. His apologia for the corrupt Chinese government is an outstanding example. For all that, Luce built a formidable and powerful media empire. After his death, the heirs to Time Inc., for mercenary reasons, merged with Warner Communications and Time-Warner was run by Warner people. That entity was eventually merged into AOL Time Warner, the nation's largest media conglomerate. Magazines are less than one-quarter of the corporate entity; *Life* is gone, *Time* is just another magazine, and it is difficult for a modern generation to appreciate the influence these two publications had on the daily lives of Americans. The "Jesuit persuader," as Luce described himself, left two books: *The American Century, The Ideas of Henry Luce.*

Peter Maas (1929-2001), one of the so-called "new wave" journalists–others were people such as Jimmy Breslin, Tom Wolfe, and Hunter Thompson–chronicled the life and times of the underworld and the police. He wrote of the incorruptible New York policeman, Frank Serpico, and the exploits of the Mafia's Joe Vallachi. Maas's investigative news reporting reflected the zest of fiction writing, a narrow line frequently overstepped in modern news writing by other less-skilled writers. Maas began his journalism career while still a student at Duke University; he obtained an interview with labor leader Walter Reuther, and sold it to the Associated Press for $100. He moved to the New York *Herald Tribune* in Paris before joining *Collier's* in 1955. He also wrote for *Look, New York,* and the *Saturday Evening Post.* His work was distinctive for its thorough research and documentation. Maas' more than a dozen books include: *The Vallachi Papers, Serpico, Manhunt, The King of Gypsies, Marie: A True Story, Made in America.*

S(amuel) S(idney) McClure (1857-1949) deserves singular credit for his sponsorship and development of muckraking; *McClure's Magazine* was its leading exponent. McClure was an idea man, an organizer. Even before he graduated from Knox College in 1874, he formed a syndicate–the Western College Associated Press–and launched a bicycling magazine, the *Wheeler.* In 1887 he canvassed Europe in search of writing talent; McClure never ceased to seek and attract talented writers. He established *McClure's* in 1893, and by 1903 muckraking was a major element of that publication with the best talent McClure could assemble: Ida Tarbell, Lincoln Steffens, Roy Stannard Baker, Willa Cather, John Mitchell, and Samuel Hopkins Adams were on his staff. McClure claimed that "bad business practices" lost him his magazine in 1912. That was true, but other factors contributed. Whatever the reasons, the magazine and muckraking were finished. McClure's contribution cannot be questioned; he stimulated writers to chronicle the ills of American society and was one of the most influential editors of American journalism. In 1944 McClure was awarded the gold medal Order of Merit by the National Institute of Arts and Letters. His books include his autobiography (ghostwritten by Willa Cather), *My Autobiography,* and *Obstacles to Peace.*

Anne O'Hare McCormick (1882-1954) was a foreign correspondent and the first woman to serve on the editorial board of the *New York Times.* She was one of the few to credit Mussolini's rise as a danger when others were dismissing him as a street thug. Her thrice-weekly column, "Abroad," in the *Times,* and her editorials were distinguished by clear and precise analysis; she was awarded a Pulitzer prize in 1937. Her only journalism training before joining the *Times* in 1922 was as associate editor of the weekly *Catholic Universe Bulletin.* She submitted free-lance articles to the *Times* and before a trip to Europe in 1921, asked Carr V. Van Anda, managing editor, if she could submit articles. She did and she was hired. In 1936, she joined the editorial staff, the first woman to have that post. Her work won her a number of journalistic and civic awards. Book: *The Hammer and the Scythe.*

Robert Rutherford McCormick (1880-1955), who wished always to be addressed as "Colonel," developed a great newspaper, the Chicago *Tribune,* into a newspaper empire. McCormick inherited wealth. When he gained formal control of the family-owned *Tribune* in 1914–his earlier activities had been in Chicago public service–he began to assemble people–an able staff, well-paid and competent–and the properties, timberland for pulp paper resources and facilities for hydroelectric power. The *Tribune* entered radio in 1931, and in 1939 McCormick assembled a staff of able foreign correspondents. The eccentric (if not slightly mad) publisher took a close and personal interest in building his overseas bureaus. Colonel McCormick, who served in World War I, was a zealot, an isolationist who deemed anyone who opposed his ideas unpatriotic. He was a vehement foe of President Franklin Roosevelt, and felt that the safety of the Republic lay with the Republican Party. He spread that doctrine through his communication empire that includes newspapers nationwide, radio, television, and a vast news-feature syndicate. The syndicate is thriving and recent newspapers acquisitions include the Baltimore *Sun* and the Times-Mirror flagship newspaper, the *Los Angles Times.* McCormick was controversial, unquestionably, but a major influence on twentieth century journalism, even if the *Tribune* was not "the world's greatest newspaper," as he claimed it to be through his lifetime.

John Tinney McCutcheon (1870-1949) began as an editorial cartoonist for the Chicago *News* in 1889, then joined the Chicago *Tribune* shortly thereafter and remained for the next forty years. His editorial cartoons appeared on the front page of the *Tribune* and were often colorized. His cartoon art illustrated many books, including those of popular columnist George Ade. McCutcheon was an adventurer who served with Admiral George Dewey at Manila Bay during the Spanish-American War, became a war correspondent with General Pershing during the Mexican War in 1916, served as a European correspondent during the Great War, and hunted big game with Theodore Roosevelt in Africa. He was among the first party to cross the Gobi Desert in an automobile. His cartoon fame came from his nostalgic art that depicted homey Midwestern sentiments of a by-gone era. His famous "Injun Summer" cartoon, first published in 1907, was reprinted annually by the *Tribune* for four decades. Ironically, his Pulitzer prize-winning cartoon was an acerbic, atypical commentary on the Great Depression. A museum honors his memory in Chicago. Books include: *Drawn from Memory, The Mysterious Stranger and Other Cartoons.*

Bernarr McFadden (Bernard Adolphus MacFadden) [at times Macfadden–he used several versions during his lifetime] (1868-1955) is remembered primarily as a physical culture enthusiast–a "health nut" to some–but he made a major contribution to American journalism. McFadden founded the New York *Evening Graphic.* The tabloid newspaper was not the pornographic sheet decried by many today. The *Graphic* was an innovative experiment; it used photographs (often of dubious veracity) freely but avoided gossip, curbed the excesses of Walter Winchell, and printed no advertisements, claiming this allowed editorial freedom. McFadden began the magazine *Physical Culture* and was one of the first to expose the dangers of smoking and tobacco, the ills of sugar, and poor eating habits. Many "victims" of cigarette smoking would be well-advised to read his many books, especially, *Truth About Tobacco,* Others of his dozen books: *The Miracle of Milk, Home Health Manual.*

William O. McGeehan (1879-1933) was a popular sportswriter who helped create the myth of Tex Rickard, the sports promoter. Young McGeehan was a volunteer in the Spanish-American War with the First California brigade. After that experience, he joined the San Francisco *Call* as a reporter in 1901, and served as city editor and managing editor of the San Francisco *Post* until he joined the New York *Tribune* in 1915. He served in the A.E.F. as an infantryman from 1917-18, and worked as a sports editor from 1922 until his death. McGeehan was typical of the hometown "cheerleader" type sportswriter found in many newspapers today.

Ralph (Emerson) McGill (1898-1969), who was awarded a Pulitzer prize in 1959, was a life-long proponent of civil rights, a crusading columnist and publisher of the *Atlanta Constitution.* He was often referred to "as the conscience of the South." McGill believed that "newspapers must come down and live with the people...." He attended Vanderbilt University, interrupted by service in the Marine Corps. He left college before graduating in 1922 and work with the Nashville (Tenn.) *Banner,* as a reporter and sportswriter. He joined the *Constitution* in 1929 as sports editor. In 1937 he won a fellowship to travel in Europe and on his return to Atlanta, was named executive editor and, in 1942, editor of the *Constitution.* In 1960 he became publisher and continued his front-page signed column. In 1964 he was awarded the Presidential Medal of Freedom. Books: *The South and the Southerner.*

Jeff (Jeffrey) MacNelly (1947-2000) was one of only five cartoonists to win three Pulitzer prizes–in 1971, 1978 and 1985. A self-professed conservative in a field dominated by liberal-leaning colleagues, MacNelly was one of America's most influential and imitated, cartoonists; his work was widely syndicated. In addition to his editorial work, MacNelly drew a popular comic strip, "Shoe," syndicated to more than 1,000 newspapers. (After MacNelly's death, Tribune Media Services continued the strip with Chris Cassalt and Gary Brookins.) MacNelly dropped out of college (University of North Carolina) to work for a local Chapel Hill newspaper before joining the Richmond *News-Leader* in 1970. He later joined the Chicago *Tribune.* MacNelly, in the age of Internet, disapproved of computer cartoons and television, preferring the newspaper page exclusively. Books include *Shoe, MacNelly, The Pulitzer Prize-Winning Cartoonist.*

Carey McWilliams (1905-80) was for twenty years editor of the *Nation,* a liberal magazine, the contents of which reflected his views as a crusader for the underprivileged. Trained in law at the University of Southern California, McWilliams served as Commissioner of Immigration and Housing. After he lost this post, he moved to New York and wrote for the *New Republic* and the liberal newspaper *PM.* He became editor of the *Nation* in 1955 until his retirement in 1975. He continued with regular weekly contributions until his death. McWilliams made many powerful enemies as he fought for government reform and opposed the hysteria of the McCarthy movement. His books include: *Factories in the Field, What About Our Japanese Americans?, A Mask for Privilege: Anti-Semitism in America, Brothers Under the Skin: Witch Hunt, The Education of Carey McWilliams.*

William Manchester (1922-) wrote his master's thesis (University of Missouri) on H.L. Mencken and the Sage of Baltimore arranged a job for him on the Baltimore *Evening Sun.* The result was an excellent biography of HLM, *Disturber of the Peace.* Manchester's undergraduate education at the University of Massachusetts was interrupted by World War II; he enlisted in the Marine Corps, and saw service in the South Pacific. He was awarded a Purple Heart for action at Okinawa. The G.I. Bill of Rights helped with his education after the war. At the *Evening Sun* after his work with Mencken was complete, Manchester served as a foreign correspondent in India and Vietnam. His several novels met with limited success. In 1955 Manchester accepted a position as managing editor of the Wesleyan University Press. His *Death of a President* generated controversy when Mrs. Kennedy objected to portions of the text, but *Look* magazine published it in serial form and the book followed with some deletions and modifications. After Manchester left newspaper work, he distinguished himself with a number of outstanding biographies. After completing two volumes of his planned trilogy of Winston Churchill, ill-health prevented completion. His earlier novels, *City of Anger* and *The Long Gainer,* depicting the corruption of Baltimore politics and the football-happy president of a state university, were less successful. Other books include: *Portrait of a President, American Caesar: Douglas MacArthur, The Last Lion: William Spencer Churchill, The Arms of Krupp, Goodbye Darkness.*

William d'Alton Mann (1839-1920) was the nefarious publisher of *Town Topics,* whose column, "Saunterings," was allegedly used to blackmail New York's society elite. *Collier's Weekly,* and newspapers including the *World,* exposed Mann's scheme to elicit funds–via advertisements, stock sales, or gift "loans." Mann was never indicted; a judge and the district attorney were on his payroll. The Colonel, as he liked to be called, was also proprietor of the *Smart Set* (1900-11), the magazine that employed H.L. Mencken and George Jean Nathan as editors. Mann had a sketchy background; his education, if any, is unknown. Mann served as a Union officer during the Civil War and saw action at Bull Run and Gettysburg, serving with General George A. Custer. His patent for cavalry accouterments earned him $50,000 in 1863 and the next year he hatched an oil scheme on worthless land. Swindled investors brought suit, but Mann escaped conviction. He next surfaced as a federal revenue officer in Mobile, Ala. His career as a carpetbagger was successful; by 1866, Mann was owner and publisher of the Mobile *Register,* successor to the four newspapers closed down for tax arrears. Mann was accused but never indicted for "tax diversion." Mann had $100,000 to invest in a cotton seed refinery and railroad speculation. Mann's patent for a railroad "boudier car" brought few sales but his million dollar stock scheme enabled him to purchase *Town Topics* in 1891. His "Saunterings" column was a popular feature and Mann prospered. In 1900 Mann purchased the *Smart Set* and coined its motto, "The magazine of Cleverness" and designed its distinctive cover logo with the double S swath. He sold the magazine to John Adam Thayer in 1911 for $100,000. Mann also published *Tales from Town Topics, Tom Watson's Magazine, Tales,* and *Transatlantic Tales.* After Mann's death, *Town Topics* was sold to Hearst in 1930 and ended its life as the title for a column in the New York *Journal-American.* Colonel Mann's enterprise paved the way for the gossip fare focused on society's leaders that pervades much of modern media.

Don (Donald Robert Perry) Marquis (1878-1937), for all his fame as a newspaper columnist, Broadway playwright, and Hollywood screenwriter, is destined to be remembered, as he feared, as the creator of, in his own words, "that goddamned cockroach." That roach was the inimitable Archy, denizen of the after dark *Sun* newsroom who left typewritten messages (lowercase only) by slamming his head against the keys of a typewriter. Marquis had little college, only one semester at Knox College in 1894 when a football scholarship was not forthcoming. He worked at odd jobs until a brief political appointment landed him a job with the Census Bureau in Washington, in 1900. From 1902-07, he worked at various newspapers in Washington, Philadelphia, and Atlanta. He enjoyed brief success at the Atlanta *News* and later the Atlanta *Journal,* trying to establish a column. In 1907, Marquis found some stability with the *Uncle Remus' Magazine,* but after Joel Chandler Harris's death, Marquis left when the magazine folded.

He free-lanced in New York City until he joined the *Sun* and began, the "Sun Dial" column. Archy appeared in March 1916, joining a cast of other characters, but Archy and his cat friend, Mehitabel, became reader favorites. Archy expounded on everything from religion and politics to philosophy and metaphysics. Marquis was writing books, Broadway plays, and magazine free-lance. Marquis moved to the New York *Herald Tribune* in 1922 and his column became "The Lantern." He bought out his contract in 1925 to devote full time to playwriting, books, and Hollywood screen writing. One reason for leaving newspaper work was because Marquis agonized over the production of his column and used few contributions to fill the space. He envied Heywood Broun, who could bat out a column in a hour. Away from newspaper work, Marquis prospered over the next several years, but lost most of his money backing his own play (always a gamble for any writer and especially for a religious allegory). "The Dark Hours" held an obscure, devoutly Roman Catholic message. Most of his screen work is forgotten, few of his books retain the humor of the time that sustained them, but Archy lives on, as Marquis feared. Books include *Archy and Mehitabel, Revolt of the Oyster The Life and Times of Archy and Mehitabel, The Old Soak, A Variety of People.*

Abe (Frank McKinney) Martin (1868-1930) wrote the long-running syndicated "Abe Martin's Almanac" that originated in the Indianapolis (Ind.) *News.* Abe Martin imparted down-home Hoosier observations, a feature that perpetuated the American rural myth long after it disappeared. Books include: *Abe Martin, Hoss Sense and Nonsense, Abe Martin's Town Pump.*

H[enry] L[ouis] Mencken (1880-1956), the Baltimore newspaperman who Walter Lippmann described in 1925 as "the most powerful personal influence on this whole generation of educated people," remains one of the most quoted (if largely unread) individuals. Mencken's influence was profound on literary taste in mid-century American; his war against Puritanism and censorship–and his battles for First Amendment rights should have earned him the profound gratitude of the Fourth Estate. It did not. Nor is any journalism school likely to bear his name—he attacked academic frauds relentlessly. His outspoken, sometimes harsh assessment of "idiots and charlatans," his incessant, intemperate descriptions of people as "boobs" infuriated readers in his time and today stirs the enmity of the politically correct. Mencken decided to forego college, even with the grades and financial resources to do so. After a brief foray into his father's tobacco business, Mencken went to work for the Baltimore *Evening Herald* in 1903 as a reporter and rose to managing editor two years later. Hardworking, Mencken wrote books and contributed to a number of magazines. When the *Herald* folded in 1906, Mencken joined the Baltimore *Sunpapers,* an association that was to last for the next fifty years. In 1908, he became book review editor for the *Smart Set,* but maintained his headquarters from Baltimore, a practice he followed for the rest of his life. His review page helped make the *Smart Set* a literary attack dog. By 1910, Mencken was associate editor of the *Evening Sun* and began his "Free Lance" column the next year. He targeted every foible and fatuous practice he could detect in the body politic. He was named co-editor (with George Jean Nathan) of the *Smart Set* in 1914 and the magazine became noticed for its content. In 1915 *Sunpapers* management canceled the "Free Lance" for its vitriolic anti-British content and Mencken found an outlet in the New York *Evening Mail* that continued until 1918. During the war years, books occupied Mencken capped with *The American Language* in 1919, a monumental contribution that earned him literary and academic plaudits. He rejoined the *Sunpapers* and began his "Monday Articles" column in 1920. Three years later he severed his relations with the *Smart Set,* and in 1924 launched the *American Mercury* that quickly established itself as a major critical voice in American letters. The same year Mencken began a series of columns for the Chicago *Tribune* that continued through 1928. Mencken was the major instigator of the hullaboo surrounding the famous Scopes "Monkey Trial"; he was the ringmaster of that media circus and earned the enmity of the South for attacking its anti-Darwinian views. In his columns and through the pages of the *Mercury,* Mencken continued his war on the Puritan influence in literature and American life. He resigned his post with the *Mercury* in late 1933; the Great Depression and economic problems prompted his departure. More important, the public grew weary of Mencken's anti-New Deal assaults. Unquestionably, the *American Mercury* lost something after Nathan left Mencken in full charge. The magazine was Mencken's no matter who wrote for its pages; quite simply, he lost his audience. Books primarily occupied Mencken, except for one brief episode as editorial page editor of the *Evening Sun* in 1938. A charming series of articles in the *New Yorker* became his *Days* book trilogy. His last hurrah was staged at the presidential nominating conventions of 1948, before a massive stroke silenced him until his death in 1956. Mencken's more than thirty books also include: *Notes on Democracy, Prejudices* [a series], *In Defense of Women, Damn! A Book of Calumny, A Book of Burlesques, Happy Days, Newspaper Days, Heathen Days.*

Frank A. Munsey (1854-1925) earned his early fame with magazines. He originated the *Golden Argosy,* a boy's publication (eventually it became a men's magazine, *Argosy*), and the *Puritan.* He later found success with *Munsey's Magazine* in the 1880s, opening the era of mass-circulation magazines. He increased sales ten-fold, to one million. No journalist, Munsey nevertheless wrote a number of serials for his magazines. His primary concern, however, was to make money. By the 1900s, Munsey turned to newspapers; he bought, merged and sold some seventeen newspapers with little thought to the intrinsic values of journalism. Munsey bought newspapers to improve journalism, he explained: "...there is no greater menace to a community than newspapers that are struggling to keep alive in an overcrowded newspaper field." Despite his unctuous defense of this "public service," critics thought otherwise. Upon Munsey's death, the usually gentle William Allen White commented editorially in the Emporia (Kansas) *Gazette* that Munsey "contributed to journalism of his day the talent of a meat-packer, the morals of a money-changer and the manners of an undertaker." Munsey was not a pleasant man to many, but his major contribution cannot be dismissed. He made clear the harsh reality that newspaper publishing is an industry–big business and not a crusading venture to do good–a lesson still lacking in many newsrooms and journalism classes.

Edward [Egbert] R(oscoe) Murrow (1908-65), unquestionably the major presence in radio (and television, which he disliked) in twentieth-century America, set standards for broadcast journalism that are rarely met and seldom exceeded. Murrow, with a compelling voice and acute news sense, also assembled a distinguished team of correspondents that made CBS radio a preeminent organization. Murrow, a speech major at Washington State, joined CBS's "Radio of the Air" in 1930 and was in Europe at the outbreak of war. His on-the-scene broadcasts of the London blitz earned him an assignment to hire a radio news team; it was one of the best aggregations of adept and literate reporters ever assembled. "Murrow's Boys" became the stuff of legend. After the war, Murrow returned as a vice president of CBS Public Affairs. In 1947, he began his program, "Edward R. Murrow and the News." He moved into television reluctantly, but his "See It Now" and "CBS Reports" programs set standards for excellence. Murrow's power and prestige brought about his downfall; CBS owner William Paley, alarmed over Murrow's stand on controversial issues, felt Morrow was a threat to network dominance. News took a backseat at CBS. Murrow took a "leave of absence" and accepted President John F. Kennedy's invitation to head the USIA. Ill health forced Murrow to resign in 1964. Murrow was a significant influence in broadcast journalism–for his integrity and standards of excellence. Murrow is the measure by which electronic news reporting is judged: few practitioners meet his standards. Book: *In Search of Light: The Broadcasts of Edward R. Murrow, 1938-1961.*

George Jean Nathan (1882-1958), long associated with H.L. Mencken's magazines–the *Smart Set* and the *American Mercury*–was one of the most influential forces in the transformation of American theater in the early twentieth century. After graduating from Cornell University and study at the University of Bologna, Nathan began as back-up drama critic for the New York *Herald* (1904-06). Other work included: drama critic and associate editor, *Bohemian Magazine; Burr McIntosh Monthly* (1908); drama critic for the Philadelphia *North American,* the Cleveland *Leader,* and McClure's Syndicate. Nathan also served as drama critic for *Puck* (1915-16). He was a drama critic for the *Smart Set* from 1908 and assumed the editorship with Mencken in 1914. He and Mencken together wrote articles on American culture as Owen Hatteras (Nathan primarily on the arts and theater). Later he joined Mencken briefly as an editor with the *American Mercury,* but Mencken wanted more politics and less theater, hastening Nathan's departure. In 1932. with several leading writers, Nathan founded the *American Spectator.* For more than fifty years Nathan was a force in the theater world (it was said that a bad review from Nathan could close a show overnight). Nathan wrote more than forty books and published for almost a decade the *Annual Theater Book.* Other works include: *Art of the Night, Comedians All, Materia Critica, The Popular Theater, The World of Falsface.*

Allen H. (Al) Neuharth (1927-), a self-described S.O.B., and he should know, originated a newspaper suited to twentieth-century tastes. The "product" was *USA Today.* In essence, *USA Today* is a national newspaper, with brief, pithy, up-beat stories tailored to hold the limited attention-span of readers in a hurry; in short, the television screen adopted to the printed page. Fred Friendly, chief of CBS News, described the newspaper accurately as "television to wrap fish in." Nevertheless, Neuharth's innovations have proved to be successful and are now imitated widely. For example, weather news, once summarized in a few lines on the upper-ear front page, is in *USA Today,* a full page, four color display of maps and forecasts featuring major regions and cities, and many newspapers have adapted this format. Neuharth's beginnings were modest. After service in World War II in Europe with General George Patton's Third Army, and later in the Pacific Theater, Neuharth attended the University of South Dakota on the G.I. Bill and became an active campus leader as a sportswriter and editor of the school paper, *Volante.* After graduation, Neuharth undertook a learning interlude to work as an Associated Press sportswriter. Neuharth and a college colleague launched a sports publishing venture, *SoDak Sports.* When the venture folded after two years, Neuharth set his sights on Florida. He ended up at the *Miami Herald,* a newspaper he decided could use help. Success as a reporter, editor and Washington bureau chief, resulted in an assignment for the Knight chain as a management troubleshooter with the Detroit *Free Press.* An offer from Gannett Newspapers led to a position as general manager in Rochester, New York. Neuharth recognized the rich opportunities for exploitation of the space-age Florida prospects with the founding of *Florida Today,* geared to the Space Coast audience. After he eventually won control of Gannett, he introduced *USA Today* in 1982 and made it a paying enterprise through adroit marketing–free copies at every airport, for example. Book: *Confessions of an S.O.B.*

M(orton) W(illiams) Newman (1917-2001), a Chicago newsman, reported all the big stories–race relations, the Mob, and city corruption–for Chicago newspapers, the *Daily News* and the *Sun-Times.* Newman was described as "being to urban reporting what Mike Royko was to column writing," a major compliment for Chicago. After graduation from the University of Wisconsin in 1938, Newman worked for small newspapers in North Carolina, Indiana, and New Jersey. He joined the *Daily News* as a copy reader in 1945, became a rewrite man, then a roving reporter and over three decades rose to be recognized as one of the *Daily News'* top reporters. After that newspaper closed in 1978, Newman joined the *Sun-Times* until 1994. From 1969-80, he was the editor of *Inland Architect* magazine. The recipient of dozens of awards, Newman was elected to the Chicago Journalism Hall of Fame in 1993.

Frank Norris (1870-1902) was one of the early realists and one of the first muckrakers. After a year at Harvard, Norris dropped college to visit Africa as a correspondent for the San Francisco *Chronicle,* and then wrote weekly contributions for the San Francisco *Wave.* S.S. McClure recruited him to *McClure's Magazine* as assistant editor. *McTeague* helped pave the way for the gritty realist school. His novel, *The Octopus,* first of a proposed trilogy, is one of the best muckraking examples–an expose of railroad price-fixing and exploitation of the farmers. Norris published articles and stories in well-known magazines such as *Collier's Weekly* and *Everybody's.* In addition to *The Octopus,* his books include *McTeague, The Pit,* and *The Collected Short Stories of Frank Norris.*

Joseph North (1904-75), a prominent writer and editor in the left-wing press, made a major contribution to the Communist-backed *New Masses.* He was born in Russia, and was brought to the United States at an early age and was graduated from the University of Pennsylvania. Strongly influenced by Marxist doctrine, North became a member of the Communist Party in 1927. He went to work for the left-leaning magazine, *New Masses,* as its "political" editor to make certain that articles adhered to a party line (the *New Masses* was funded, at least partially, with periodic assistance from the Soviet Union). One of his writing discoveries was Mike Gold, and North was influential in developing other young writers. He covered the Spanish Civil War and in 1949, the magazine became *Masses and Mainstream.* He was a correspondent for the *Daily Worker* as well and in that capacity covered the Cuban revolution. North was an ardent admirer of Fidel Castro and Cuba's Communist cause. North maintained through his career that "there is no such thing as Free Speech in America." His books include: *What Are We Doing in China?, Robert Minor: Artist and Crusader, Cuba: Hope of a Hemisphere, New Masses: An Anthology of the Rebel Thirties.*

John B. Oakes (1913-2001) made a major contribution to the *New York Times,* particularly on its editorial page and specifically its op-ed page. He moved the *Times* editorial voice from a wishy-washy on-the-one-hand, but on-the other-hand stance to positions of principle. Oakes was born of rank (a product of the Ochs-Sulzberger clan) and privilege–Lawrenceville School, Princeton, University of Dijon, and a Rhodes Scholar at Oxford. He began his newspaper career with the Trenton *Times* in 1934, then moved to the *Washington Post,* covering politics from 1937-41. During 1941-46, he served in the Army, rising from private to major; his service in Europe earned him a Bronze Star, an O.B.E. and a Croix de Guerre. He joined the *Times* in 1946 as an editor of "The Week in Review." Oakes was an editorial writer from 1949 on, and became editor of the editorial page in 1961. His major contribution was to infuse the *Times'* voice with a firm, even passionate, point of view. His strong views brought contention and controversy within the *Times* ownership. Oakes was replaced in 1976, but his legacy prevails and he continued to contribute columns and his liberal views on politics and the environment until he retired. He received a George Polk Award shortly before his death. Oakes also served as a visiting professor at Syracuse University (1977-78). Books include *The Edge of Freedom.*

Jack [John Dennis Patrick] O'Brian (1914-2000), one of he first to write about television, conducted a nationally syndicated column, with commentary in the gossipy style, minus the vitriol, of Walter Winchell. He was also a coiner of words–"splitsville" was his description of divorce. Born in Buffalo, he dropped out of grammar school to become a cub reporter with the Buffalo *Courier-Express* and early earned a reputation as a cantankerous commentator. O'Brian joined the Associated Press in 1943 as a drama and theater critic. Three years later he moved to the New York *Journal-American* to start a radio-television column. He inherited Dorothy Killgallen's column, "Voice of Broadway," in 1967 shortly after her death. After his last newspaper, the *World Journal Tribune* shut down, he turned to radio on WOR-AM and continued a nationally syndicated column.

Adolph S. Ochs (1858-1935) is responsible for making the *New York Times* the newspaper that it is today–one of the finest in the world. His career began in Chattanooga in 1878 with the *Dispatch,* where he learned one important lesson: control is critical. After that venture failed, he bought control of the *Chattanooga Times.* In 1896, Ochs bought the debt-ridden *New York Times* and made it into a profitable enterprise. With managing editor Carr C. Van Anda, Ochs directed his newspaper toward fair, impartial coverage, foregoing the theatrics of Pulitzer and Hearst–the *Times* became "the newspaper of record." Ochs laid the foundation for one of the most successful newspapers of twentieth-century America.

Fremont Older (1856-1935), an outspoken opponent of the death penalty, was one of America's most controversial editors. His beginnings were modest; he began as a printer's apprentice with the Berlin (Wis.) *Courant,* but from 1895 until 1918, he was managing editor of the San Francisco *Bulletin.* Older was involved in the exposure of municipal graft, corruption and election scandal–his was a stormy tenure. As an editor, Older was kidnapped, shot at, and threatened in an effort to muzzle his newspaper. His most controversial stance, however, was his unremitting opposition to the death penalty. Older staged protests that generated publicity nationwide By 1918 he was editor of the San Francisco *Call-Bulletin* and continued his crusade until his death. Books include *My Own Story, Growing Up.*

Kyle D. Palmer (1891-1962), as political editor of the *Los Angles Times,* was a powerful political influence in California. A close friend and confident of Earl Warren, it was Palmer who persuaded Warren to accept the Republican vice-presidential nomination in 1948 with Thomas E. Dewey in the 1948 contest with President Harry S Truman. Palmer was a state kingmaker and directed the position of the *Times.* Palmer, born in Tennessee, was educated at Staunton Military Academy and Throop Polytechnic Institute, predecessor to the California Institute of Technology. He joined the *Times* in 1910. After service as Washington correspondent, he became the *Times'* political editor until his retirement almost a half-century later.

Louella (Lolly) Parsons (1881-1972) was a Hollywood gossip columnist who in her day could make or break careers. What Parsons wrote was important to movie fans by the millions, but also to actors, producers, writers, directors, and owners. She kept the nation informed about actors' lives and loves, the motion picture industry and was important to studio heads as a source of control on the conduct of the film colony. It was said that she used fear as a weapon to get copy for her syndicated column In any event, she earned a reputation as a driven, hard-boiled professional. Her salary in Depression-era America, exceeded $50,000 annually and she had a contract that prohibited any editor from altering a word. Her professional career began in Chicago as a publicity writer for Essanay Studio in 1911 and she shortly thereafter wrote the Chicago *Herald's* first movie column. She later moved to the New York *Morning Telegram.* In 1922 Parsons moved to Hearst's New York *American.* When she became ill with tuberculosis, Hearst sent her to Palm Springs on full salary. When she recovered after a year, Hearst instructed her to write a Hollywood column, which he syndicated to seventy newspapers with an estimated twenty million readers. Parsons was the foremost of the gossip reporters–Hedda Hopper and Sheila Graham were two other notable columnists. Parsons continued her column until her retirement in 1965. Books: *Tell It to Louella, The Gay Illiterate.*

Alicia Patterson (Guggenheim) (1906-63), the founder, editor and publisher of *Newsday*–the "respectable" tabloid–the largest circulation daily on Long Island, was the daughter of Joseph Medill Patterson, founder of the the New York *Daily News.* Her only newspaper experience was with her father's *Daily News,* and as a cub reporter she involved the newspaper in a libel suit. She also worked briefly for *Liberty* magazine, another family publication. She and her husband founded the newspaper for $750,000 and it began publication in 1940. The paper was awarded a Pulitzer prize in 1954. Patterson's liberal views enabled her to support the New Deal and other Democratic causes. Patterson was an owner who wanted things her way; her views of what should be in an editorial page cartoon cost her the services of three-time Pulitzer winner Edmund Duffy.

Eleanor Medill (Cissy) Patterson (1884-1948), a forceful and dynamic publisher of the Washington *Times-Herald,* maintained a firm control over the newspaper's editorial and news policies, that often reflected her own temperamental personality. Her newspaper was one of the most successful, and controversial, in the nation. The formula for success was simple: circulation and advertising. With a formidable social and journalistic background–her brother was Joseph Medill Patterson, founder of the New York *Daily News* and her maternal grandfather the founder of the Chicago *Tribune*–she began in 1930 at the top, as editor of Hearst's Washington *Herald.* Patterson worked as reporter, posing as a homeless, penniless "Maude Martin" to write a series of articles that boosted circulation. Her feud with Eugene Meyer, owner of the *Washington Post,* over comic strip publication, created national interest. She also used her newspaper to attack other foes, including, but not limited to: President Franklin Roosevelt, Walter Winchell, Drew Pearson, and Interior Secretary Harold Ickes. In 1939, she purchased the *Times* and the *Herald* from Hearst and merged the two in order to create an "around-the-clock" newspaper. Patterson was described by many adjectives–good and bad, and probably deserved each–but this mercurial, imaginative woman was never dull and she was one amazing journalist. She also served as a director of the Chicago *Tribune* and Board Chairman of the New York *Daily News.* During her lifetime Patterson's newspaper dominated Washington (it was eventually absorbed by the *Washington Post*). Her books include two novels: *Glass Houses, Fall Flight.*

Joseph Medill Patterson (1879-1946) founded the New York *Daily News,* the first successful tabloid newspaper and guided it to the largest-circulation daily in the nation. He and his cousin, Robert McCormick, publisher of the Chicago *Tribune,* and his sister Eleanor (Cissy) Patterson, constituted a strong triumvirate of New Deal opposition and bitterness toward President Franklin Roosevelt. Patterson was educated at Yale, but interrupted his education to cover the Boxer Rebellion in China for the *Tribune;* he graduated in 1901. At age twenty-four he was elected to the Illinois State legislature; two years later he was Chicago's Commissioner of Public Works. He served with the Army in the Mexican border patrol wars and during World War I, he saw action with the Rainbow Division and rose to captain. He and his cousin McCormick began the *Daily News* in 1919, based on his experience with the British tabloids. He took an active hand in every facet of his newspaper–he originated comic strips that reflected his themes and guided carefully the artists' development. "Little Orphan Annie" was a strip that reflected the rewards of the capitalistic system; "Dick Tracy," the crime-fighter, was another of Patterson's comic creations; he was also instrumental in the formulation of "Gasoline Alley," a strip that reflects strong middle-class values. Patterson took an active and continuing interest in his newspaper and its contents reflected his personality and interests. He, with Robert McCormick, also created *Liberty* magazine, which was later sold to Bernarr McFadden. Books: *A Little Brother of the Rich, Rebellion.*

Ethel L. Payne (1911-91) was for many years (1953-78) a reporter and eventually Washington correspondent for the Chicago *Defender.* Hers was a prominent black voice during a period when few newspapers employed blacks on their staff Payne left the *Defender* for radio and television work and to write a syndicated column for a number of newspapers nationwide. Her professed goal as a reporter was "to be an agent of change," as indeed she was, covering civil rights issues across the South.

Drew [Andrew Russell] Pearson (1897-1969) proclaimed himself a "modern muckraker," and his books and newspaper columns exposed graft, wrong-doing, and corruption in national politics and government. He worked for the *United States Daily* (1926-29) and the Baltimore *Sun* (1929-32). His anonymous collaboration on a book (with Robert Allen) led to his popular syndicated column, "Washington Merry-Go-Round" which castigated government's misdeeds. Pearson, as a gadfly, was not beloved; President Harry S Truman, no admirer, described Pearson as a "son-of-bitch." His mother-in-law had more invective. Cissy Patterson, publisher of the Washington *Times-Herald,* banned his column from her newspaper. Books include: *Washington Merry-Go-Round, The Nine Old Men, The President, The Case Against Congress.*

Westbrook Pegler (1894-1969) was a good sportswriter early in his career who later became an acerbic political commentator notorious for his brutal denunciations of real and imagined enemies. Pegler began his career at age twenty for Scripps-Howard, covered World War I in Europe, and then enlisted in the Navy. In 1919 he joined United Press in New York, then the Chicago Tribune Syndicate, writing sports. He turned to political writing in 1933 for the New York *World-Telegram.* Pegler was usually either lauded or despised; liberals loathed him when he defended a lynch mob in California; intellectuals loved him when he attacked Mussolini and Hitler. His exposure of racketeering in Hollywood won him a Pulitzer prize in 1941. Pegler lost a disastrous $175,000 libel suit when he attacked Quentin Reynolds (for a book review of Heywood Broun, a supposed friend whom Pegler envied). His *Journal-American* column was terminated when he attacked publisher Hearst in 1962. Pegler was journalism's "angry man" whose last submissions were cut or altered even by his sympathizers. Books include *T'Aint Right, The Dissenting Opinions of Mr. Westbrook Pegler.*

S(idney) J(oseph) Perelman (1904-79) contributed articles and art to *Judge* and *College Humor* before he graduated from Brown University; thereafter he wrote mainly for the *New Yorker.* Perelman was one of America's preeminent humorists and one of the best prose stylists in the twentieth century. He also spent time in Hollywood and was scriptwriter for such Marx Brothers classics as "Animal Crackers" and "Horse Feathers." His twenty books include *The Road to Miltown, The Rising Gorge, Eastward Ha!*

David Graham Phillips (1867-1911) is one of the lesser-known muckrakers, but it was his series of articles, "The Treason of the Senate," dealing with the corruption of the United States Senate, that prompted President Theodore Roosevelt to give that pejorative name to the group of reform-minded journalists. The magazine articles led to a book, and that book helped bring about the direct election of senators. Phillips worked as a reporter for several Cincinnati newspapers, the New York *Sun,* and the New York *World.* Phillips' articles in *Cosmopolitan* magazine, commissioned by William Randolph Hearst, led to his famous book concerning the domination of the Senate by big business and the trusts. Phillips, an editorial writer for the New York *World,* once said, "I'd rather be a reporter than President of the United States." But he turned to full-time writing in 1902 and produced some two dozen books to great acclaim and success (each averaged 100,000 sales)–now mostly forgotten. Young H.L. Mencken, in a burst of misplaced enthusiasm, praised Phillips as "the greatest living novelist." Phillips was assassinated by a deranged reader in 1911 who deluded himself that his sister had been defamed in one of Phillips' novels. Books include *The Treason of the Senate, The Great God Success, Susan Lenox: Her Rise and Fall.*

Shirley Povich (1905-98), through his seventy-five year career at the *Washington Post,* lived the novelist's dream scenario of rising from copyboy to editor and nationally-known columnist. Publisher Edward (Ned) McLean liked Povich as a caddy and gave him a job on the *Washington Post* as a copyboy and paid Povich's tuition to Georgetown University. Povich was a full-time reporter and earned a by-line for his story on the 1924 pennant-winning Washington Senators. By 1926 Povich became the youngest sports editor in America. He relinquished that post in 1933 to devote full-time to his six-times weekly column, "This Morning with Shirley Povich." He was an early supporter for desegregation of major sports–baseball beginning in 1941 and later that decade with George Marshall's Washington football Redskins. Povich saw active service as a war correspondent–he landed with the Marines in the invasions of Okinawa and Iwo Jima. His reporting won Povich many awards, including membership in *Who's Who of American Women* ("Shirley" confused readers, as well). In 1974 Povich retired from the *Post,* but continued to contribute his column; the last published the day of his death. He is enshrined in the Baseball Hall of Fame, befitting a sportswriter who was one of the best. Books: *The Washington Senators, All These Mornings.*

Joseph Pulitzer (1847-1911) left a legacy–the Pulitzer prizes for excellence in journalism, administered by Columbia University–that ensures the recognition of quality for American newspapers of excellence, regardless of size. Pulitzer owned and operated two great newspapers–the St. Louis *Post-Dispatch* and the now-defunct New York *World.* He is today associated with the birth of "yellow journalism"–a misnomer, usually applied to a shoddy product. The *World* was a liberal, crusading newspaper and the comic page was but one means to increase circulation. Pulitzer, through his newspaper, was responsible for the public funding for the building of the base for the Statue of Liberty on Bedloe Island in 1886. His standard was "accuracy, accuracy, accuracy." The *World* is generally acknowledged to have been the greatest newspaper of its time, perhaps one of the best of all time. Even his partial blindness did not prevent Pulitzer from active direction. Despite specific directions to the contrary in his will, Pulitzer's heirs sold the *World* and destroyed a great newspaper. The employees matched and exceeded the purchase price, but Roy Howard's *Telegram* held a secret agreement and absorbed the assets of the *World.* Pulitzer's encouragement of excellence continues through the awards he founded. The measure of "excellence" eroded, and over the years endured blatant favoritism, bias and political log-rolling by the judges. Many deserving newspaper workers went unrecognized by a Pulitzer prize.

Ernie [Ernest Taylor] Pyle (1900-45) was the most renowned–and the best-loved–war correspondent of World War II. Pyle was a newsman who knew America and its people, and he reported the wretched war years from the battle fields in human terms. The troops who fought were his focus, not grand strategy or sweeping military tactics. Pyle was well-known before he became famous. His early experience included writing travel stories for the Washington *Daily News* in 1923. Pyle also worked in New York for the *World* and later the *Post.* He rejoined the *Daily News* in 1927 as telegraph editor and rose to managing editor. In 1933 Pyle began a travel column for Scripps-Howard and visited all forty-eight states, Canada, and Latin America. In 1940 he covered the war and the German bombing of London. Pyle landed with the American troops in the invasion of North Africa and reported campaigns in Tunisia, Italy, and later the invasion of Normandy and across Europe. Pyle wrote of the troops, the "grunts" and their war. Readers loved his stories with names, addresses and home towns carefully noted, along with the grim details of ground war. His dispatches were memorably poignant. Awarded a Pulitzer prize in 1944, Pyle was America's preeminent war correspondent. After VE-Day, he followed the troops to cover the war in the Pacific and was killed by a Japanese sniper. Pyle was as brave as any of the men whose battles he chronicled. Books include: *Brave Men, Here is Your War, Ernie Pyle in England, Home Country, The Last Chapter.*

Terry Ramsaye (1885-1954) graduated from the University of Kansas (1905) and worked for a number of newspapers until 1914: the Kansas City (Mo.) *Star,* the Kansas City *Times,* the Leavenworth (Kansas) *Times,* the Omaha (Neb.) *Bee,* the St. Paul (Minn.) *Pioneer Press,* and in Chicago, the *American* and the rival *Tribune.* He then produced motion pictures for the United States Treasury, including "The Price of Peace" and contributed "Profiles" to the *New Yorker.* Books include: *A Million and One Nights* (2 vols.), and he was editor of *Pathe News, Pathe Review, Motion Picture Herald, Hall of Fame, Motion Picture Almanac.*

Dan Rather (1931-) earned a Journalism B.S. from Sam Houston State Teachers College (Tex.) in 1953 and taught journalism briefly. He began work for the Associated Press in Huntsville, before joining KHOU-TV, a CBS affiliate in Houston. In 1962, Rather became chief of the bureau. Coverage of the assassination of President John F. Kennedy, November 1963, proved to be Rather's big break. At CBS, Rather was White House correspondent, appeared on "60 Minutes," "48 Hours," and other national shows. He succeeded Walter Cronkite in 1981 as anchor for the coveted "CBS News" segment. Rather long associated himself with the Edward R. Murrow tradition at CBS (Eric Sevareid, no admirer, reminded Rather that much of his aura was self-invented). Despite a lapse into rustic homilies from time to time, Rather remains one of the few at CBS to attempt to retain a heritage of genuine news, as news becomes increasingly mere infotainment and public relations pizzazz. Books include: *The Camera Never Blinks, I Remember, Deadlines and Datelines.*

John Reed (1887-1920) was a Harvard poet, a war correspondent, a battler against social injustice, and a journalist whose ideology fueled his work. After Harvard College, he went to work for the *Everybody's* magazine with Lincoln Steffens in 1911. He joined the *Masses* in 1913, and covered the Mexican revolution and the Ludlow strike the next year for *Metropolitan* magazine. In 1917 he was writing also for the pro-German New York *Evening Mail* to report on the Russian revolution and wrote extensively for the *Liberator.* Reed covered the Communist cause with sympathy; he contracted typus in Baku, died in Moscow and is buried in the Kremlin Wall with other Soviet heroes. John Reed clubs, promoted by the *New Masses,* a pro-Communist magazine, influenced many writers of the left in the 1930s. Books include: *The Day in Bohemian New York, Insurgent Mexico, The War and Eastern Europe, Ten Days that Shook the World.*

Scotty [James Barrett] Reston (1910-95) was the consummate "insider" as a newsman and columnist; he rewarded his friends, cultivated his sources, and protected his newspaper, the *New York Times.* After a beginning career as a sportswriter and sports publicist, the landed a job as assistant to *Times* publisher Hays Sulzberger, and became a propagandist for the U.S. Embassy in London. Reston was named chief Washington correspondent for the *Times* in 1939, and was awarded Pulitzer prizes in 1945 and 1957 for excellence in reporting. His column, "Washington," was syndicated by the *Times* to several hundred newspapers and was known for its reliable inside information from officialdom. The *Times* rewarded Reston: associate editor in Washington, 1939; executive editor in 1968, vice president; and columnist in 1974. Reston was an influential newspaperman who helped to guide American foreign policy. Books include: *Artillery of the Press, Prelude to Victory, Sketches in the Sand, Deadline: A Memoir.*

Quentin Reynolds (1902-64) should be remembered as one of the best correspondents reporting World War II. He was a prolific writer and a reporter who prided himself for being on the scene. His career began in 1930 with the New York *World* and after its demise, the *World-Telegram.* Damon Runyon helped him land a job with the International News Service and in 1932 he joined *Collier's* magazine as Berlin correspondent During the war years, Reynolds covered the air battles over London, the early action in France, American campaigns in North Africa, and the invasion of Europe. His thirty books include: *Convoy, London Diary, Wounded Don't Cry, Only the Stars are Neutral.*

[Henry] Grantland Rice (1880-1954) entertained and informed sports fans for more than fifty years with his nationally syndicated column, "The Sports Light." Rice's colorful phrases have entered the sports lexicon–the Four Horsemen, the Manassas Mauler, the Galloping Ghost–and his florid prose was popular. One piece of doggerel he wrote is remembered: "When the One Great Scorer comes to write against your name, He marks–not whether you won or lost–but how you played the game." In these cynical times, that kind of thought might not meet approval–it *is* all about winning and for the big bucks. He wrote in a time when standards meant something. Rice was a man of rectitude and unquestioned integrity and his half-century of newspaper observation won him the title "Dean of American Sportswriters." Books include *The Tulmult and the Shouting, My Life in Sports.*

Jacob A. Riis (1849-1914) was a photojournalist before the term was invented; he chronicled the lives and conditions of the poor in New York City. Riis became a police reporter for the New York *Tribune* and portrayed the daily life in the slums with photographs. His photography, sometimes secret and clandestine, would be considered unethical by today's standards, but he recorded life, not posed portraits. This led to his selfless career as a crusading newspaperman to expose slum conditions. In 1903 President Theodore Roosevelt described Riis as "four-square" and New York's "most useful citizen." Riis's work has been condemned as racist. Riis may have been an elitist, but he was not a racist. His important books are: *How The Other Half Lives, The Children of the Poor, A Ten Years' War, The Children of the Tenements, The Making of an American.*

Inez (Callaway) Robb (1901-79) regularly produced a five-day-a-week column and seized the opportunity of World War II to become one of the few female war correspondents–and a good one. She began with the Boise (Ida.) *Evening Capitol News* and by the 1920s was with the Sunday New York *Daily News* as assistant editor for the women's pages. In 1928, she was named society editor and took over a daily column as "Nancy Randolph." In 1938 Robb joined Hearst's International News Service and began her column, "Assignment America" and visited more than forty foreign countries. By 1953, she was with the Scripps-Howard Newspapers and United Features syndicated her column to more than 140 newspapers. Her autobiography is *Don't Just Stand There.*

Maxie (Max) Robinson (1939-88) was the first black broadcaster to serve as anchorman for a national television network, for ABC in 1978. His broadcast beginnings were modest; he swept floors at the studio. After Oberlin College, his first job was in Portsmouth, Va., where he read the news with his face hidden from viewers by the station logo. In 1965 Robinson held jobs in Washington D.C., with WRC and WTOP and served as mid-day anchor and later teamed with Gordon Peterson at WTOP. Robinson's career was not without news-making incidents of his own–he was arrested for firing a .347 Magnum mourning his father's death. He joined ABC in 1978 and was part of its tripartite news team with Frank Reynolds and Peter

Jennings. Robinson's erratic behavior probably cost him advancement. In 1981, in a public speech at Smith College, he accused ABC and the networks of racism. When Reynolds died in 1983 Robinson refused to attend the funeral because he was scheduled to sit beside first lady Nancy Reagan. Two months later Jennings was named sole anchor for ABC. Robinson then joined NBC in Chicago (1984-85) and later left to work on *Essence* magazine. Robinson died of AIDS in 1988 and a number of treatment centers honor his memory.

Andy (Andrew A.) Rooney (1919-) is known to millions of viewers as the resident curmudgeon of the CBS weekly television show "60 Minutes." Unknown to many, however, is that Rooney has a solid background as a print journalist; his syndicated column reaches more than 200 newspapers. After graduating from Colgate College in 1942, he went into the U.S. Army and became a staff member of the wartime newspaper *Stars and Stripes.* He tried magazine free-lancing after the war, but turned to radio and television–writing for Garry Moore and Arthur Godfrey, among others. He also wrote scripts for Harry Reasoner and Walter Cronkite. His essays are well-written, opinionated points of view that have delighted audiences for thirty years. Rooney has won four Emmys, six Writers Guild Awards, and a George Foster Peabody award. Books include: *Word for Word, A Few Minutes with Andy Rooney, Pieces of My Mind, And More by Andy Rooney, My War.*

Eleanor Roosevelt (1884-1962) was not primarily a journalist, but made a notable media contribution as a trailblazing first lady who made her opinions known to a wide audience. After her husband Franklin Delano Roosevelt became a New York state senator, she wrote articles in 1920 for the League of Women Voters' *Weekly News* and articles for the *North American Review.* From 1925-1928, she served actively as editor of the monthly *Women's Democratic News.* After FDR became President, she began a syndicated column in 1933 for the North American Newspaper Alliance, and a monthly column for *Woman's Home Companion,* 1933 through 1935. As first lady, she opened opportunities for women when she restricted her press conferences to female reporters only. Mrs. Roosevelt began weekly radio broadcasts in 1934. A year later, she began her six-times weekly newspaper syndicated column, "My Day" which continued until 1962. Books include: *It's Up to the Women, If You Ask Me, My Days, On My Own, This is My Story.*

A(braham) M(ichael) Rosenthal (1922-), as executive editor of the *New York Times* for two decades, wielded the powers of a Caesar and exerted vast influence over the people and policies of the newspaper. His association with the *Times* lasted for forty-two years, beginning in 1944 until his retirement in late 1986. He was arrogant, profane, thin-skinned, vindictive, and quirky, but an outstanding newspaperman. A New Yorker, he attended DeWitt Clinton High School and went on to CCNY (City College of New York), the only college he could afford, in 1941. He worked on the school newspaper, *The Campus,* and became a stringer for the *Herald Tribune* and later the *Times.* Rosenthal dropped out of college to work full-time as a "temporary" employee covering the United Nations for the *Times.* He stayed nine years (his work earned Rosenthal a journalism degree from CCNY). Rosenthal finally won an assignment as a foreign correspondent, first in India (1955-57) and then in Poland (1958-60)–where his reports had him expelled and earned a Pulitzer prize. From 1960-62 he served in Tokyo. Brought back to New York, Rosenthal was appointed metropolitan (city) editor and ruled with a profane, brutal style in his efforts to improve the newspaper. With strong support from Turner Catledge, Rosenthal was promoted to assistant managing editor for news in 1967, by 1976 he moved to the pinnacle–executive editor–and began to remake the *Times.* Rosenthal's career was stormy though productive, but no exception was made for him when he reached the mandatory retirement age. He was shunted off to a twice-weekly column until his contract expired. He later became an editorial consultant for Putnam books. Book: *Thirty-Eight Witnesses.*

Harold W. Ross (1892-1951), a self-described "hobo newsman," created the *New Yorker* magazine in 1925. Ross was a journalistic genius based on that creation alone. Lacking a college degree, Ross began in 1911 with the Salt Lake City *Tribune.* By 1917 he had worked at newspapers in six states, never holding any one job for very long. After he enlisted in the Army in 1917, Ross managed to land the job of editing the A.E.F. newspaper for the troops, the *Stars and Stripes.* His staff was comprised of a distinguished group of soldier contributors, including commissioned officers. Back home, Ross began a version for the returned veterans, the *Home Sector,* later incorporated by the American Legion into its publication *The Weekly.* Ross' dream was a magazine of sophistication, which he managed to bankroll on a shoestring in 1925. After an uneven beginning, the *New Yorker* managed to become one of America's most literate and talked-about publications. Ross edited every word and questioned every fact. He assembled a team of unique talent, including E.B. White and James Thurber, plus a stable of artists who helped give the magazine its distinctive identity. After Ross' death in 1951, William Shawn succeeded him as editor, but the sale of the *New Yorker* to Samuel I. Newhouse in 1958 marked the end of the unique role of the *New Yorker;* today it is just another glossy magazine. Ross died one year after the *New Yorker's* first quarter-century, and no publication since those years has matched its early creative excellence.

Richard H. Rovere (1915-79) distinguished himself as an outspoken protester during the press intimidation of the McCarthy era. After graduating from Bard College in 1937, he joined the *New Masses* as associate editor, then was assistant editor (1940-43) with the *Nation.* He was with *Common Sense* from 1943-44, and joined the *New Yorker* from 1944-79. Rovere was contributing editor-book critic with *Harper's* (1949-50); contributing editor to the *Spectator* (1954-62); and editorial board member of the *American Scholar* and the *Washington Monthly.* Books include: *Affairs of State, The Eisenhower Years, Senator Joe McCarthy, The American Establishment, The Goldwater Caper, Waist Deep in the Big Muddy.*

Carl Rowan (1925-2000), a leading liberal black writer, served in government and became a well-known panelist on television. Rowan's wartime service with the U.S. Navy enabled him to attend Oberlin College on the G.I. Bill of Rights. His first job was with the Minneapolis *Tribune,* where he covered the civil rights movement. His passionate reporting prompted President John F. Kennedy to appoint him as assistant secretary in the Department of State to aid in its integration. He also served as a delegate to the United Nations, and under President Lyndon B. Johnson, as director of the U.S. Information Agency, the highest ranking black individual in the government in 1964. He appeared on television's "Inside Washington," for thirty years until his retirement in 1996. His column, distributed by King Features to sixty newspapers, was published three times weekly until his death. Rowan's eight books include *Breaking Barriers, Wait Till Next Year, The Coming Race War in America.*

Mike Royko (1932-96), a throw-back to an earlier era–the old Chicago school of rough-and-tumble newspaperman–was a regional columnist who entertained millions of readers. His citation for a 1972 Pulitzer prize said as much. With no college, and scant Air Force experience during the Korean War, Royko began with the Lincoln-Belmont (Ill.) *Booster,* and later with the Chicago City News Bureau. In 1959, Royko joined the Chicago *Daily News* and gained a column in January 1964. He moved to the *Sun-Times* after the *News* folded. He joined the Chicago *Tribune* in 1981. His hour-long "Royko on Tap" was a popular television show. Royko wrote of the people in bars and the working world; in later years, a politically-sensitive generation complained of the descriptive terms he used, such as Polack and Bohunk. Royko's gritty satire was sometimes misunderstood, but he was an eloquent voice for a disappearing blue-collar, working-class smoke-stack, industrialized America. Books: *Boss; Up Against It; I May Be Wrong, But I Doubt It; Slats Grobnik and Some Other Folks; Sez Who? Sez Me.*

[Alfred] Damon Runyon (1884-1946), writing in the 1920s, '30s and early '40s, depicted an arcane world of Broadway characters who captured the imagination of America. Runyon's gamblers and gangsters, hoodlums and grifters, became the "Guys and Dolls" that enchanted readers. His apprenticeship began in 1895 with the Pueblo (Colo.) *Advertiser.* After service in the Spanish-American War, he wrote short stories and joined the San Francisco *Post* and later the *Rocky Mountain News.* In 1911 he joined William Randolph Hearst's New York *American* as a sportswriter. Runyon covered America's foray into Mexico and in 1918 served as a war correspondent in Europe. King Features and International News Service syndicated his column, "The Brighter Side." A number of his books became popular motion pictures. Runyon entertained and enlivened America with a now-vanished Broadway world that some claimed existed only in Runyon's imagination. Books include: *The Blue Plate Special, The Best of Damon Runyon, Take It Easy, Runyon First and Last, Guys and Dolls, Money From Home.*

Adela Rogers St. Johns (1894-1988) grew up in the shadow of her father, a well-known lawyer, but made her own reputation as one of the best-known reporters of the era. She began as a cub reporter with Hearst's San Francisco *Examiner,* and later with the Los Angeles *Herald,* where she covered a number of sensational events–the Leopold and Loeb trial and the Lindbergh kidnapping trial. St. Johns was a "sob-sister" who wrote stories laden with emotion and frequent use of the personal pronoun. Later, in Hollywood, where she worked for Hearst's International News Service, she was dubbed "the Mother Confessor of Hollywood." In the 1950s she taught journalism at the University of California at Los Angeles, and other colleges. Although retired from active journalism, she returned in 1982 to cover the conspiracy trial of Patricia Hearst for the *Examiner.* Her many books include: *Sky Rocket, Free Soul, Final Verdict, The Honeycomb.*

George S. Schuyler (1895-1982) angered a great many people, especially readers of the black press, as a columnist for the Pittsburgh *Courier.* For forty-one years his column, "Views and Reviews," took an iconoclastic stand against many of the black shibboleths. No less a critic than H.L. Mencken described Schuyler as a man of "intelligence, independence, and courage" and "one of America's best columnists." Schuyler did not hesitate to attack anyone, regardless of race; he deplored "white do-gooders and dreamers" as well as "black apologists and agitators." Schuyler employed satire, parody, and invective to castigate his targets. He saw himself as "an aristocrat in the colored community;" black, but thorough Yankee. After public education in local high school, Schuyler enlisted in the Army and served from 1912-19, with the 25th Infantry Division, an elite black unit, where he rose to first lieutenant. He wrote articles for service publications and the

Honolulu *Commercial Appeal.* After his discharge, Schuyler could find only odd-jobs. A meeting with A. Philip Randolph led to a job with his publication, the *Messenger.* Schuyler was given a column in 1923, "Shafts and Darts: A Page of Calumny and Satire," in 1923 and he served as an assistant editor through 1928. His commentary drew attention, and in 1925 he was invited to write a column, "Views and Reviews," for the Pittsburgh *Courier,* the second-largest circulation black newspaper in America. Schuyler began investigative reporting before the term was coined; a series of cross-country interviews through thirteen states found that "white hatred of the Negro was a myth." A later article for the *Nation* that ridiculed"The Negro Art Hokum" made Schuyler a celebrity. Schuyler wrote widely for publications, black and white: the *American Mercury, Nation,* the *New Masses, Ebony,* and *Topaz.* In 1930 Schuyler investigated the black slave trade for a series of articles for the New York *Evening Post.* His well-documented findings disclosed that African blacks conducted the African slave trade and profited from the practice. These findings irritated black readers, who also objected to Schuyler's point that "light blacks" discriminate against "black blacks." He also published articles in leading white newspapers–the *Washington Post,* the Philadelphia *Public Ledger*–a first for a black writer. Schuyler's book, *Black No More,* was praised by critics of both races, but his often intemperate attacks aroused enmity. In the 1930s Schuyler went to war on the Communists and the *Daily Worker* for exploiting blacks and pitting blacks and whites against each other. His attack on black churches and their leaders aroused opposition from the Chicago *Defender* (a leading black newspaper), and the influential chain of *Afro-American* newspapers. In 1937 a Schuyler survey of forty-two cities in seventeen states, found that Communist influence in industrial unions harmed blacks; increasingly, in the 1950s, Schuyler saw a vast Communist conspiracy undermining American society and became an avid supporter of the anti-Communist movement. In 1944, the *Courier* asked Schuyler to become New York editor; he also was a contributing editor to *Plain Talk,* an anti-Communist magazine. He dismissed prominent Negro leaders, such as Paul Robeson, as "lame-brains" and warned incessantly of the Red menace. His weekly broadcasts, "The Negro World," and "The Editors Speak," gave Schuyler a larger audience. In September 1960, management relieved him as New York editor and refused to print his attack on Dr. Martin Luther King's Nobel Prize. Schuyler found an outlet in William Loeb's Manchester (N.H.) *Union-Leader,* which thereafter became his newspaper outlet. He also attracted a contract with NANA (North American Newspaper Alliance) for a syndicated column. He continued with his iconoclastic viewpoint until his death in 1982. His opinion were not popular, but Schuyler cared little. What others did not wish to hear, he felt compelled to write. He attacked without fear or favor Negro apologists and white liberals as paternalistic do-gooders. Schuyler made an achievement in American journalism that one day may be recognized. Books include: *Black and Conservative, Slaves Today: A Story of Liberia, Black No More.*

E(dward) W(yllis) Scripps (1854-1926), founder of United Press, built America's first newspaper chain which became the Scripps-Howard organization. Long before the innovative tabloid *PM,* Scripps published a mini-adless newspaper, *Day Book,* in Chicago (Carl Sandburg was a staff member); it lasted for six years before expiring prior to World War I. Scripps publicly was an early advocate of labor reform through his Cincinnati newspapers. Scripps was no liberal, but he believed in a fair working wage. His public principle was "to make it harder for the rich to grow richer and easier for the poor [to keep] from growing poorer." His primary credo for his editors was simple and direct: "Do no business except at a profit." His life and work is worth remembering, but he was no Pulitzer or Hearst and Scripps' legacy is neglected by most newspaper historians. When he died at sea aboard his yacht, Scripps' media empire included the United Press, NEA (Newspaper Enterprise Association), Acme Newsphotos, United Features Syndicate, and controlling interest in daily newspapers in fifteen states that included the Cleveland *Press,* the Pittsburgh *Press,* and the San Francisco *News*. Books: *Self-Portrait, Damned Old Crank.*

Ellery Sedgwick (1872-1960) enjoyed a long editorial career, most notably for the *Atlantic.* Blessed with background, privilege, and family connections, Sedgwick–after an education at Groton and Harvard and a brief apprenticeship with the *Worcester* (Mass.) *Gazette*–became an assistant editor for the *Youth's Companion.* He was appointed editor of *Frank Leslie's Popular Monthly* in 1904. He changed the name to *Leslie's Monthly,* and with an artful mix of articles and stories, made the magazine into a successful venture. Sedgwick reaped a windfall when Hearst bought his copyrighted title, the *American* magazine, and further capitalized on that venture when he applied for a job after the talented group at *McClure's* jumped ship. Sedgwick became editor of *McClure's.* That experience lasted a year, but McClure inspired Sedgwick ever after. Family connections helped him become a book editor for D. Appleton and Company. Sedgwick became editor of the *Atlantic* in 1908 though the best possible means: he bought the magazine and served as its editor for the next thirty years. After he published a series of laudatory articles on Generalissimo Francisco Franco and the Spanish Civil war, he resigned as editor. Books include *The Happy Profession, Atlantic Harvest.*

George Seldes (1890-1995) is distinguished through his long journalism career for his unremitting effort to tell the truth, an effort frequently thwarted by his publishers. Seldes' magazine, *In Fact,* published in the 1940s, sought to correct newspaper errors and omissions. Seldes' long career began with the Pittsburgh *Leader* in 1909, and he later moved to the Pittsburgh *Post.* He departed when his story on Billy Sunday, the ballplayer evangelist, was deemed sacrilegious. He tried Harvard for a year, but went on to the New York *World* and the United Press. During the war years, Seldes worked for Floyd Gibbons in the Paris office of the Chicago *Tribune's* Army Edition and performed war work for the Wilson Administration. He worked for the *Tribune* after war's end. A number of his stories were spiked for not following the *Tribune's* anti-Soviet editorial policy. Ironically, Seldes was expelled from Russia in 1924 for his unfavorable stories of the Soviet regime. By 1928, when Seldes resigned from the *Tribune,* he had also quarrelled with a number of news sources: the Vatican, Mexico, Mussolini, the United States diplomatic corps, and his bosses at the *Tribune,* for stories that were unfavorable to the powers that be. During the 1930s Seldes wrote a number of books that reflected his views: *Lords of the Press, You Can't Print That, Can These Things Be!* and *Vatican.* From 1940-50 he was editor and publisher of his own weekly publication, *In Fact,* dedicated to truth-telling and exposing corruption. Poor health and charges that he was a Communist (Red-baiting was revived in the postwar years) led to the closing of *In Fact,* one of the few journals that sought to critically examine the workings of the press in America. His exposure of big business influence and advertisers' censorship of much of the nation's press was not met with favor by his peers. Seldes' temperament and his scathing criticisms (even if true) did not win favor with his colleagues or his employers. Nevertheless, Seldes' role was a significant one in defining what the role of the press should be given its First Amendment protections. In addition to those mentioned, Seldes' many books include: *You Can't Do That, Catholic Crisis, Witch Hunt, Facts and Fascism, Tell the Truth and Run, Witness to a Century.*

Eric Sevareid (1912-92), who was one of "Murrow's Boys," said of Edward R. Murrow, "He invented me." Sevareid invented himself. After his studies at the University of Minnesota, the London School of Economics, and the Alliance Francaise (Paris), Sevareid joined the staff of the Minneapolis *Journal* in 1936. By 1938 he was a reporter for the Paris edition of the New York *Herald Tribune.* Murrow hired him as a radio correspondent for CBS because he could write. Sevareid suffered from "mike fright" terribly throughout his career. In his subsequent years as a broadcaster, Sevareid distinguished himself as a writer of excellence. He covered the war in France and witnessed the French capitulation. From 1941-43, Sevareid served with CBS in Washington, then served as a correspondent in China. Later, he was with CBS, London. From 1946 through 1977, Sevareid served as news commentator, on radio and later television, in various capacities. Savareid, who provided commentary as part of Walter Cronkite's news broadcasts, was often seen as a Cassandra-like voice of doom. In an effort to present both sides, Sevareid often resorted to the "on the one hand" approach; for his troubles, he earned the name "Eric Severalsides." His outstanding television work earned him three Peabody Awards. Books include: *Not So Wild a Dream, In One Ear, Small Sounds in the Night, This is Eric Sevareid.*

Eileen Shanahan (1924-2001) broke ground in a male-dominated area of economic reporting in the Washington bureau of the *New York Times*–and she was one of the best. The *Times,* to its discredit, rewarded Shanahan with a less-than-adequate salary, far below the levels of her male colleagues, Shanahan was the first female reporter hired by the *Times'* Washington bureau to cover government beyond presidential wives and her work dealing with finance and the federal budget was outstanding. She became one of the leading plaintiffs in a discrimination suit that cost the *Times* $350,000. She left that newspaper in 1977 (she suspected, probably accurately, that management would punish her for the lawsuit) to become an official in the Carter administration as top public affairs officer in the Department of Health, Education and Welfare. She returned to newspaper work in 1977 as assistant managing editor of the Washington *Evening Star.* When that newspaper folded in 1981, she took a similar post with the Pittsburgh *Post-Gazette.* In 1987, Shanahan became founding editor of *Governing,* the first national publication devoted exclusively to state and local governments. Prior to joining the *Times* (1962-77), Shanahan worked for the United Press, the *Journal of Commerce,* and the Research Institute of America. She closed out her journalism career in 1994 as Washington correspondent for the St. Petersburg (Fla.) *Times.* In all her positions Shanahan worked for the advancement of minority and women reporters.

Lloyd Shearer (Walter Scott) (1916-2001) wrote the popular "Personality Parade" column that informed fifty million readers of celebrity trivia (under the name of Walter Scott) for *Parade* magazine from 1958 until 1991. After graduation from the University of North Carolina, Shearer was drafted into the Army in 1941 and spent the war years in New York and Los Angeles, as a writer for the Army magazine *Yank,* and then for Armed Forces Radio. He was a free-lance contributor to the *New York Times* with articles describing the lighter side of military life. He became West Coast correspondent for *Parade* in 1953, and started "Personality Parade" in 1958. He was astute enough to copyright the feature, which he later sold to *Parade* in 1991. The content of the column was prompted by the more than 5,000 questions readers sent–when readers were lax, Shearer-Scott supplied his own questions. Under his own by-line, Shearer wrote magazine interviews and profiles of national and movie-town celebrities.

William L. Shirer (1904-93) distinguished himself as a print reporter, a broadcast journalist, and as an historian. Early in his career, after graduation from Coe College (Iowa), his newspaper experience was part-time and summer work covering sports. Shirer was a personification of the hard-boiled Chicago newspaperman; in 1925 he landed a job on the copy desk of the Paris edition of the Chicago *Tribune,* where one of his colleagues was James Thurber. From 1929-32 he served as the *Tribune's* reporter in Italy (where Col. McCormick objected to his "heavy," i.e., dull writing), England, and France specializing in sports events. Later, he was the bureau chief in Vienna. In 1934, Shirer worked for the New York *Herald Tribune* as their European correspondent. From 1935-37, he was Berlin correspondent for Hearst's Universal News Service. His reports covered the rise of Nazism, Hitler, and the growing unrest in Europe. His reporting of the Berlin Olympics roused the ire of Hitler and when Hearst closed down UNS, Shirer looked for work elsewhere. Edward R. Murrow, who admired his writing and perceptive reporting, invited Shirer to open an office in Vienna for CBS radio. Shirer began his radio career despite the fact that he lacked a "radio voice." Until 1941 Shirer roamed Europe's capitals reporting war developments on the scene. After publication of *Berlin Diary,* Shirer left England to promote his book amid much celebrity in America. Shirer's abandonment of his wartime post with CBS caused a rift with Murrow, who wanted Shirer to continue broadcasting and felt that Shirer had deserted his wartime job for celebrity. Shirer continued to broadcast for CBS News at home with a daily newscast and produced books that sold well and earned more acclaim. His news program was canceled in 1947, CBS claimed because of low ratings. Shirer claimed the cause was his liberal views. (Shirer was correct, but the Sunday slot given him was weak in listeners, however.) Shirer felt that Murrow, now in charge of CBS News, should have defended him, but Morrow remembered Shirer's wartime abandonment, and a clear break occurred in their relationship. Shirer turned to a full-time career as an historian and produced more than a dozen books. These include: *Berlin Diary, Midcentury Journey, The Sinking of the Bismark, The Rise and Fall of the Third Reich. The Nightmare Years.*

Red (Walter Wellesley) Smith (1905-82) was for thirty-seven years one of the most erudite sports commentators for the *New York Times,* and his superb command of the language earned him a Pulitzer prize in 1972. At the time of his death, his three-time-a-week column was syndicated to 500 newspapers. Smith's career began after his graduation from Notre Dame in 1927, with the Milwaukee *Sentinel.* A year later, he joined the St. Louis *Star.* In 1936, Smith joined the Philadelphia *Enquirer,* and stayed until 1945, when he accepted an offer from the New York *Herald Tribune.* He became sports columnist for the *World Journal Tribune* in 1966 until the newspaper folded the next year. Until he joined the *Times* in 1971, Smith continued to produce his syndicated column independently. His newspaper career spanned fifty-five years and Smith chronicled the sporting events of those years in memorable fashion; he was virtually without peer in his profession. Smith's books include: *Remembered Friends, Out of the Red, Views of Sport, Strawberries in the Winter, The Best of Red Smith.*

Hartzell Spence (1908-2001), executive editor and founder of *Yank* magazine, was the man who brought the World War II pinup to the American lexicon. After graduating from the University of Iowa in 1930, Spence served as Iowa bureau manager of the United Press Association. He was promoted to oversee the New York special services office. Spence won fame in 1941 with his best-selling book and motion picture, *One Foot in Heaven.* He joined the Army the next year and founded and served as the editor of *Yank,* a weekly magazine for servicemen. Spence's major contribution was the introduction of the pinup, a photograph of a provocatively-clad female, usually a movie star. He also popularized George Baker's "Sad Sack" cartoon feature, which was syndicated nationally. After his service with *Yank,* Spence transferred to the Army Air Force and was awarded the Legion of Merit in 1945. He resumed his career as a writer after the war and wrote more than 200 articles for leading magazines such as the *Saturday Evening Post, Look,* and the *Reader's Digest.* Spence's other books include: *The Big Top, Marcos of the Philippines.*

[Joseph] Lincoln Steffens (1866-1936), an early muckraker, and an editor of *McClure's* magazine, was a major force in that movement. Steffens helped goad President Theodore Roosevelt's attack on "muckrakers." Steffens was well-educated and well-to-do–the family home later became the California Governor's Mansion. After graduating from the University of California at Berkeley, he attended Berlin University and the Sorbonne. In 1897, Steffens joined the New York *Post,* and then the *City Advertiser,* as city editor. In 1901 he was appointed editor of *McClure's* magazine and began his "shame of the cities" series documenting corruption in a dozen American cities. In 1906, disturbed by publisher S.S. McClure's megalomania, he and the core group of muckrakers founded the *American* magazine. He resigned in 1908 to be an advisor to Boston's Good Government Group. As editor of *Everybody's* magazine in 1910, he hired two of his proteges from Harvard: Walter Lippmann and John Reed, launching the careers of two major American journalists. Steffens wrote for various publications, but his career in muckraking ended in 1910. Steffens reported the revolutions in Mexico and Russia; he admired Stalin as a "scholar" and Mussolini because he was "efficient." His 1918 observation on the Soviet Union, "I have seen the future and it works," haunted him for the rest of his life. Books include: *The Shame of the Cities, The Struggle for Self-Government, Upholders, The Red Moses, The Autobiography of Lincoln Steffens.*

John Steinbeck (1902-68), a prize-winning novelist–whose work was recognized with the Nobel Prize and a Pulitzer prize–gained early fame as a journalist when he published the articles that grew into *The Grapes of Wrath,* the story of Depression-era displaced "Oakies." Educated at Stanford University, he began his career with the New York *American,* then returned to California to write novels. Steinbeck worked for the Monterey *Beacon* that published his articles dealing with the dispossessed share-croppers; he published similar work for the *Nation* and the San Francisco *News.* His journalism includes wartime service as a correspondent for *Collier's Weekly*, and those wartime dispatches were collected into the book, *Once There Was a War.* Other books include: *The Grapes of Wrath, In Dubious Battle, Travels with Charlie, In Search of America, Of Mice and Men, The Pearl, Cannery Row.*

Thomas Lundsford Stokes (1898-1958) won a Pulitzer prize in 1939 for his exposure of graft and corruption in the WPA (Works Progress Administration) in Kentucky. A disillusioned conservative, Stokes was an ardent supporter of President Roosevelt's New Deal program, but he was a conscientious newspaperman through his long career. During college at the University of Georgia, Stokes worked for the Atlanta *Constitution* and the *Georgian.* After graduation, he worked for a number of Georgia newspapers: the Atlanta *Press,* the Athens *Herald,* and the Macon *News* before going to work in Washington for United Press. In 1933 he became Washington correspondent for the New York *World-Telegram* and the Scripps-Howard Newspaper Alliance. In 1941 he joined the United Features Syndicate as a columnist supplying more than 100 newspapers. Books include: *Chip Off My Shoulder, The Savannah.*

I(sadore) F(einstein) Stone (1907-89) described himself as a "guerilla" with regard to reporting. Stone was a liberal, outspoken, and utterly fearless newsman. In 1931 he managed to get a job with the Philadelphia *Record,* by 1933 he was the top editorial writer for the New York *Post.* Off and on, Stone worked for the more liberal New York newspapers–*PM,* the *Star,* and the *Compass* until it folded. In 1953 Stone began his own newspaper, the *I.F. Stone Weekly.* For the next twenty years, his *Weekly* was one of the nation's most outspoken newspapers that exposed the worst of government suppression of civil rights and coverups by the Washington bureaucracy. Ill health forced Stone to publish on a biweekly basis in 1971, then he closed the *Weekly.* Stone continued as a contributing editor for the *New York Review of Books* (1964-76). Iconoclastic, independent and a nonconformist, Stone added a valuable and provocative voice to American journalism. Books include: *The Haunted Fifties, The Hidden History of the Korean War, In a Time of Torment, The Truman Era.*

Melville E. Stone (1848-1929) expanded American journalism into the twentieth century and is best remembered as the man responsible for the growth of the Associated Press. When fire wiped out his iron foundry, Stone turned to newspaper work: first with the Chicago *Republican,* and then the *Inter-Ocean,* where he rose to editor. After a period with the Washington *Mail* and the New York *Herald,* he returned to Chicago and established the *Daily News.* It became the first successful penny press, so successful that Stone acted to bring more pennies into the city to ensure sales. He sold the paper in 1888, and traveled abroad for two years. Upon his return, Stone went into banking; in 1893 he became general manager of the Associated Press and used his banking and business acumen to expand the enterprise. An adverse court ruling in Illinois (affirming that AP news was not proprietary) prompted Stone to move AP's headquarters to New York, thus avoiding the Illinois ruling. Journalism owes Stone a debt of gratitude for its growth and stability. His only book: *Fifty Years a Journalist: Autobiography of Melville E. Stone.*

Ed (Edward Vincent) Sullivan (1901-74), a newspaper gossip columnist, became one of the early television personalities as host of a weekly variety program that became widely popular. His beginnings were modest, even average. After high school, he worked for the Hartford *Post* and went on to work for a number of New York City newspapers–the *Evening Mail,* the *World,* the *Morning Telegraph,* the *Evening Graphic*–as a sportswriter and then a Broadway columnist. He joined the New York *Daily News* as a replacement for Walter Winchell. Sullivan's column, "Little Old New York," endured for the next forty years. Sullivan, who served as master of ceremonies for the newspaper's annual Harvest Moon Ball (1936-52), was tapped to host a weekly radio show on CBS in 1942. Mainly, on this background–and because no one with any stature in show business wished to appear on television–Sullivan was appointed host for the CBS television show, "Toast of the Town," in 1948. The variety show was an early favorite with viewers, despite Sullivan's stiff, sometimes grotesque, style. In 1955 it was renamed "The Ed Sullivan Show" and ran with high ratings until 1971. Sullivan, who won an Emmy, and is enshrined in the Television Hall of Fame, helped found the National Academy of Arts and Sciences. Sullivan continued his column until his death.

Frank Sullivan (1893-1976), a noted humorist, wrote for the New York *World* and, later, primarily for the *New Yorker.* He is remembered as the creator of that magazine's Mr. Arbuthnot, the cliche expert. After graduating from Cornell University in 1914, Sullivan worked for the New York state *Saratogian* before he joined the New York City *Tribune* in 1919. Three years later, Sullivan joined the *World,* and after he wrote a story about a well-known society woman's death–she was not dead–editor Herbert Bayard

Swope assigned him to humor. His column for the *World,* "A Letter from Frank Sullivan," or, alternately, "Frank Sullivan's Private Mail," ran from 1928-31. In addition, Sullivan filled-in for Heywood Broun and F.P. Adams when these columnists were absent. After the demise of the *World,* except for an occasional piece for *PM,* Sullivan never worked for another newspaper. Sullivan concentrated on books and magazine pieces and his annual Christmas message ran in the *New Yorker* for forty-two years, from 1932-74. A prolific writer, Sullivan could address any subject convincingly; for instance, his travel pieces were informative but he never traveled abroad or west of St. Louis. Although a humorist, Sullivan in a piece for *The End of the World,* wrote one of the most poignant sentiments in journalism: "When I die I want to go wherever the *World* has gone, and work on it again." Books include: *In One Ear; Innocent Bystanding; Sullivan Bites News; Well, There's No Harm in Laughing; The Night the Old Nostalgia Burned Down.*

Mark Sullivan (1874-1952) created journalism that assessed events of American life for fifty years. Educated at Harvard and with a law degree, Sullivan in 1904 was invited to join the *Ladies' Home Journal* for its campaign against patent medicine frauds. (Editor Bok rejected Sullivan's article for being "too legal.") *Collier's Weekly* did not hesitate to publish the article and won much acclaim. One of the lesser-known muckrakers, Sullivan was named editor of *Collier's Weekly* in 1914 and served through 1919. Then he moved to the New York *Evening Post* until 1923, when he joined the New York *Tribune.* He wrote a syndicated column "Our Times" until his death. Sullivan's books include the monumental six-volume *Our Times: The United States-1900-1925,* a chronicle of the times and the way they affected the average man. Other works include: *The Great Adventure at Washington, Flood Marks.*

Raymond Gram Swing (1887-1968), despite his whispery delivery, was one of America's most listened-to radio voices during World War II. Of Swing it was said: "I can talk like anything, but only God can talk like Swing." He studied at the University of Halle (Germany) and took a degree at Oberlin College.His early journalism included jobs with the Cleveland *Press,* the *Orville Courier* (Ohio), and the Indianapolis *Star* by age twenty-four. After a visit to Europe, Swing became bureau chief in Berlin for the Chicago *Daily News* as World War I began. He managed to break the news of the powerful Krupp "Big Bertha" gun. After the war, Swing held a number of jobs: with the *Nation,* the New York *Herald,* the *Wall Street Journal,* and the Philadelphia *Ledger,* where he served as Berlin bureau chief for the next ten years. In the 1930s, Swing did some radio work for NBC, CBS, and the BBC. In 1943, Swing rejoined the *Nation* and also became correspondent for the *London News Chronicle* and the *Economist,* He resumed broadcasting for CBS and the BBC, alternating on broadcasts with Elmer Davis. Swing began a radio series for Mutual with 110 stations and an international audience, estimated to be thirty-seven million listeners. In 1942, he joined the NBC Blue network with a five-night-a-week broadcast. Ill health restricted Swing to a once-a-week broadcast and in 1951 he became principal commentator for the *Voice of America.* Swing would simply omit news he disagreed with, but his delivery was intense and contained a deep perspective that listeners appreciated–at his peak, his audience was estimated to be one hundred million. His books include: *How War Came, In the Name of Sanity, Forerunners of American Fascism, Preview of History.*

Herbert Bayard Swope (1882-1958) won journalistic fame as editor of one of America's greatest newspapers, Joseph Pulitzer's New York *World.* He began his career with the St. Louis *Post-Dispatch* and in 1895 moved to Chicago, first with the *Tribune,* and later, as a reporter with the *Inter-Ocean.* Within a year, the New York *Tribune* sought him out. Gambling lost him that job and he became a press agent for a theatrical agent. Within a year he was back in New York with the *Morning Telegraph.* He returned to the *Herald,* but left because of disenchantment with management's mediocrity. He joined the *World* as a reporter in 1909. Swope was an excellent reporter–his reports on the *Titanic* disaster and his European war dispatches were distinguished– and he won the first Pulitzer prize in 1917. In 1920 he was made executive editor of the *World*–invented (and named) the op-ed page, added black reporters to the news staff, and made the *World* a world-class newspaper. He resigned in 1929 over his disgust at new management's parsimony and ineptness–and their decision to close down the *World* two years later proved him correct. Swope ended his career with newspaper journalism, but went on to serve with CBS and NBC and a number of local and national civic posts. Swope was literally a "legend in his time" and is now often remembered as a successful financier. Books include *Inside the German Empire.*

Tad (Tadeusz Witold) Szulc (1926-2001), as a *New York Times* correspondent broke the story of the "Bay of Pigs," the disastrous 1961 attempt by the Kennedy Administration to invade Cuba. Szulc was an aggressive reporter who managed to cover world events for the *Times* from 1953-72 with a way of being in the right place at the right time to get a big story. Szulc's perceptive reporting and his books earned him the CIA's enmity and he was classified as an "enemy of the agency and a suspicious foreign agent." He was neither. Szulc was an excellent newspaperman who reported facts the agency wished kept secret. Born in Poland, Szulc attended a Swiss boarding school and joined his parents in Brazil in 1941 and attended the University of Brazil 1943-45. After college, he joined the Associated Press in Rio; he came to the United States in 1949, covering the United Nations for United Press International. He joined the *Times'* night rewrite desk in

1953. After he became a correspondent, Szulc covered Argentina, Spain, Portugal, and Eastern Europe He uncovered the Cuban invasion plot on a Miami stopover between assignments–the "luck" of a good reporter, that never deserted Szulc. He left the *Times* in 1972 to write books that include: *Twilight of the Tyrants, The Illusion of Peace: Foreign Policy in the Nixon Years, Fidel: A Critical Portrait, Pope John Paul II: The Biography.*

Ida M(inerva) Tarbell (1857-1944) was a muckraker and one of the best, an investigative reporter before the term was invented. Tarbell used facts, figures, and statistics to present hard, well-reasoned indictments against unlawful business and wayward government practices. Her childhood was influenced by industrialization and practices of the oil business that affected her father's small holding. She became a foe of privilege. After graduating from Allegheny College (the only female in her class), she taught language and mathematics for two years. She joined *The Chautauquan* in 1863 as a researcher and fact-checker. She left in 1890 to study in Europe, and supported herself with free-lance fiction pieces for *Scribner's* and *McClure's Magazine.* She joined the *McClure's* staff in 1894. Research for an article led to her first books, biographies of Napoleon and Lincoln. As associate editor in 1896, she began research on Standard Oil. Her scathing indictment, backed with facts from company and court records, ran serially from 1902-04. Her *History of the Standard Oil Company* became a classic and led to the breakup of Standard Oil. Tarbell, accompanied by much of the *McClure's* staff, left in 1906, to found the *American Magazine.* Before she left the *American,* Tarbell published one of her serials, *The Tariff in Our Times,* a penetrating examination of the tariff, a subject as arcane then as it is today to most people. During the war years, Tarbell worked with the Woman's Committee on National Defense and joined the *Red Cross Magazine* in Paris, in 1919. Tarbell's views on suffrage and other women's issues did not endear her to feminists; women were not oppressed, she thought, and their role was in the home. Similarly, when her later books seemingly abondoned muckraking reform and dwelt kindly with big business and portrayed its better aspects, Tarbell was accused of being an apologist for business. Tarbell was a traditionalist who believe in the American Dream and the virtues of stewardship. Throughout her career she sought reform and equality in business and social life; her moral compass never wavered. Despite her agenda, and it was narrow, Ida Tarbell's contribution to American journalism was monumental and should not be neglected. Books include: *All in the Day's Work, The Business of Being a Woman, History of the Standard Oil Company, Life of Elbert H. Gary: The Story of Steel.*

Bert Leston Taylor (BLT) (1866-1921) originated his column, "A Line O'Type or Two," in 1901, and it influenced columnists for the next one hundred years. Taylor began his career in his native New England after graduation from City College of New York. He worked briefly for the Montpelier (Vt.) *Argus and Patriot,* the Manchester (N.H.) *Union,* and the Boston *Traveler.* In 1896 he joined the New York *Herald,* and in 1898 the Chicago *Journal* hired him and gave him a column, "A Little About Everything." That work brought him to the attention of the Chicago *Tribune* and the beginning of his famous column. After a brief time, however, Taylor returned to New York in 1903 and the *Telegraph* with a column, "The Way of the World." The next year he joined *Puck* as editor of the comic magazine. He was lured back to Chicago and resumed his column. Taylor's work was literate, and he welcomed readers' contributions; he prided himself on lucid prose and the poetry in his columns. Franklin P. Adams shamelessly copied and continued the format. Another writer who used the format to advantage was H.L. Mencken with his column, "The Free lance." After Taylor's death, his column was conducted by Richard Henry Little (RHL) Books include: *Line O'Type, Motley Measures, The So-Called Human Race, The Charlatans.*

Studs (Louis) Terkel (1912-), a journalist who captured the voice and thoughts of America with his microphone, has documented the thoughts of the "man-in-street" opinion in his many books. Educated at the University of Chicago (1930) and the Chicago Law School (1932), Terkel followed a career acting and performing. He acted in radio soap operas, was a radio disc jockey, was a sports commentator, and conducted a local television interview program. In recent years, Terkel was host of a daily radio program for WPMT, Chicago. Terkel's fame comes from his books that captured the sounds and cadence of average Americans dealing with the topics close to their hearts–working, death, and other remembrances. Books include: *Division Street: America, Hard Times, Working, Talking to Myself, American Dreams: Lost and Found, The Good War.*

Lowell Thomas (1892-1981) for almost a half-century was a radio commentator–more entertainer than newsman. He joined the Chicago *Evening Journal* in 1913 after college. His academic career included graduate work at Princeton, where he headed the Speech Department. Thomas made his early fame as a lecturer and world traveler through a meeting with Lawrence of Arabia. Thomas' first radio appearance was with KDKA, Pittsburgh, in 1929 and the next year he signed with CBS. His evening newscasts–much hyperbole, some fabricated–were pleasant listening and a staple of American radio for forty-six years. His many books include: *With Lawrence of Arabia, Raiders of the Deep, India: Land of the Black Pagoda, Wings Over Asia, Good Evening Everybody.*

Dorothy Thompson (1893-1961), one-time rated by the polls, as equal in influence to Eleanor Roosevelt, is relatively forgotten. She was the prototype for the 1942 Katharine Hepburn film, "Woman of the Year." Thompson was known for her newspaper reporting, her books and magazine columns, and her radio program. Thompson, a leading woman's suffrage advocate, lost favor with the feminists with her view that women's place is in the home. An outspoken supporter of a Jewish homeland, Thompson fell out of favor with the Zionists when she charged the Irgun as terrorists. Always outspoken and opinionated, Thompson deserves recognition for her work. After graduating from Syracuse University, Thompson became publicity director for the National Social Reform Unit in New York and free-lanced for New York newspapers in an effort to land a full-time job, without success. When she attended the World Zionist convention in 1920, she filed dispatches for the International News Service. That work led to her being paid on a space rate for the Philadelphia *Public Ledger* in Vienna. Thompson was hired full-time based on her many stories (it was cheaper for the newspaper) and was made Vienna bureau chief for the *Public Ledger.* She covered events in Austria and elsewhere in Europe and Russia. During this period she married the author, Sinclair Lewis, then at the height of his popularity. That event prompted her retirement from newspaper work; she returned home to write *The New Russia.* Her freelance writing led to a return to Europe where she managed a hard-to-get interview with Hitler. Thompson proved to be a poor prophet and saw little future for Hitler as an effective leader, and her next book in 1931, *I Saw Hitler,* condemned his anti-semitic policies. When she returned in 1934, Thompson was expelled from Germany, but her notoriety earned her a position in 1936 as a thrice-weekly columnist for the New York *Herald Tribune.* Her conservative views "On the Record" were seen by the *Herald Tribune* as an alternative for liberal-leaning Walter Lippman, and within a year she was syndicated to more than 130 newspapers. At the same time, Thompson-with the help of a press agent–managed to land a weekly radio program and a $1,000-a-month column with *Ladies' Home Journal.* By 1939, *Time* reported her annual income as $103,000. Her 1940 Broadway play, "Another Sun," depicting the plight of the Jewish refugees, was a financial and critical failure, but provided copy for her newspaper and magazine columns. Thompson was a constant reminder of the plight of the Jews. Her ardent support for Franklin Roosevelt and the New Deal cost her continued publication in the *Herald Tribune* and she moved to the New York *Post.* Thompson, despite her support for a Jewish homeland, attacked the Irgun as terrorists. This cost her the job with the *Post* and prompted condemnation by Zionists. Her *Journal* columns, less political, lauded woman's role in the garden and kitchen, a view that infuriated feminists. Her column appeared until 1958, however, when she retired because of increasing deafness. Thompson was an imposing woman who dominated conversations and wrote as she spoke, with lots of personal pronouns and exclamation points. John Hersey, then secretary to Lewis, described her as a Wagnerian Valkyrie; friends described her as a prima donna or a monster. Thompson was a self-made woman with a talent for self-promotion who exerted a powerful influence on prewar America. Her enemies outnumbered her friends and those who should have shown gratitude for her efforts on behalf of their causes chose to ignore her contributions. Her books include: *The Courage to be Happy, I Saw Hitler, Let the Record Speak, Dorothy Thompson's Political Guide.*

James Thurber (1894-1961), gifted as he was, deluded himself that he was the greatest comic writer since (if not better than) Mark Twain. His short story, "The Secret Life of Walter Mitty," became American lore, however. Thurber, after graduating from Ohio State University, worked for local newspapers in Columbus and then joined the international Chicago *Tribune,* in Paris. He met limited success with humorous free-lance pieces and returned to New York at age thirty-two. A ship-board acquaintance enabled him to meet the *New Yorker's* E.B. White. Real success did not come until he joined the *New Yorker* in 1926. Thurber's comic stories and his cartoons (salvaged from the waste basket by White), won him fame. The Thurber dogs and his series of men versus women are classic. "The Thurber Carnival" became a Broadway hit. His series for the *New Yorker,* "Where are they Now?' and "Soapland" showed Thurber at his journalistic best. Books include: *Is Sex Necessary?* (with White), *My Life and Hard Times, Thurber Country, Thurber's Dogs, The Years with Ross.*

Robert Trout [Robert Albert Blondheim] (1909-2000), whose career spanned nearly seventy years, was widely known as "the iron man" of broadcasting for his ability to stay with a breaking story. He coined the term, "fireside chat" for the radio addresses of President Franklin D. Roosevelt. Trout was a pioneer in radio broadcasting and, later at CBS, was one of the original "Murrow Boys," that group of erudite broadcasters recruited by Edward R. Murrow. Trout, who never went to college, began with WJSV, Alexandra, Va., in 1927, then moved in 1932 to CBS's WTOP, in Washington, D.C. He was invited to New York by Murrow and was the announcer for FDR's radio talks. During the 1944 D-Day invasion, Trout broadcast for one stretch of seven hours describing the landings. He served briefly as a host for a CBS quiz, "Who Said That?" From 1947-52, Trout worked for NBC and in the early 1980s with ABC. At the time of his death, Trout could be heard on National Public Radio's "All Things Considered." Every major event for the last seventy years of the twentieth century was reported by Trout factually and with consumate fairness.

Mark Twain [Samuel Langhorne Clemens] (1835-1910), author of much of America's most distinguished literary achievement, began his career as a newspaperman and many of his books reflect his perceptive journalistic skills. He became a printer's devil at the age of twelve and traveled from Iowa to New York and points in between. Beginning with his first contribution to his brother's newspaper, the Hannibal (Mo.) *Journal,* his newspaper career included: the Virginia City (Nev.) *Territorial Enterprise,* the San Francisco *Call,* the Sacramento (Calif.) *Bee,* the San Francisco *Alta California* and in New York, the *Tribune* and the *Herald.* When the Civil War interrupted his fledgling career as a Mississippi pilot, he headed West and adopted the river term "Mark Twain" as his pen name in 1863. His newspaper sketches were widely reprinted. The San Francisco *Union* sent him abroad to the Sandwich Islands (Hawaii) and later he traveled to Europe. His book, *Innocents Abroad,* helped win him fame. Sent by Horace Greeley to cover Washington for the New York *Tribune,* Twain moonlighted as an assistant to Senator William Stewart (a practice permissible in that era). That experience gave him material for short stories and *The Gilded Age,* a satiric examination of post-Civil War life in America, that exposed lobbyists, privilege, and patronage. His *Life on the Mississippi* is one of the best journalistic book-length essays ever to appear in print. Twain left daily journalism but his books liberally drawn from that experience provide America with some of its finest literature, notably, the *Adventures of Huckleberry Finn*–perhaps the great American novel. Twain reported with a journalist's eye the mores and morals of American, with a humor that was biting and sometimes bitter. Other works include: *Roughing It, Tom Sawyer, A Connecticut Yankee in King Arthur's Court, The Mysterious Stranger.*

Carr C. Van Anda (1864-1945) was without question a true "Giant of the Press." Managing editor of the *New York Times* from 1904 until 1932, Van Anda is responsible, more than anyone, for making the *Times* the foremost news gathering newspaper in America. He studied mathematics and physics at Ohio State for two years, then held several newspaper jobs: the *Auglaise Republican,* the Cleveland *Herald,* the *Plain Dealer,* and the *Evening Argus;* later he joined the Baltimore *Sun* as night editor. In 1988, he joined the New York *Sun* working for Charles A. Dana; in 1904, he joined the *Times.* Van Anda set a standard for accuracy and efficiency and a newsroom that eschewed the Hearst-Pulitzer theatrics. He won out on a number of memorable events and the *Times'* coverage of the sinking of the White Star liner *Titanic* was outstanding because of his diligence. Van Anda's legendary career was based on hard work, intelligence, and a curiosity that would not be satisfied with the mundane. The story is true that he detected an error in an Einstein equation that was corrected before the *Times* went to press. He produced no books, but every book written about the *New York Times* is indebted to the story of Van Anda's contribution.

Oswald Garrison Villard (1872-1949), as editor and publisher of the *Nation* (1918-32), was one of the most influential political journalists in the United States. He inherited ownership of the New York *Evening Post,* and before he joined that newspaper had only six months' experience on the Philadelphia *Press.* Villard held an M.A. in History and taught at Harvard. His opposition to President Woodrow Wilson's war program in 1918 prompted him to sell the *Post* and found the *Nation,* a weekly magazine. The *Nation* earned a reputation as a liberal voice that welcomed comment from a range of writers. Villard relinquished active management in 1932, but continued as a contributor to the *Nation* through 1940.

Stanley Walker (1898-1962) was an extraordinary editor of the New York *Herald Tribune* from 1928 through 1934. He began his career in 1919 at the Dallas *Morning News* and moved to the New York *Herald* in 1919. He was named night city editor in 1926 and city editor in 1928. These were the "seven sparkling years" of a newspaper that became known as a writer's newspaper. In 1936 he left the *Herald Tribune* to join the New York *Daily Mirror* briefly. He then endured a brief, unsuccessful tenure as managing editor with the *New Yorker* magazine–Walker had the temperament for newspapers' daily deadlines. In 1939 he joined the Philadelphia *Evening Public Ledger,* but left the next year to write books. In addition to his classic *City Editor,* books include: *The Night Club Era, Mrs. Astor's Horse, Dewey: An American of this Century, Home to Texas.*

Henry ("Marse Henry") Watterson (1840-1921) made his fame in the late 1860s, but his influence carried into the twentieth century. Though a relic of another era, Watterson's vigorous editorial work earned him a Pulitzer prize in 1917. For more than fifty years Watterson was editor of the Louisville *Courier-Journal* (1868-1919) and made that newspaper an influential voice of the South and his personal political points of view of nationwide interest. Watterson's career spanned time enough that he was attacked by a Thomas Nast cartoon (as an unreconstructed rebel) to urging President Woodrow Wilson to become engaged in World War I (for which Watterson won a Pulitzer). He supported the Southern cause, but advocated civil rights and a new industrialized South. Books include: *Oddities in Southern Life and Culture, History of the Spanish-American War, "Marse Henry."*

E[lwin] B[rooks] White (1899-1985) brought the short journalistic essay to a high art form in America primarily through the *New Yorker.* He graduated from Cornell in 1921, interrupted by military service in World War I. White held several jobs–writing for the United Press, the Seattle (Wash) *Times,* as a mess boy aboard a tramp steamer, and as an advertising copywriter. His free-lance poems and stories to the *New Yorker* led to a job offer in 1927. White's writing for "The Talk of the Town" and "Notes and Comment" features won him wide recognition as a writer of uncommon merit. His more than twenty books include the children's classics *Charlotte's Web* and *Stuart Little.* White reworked his Cornell English text by William Strunk in 1959 and published *The Elements of Style,* which continues to provide invaluable guidance to writers at all levels. White's elegant style championed no social issues; during the 1930s his readers were not burdened with issues of the Great Depression. He dismissed the New Deal and described President Franklin Roosevelt as an "actor" who mouthed "platitudes"–White's humorous reference to his "threadbare" Burberry coat rings hollow. He could be somewhat of a crank; during the early and mid-1940s, White's theme of one-world-brotherhood of man ideal became tiresome. Editor Ross tolerated the refrain because it was White. In addition to those mentioned, White's other books include: *Is Sex Necessary?* (with James Thurber), *The Trumpet of the Swan, One Man's Meat, Second Tree from the Corner, Farewell to Model T, Everyday Is Saturday, Points of My Compass.*

Theodore H. White (1915-86), with his exacting coverage of the 1960 presidential campaign, forever after influenced how reporters viewed–and explained–America's national electoral experience. After Harvard in 1938, where White majored in Chinese history, he free-lanced articles for the Boston *Globe* and the Manchester *Guardian.* His on-the-scene coverage of the Sino-Japanese war attracted favorable attention and he was recruited by Time Inc.'s John Hersey to cover China and East Asia for *Time* magazine; by 1944, White was chief of the bureau. After brilliant coverage for *Time* and *Life,* where he witnessed the corruption of the Chinese Nationalists, White resigned in 1946 when he learned that publisher Henry Luce allowed employees to submit whatever copy they discovered, but printed only information filtered through Luce-think with little regard for fact. White enjoyed brief celebrity with his book, *Thunder Out of China,* and served briefly as editor of the *New Republic.* In 1948, he covered Europe for the Overseas News Agency and left to become political correspondent for the *Reporter* magazine from 1950-53 He found editor Max Ascoli was as biased, from the left political perspective, as was Luce from the right. White joined *Collier's* as senior political correspondent in time to witness the demise of mass magazines. White turned to writing novels, then became a consultant for CBS News before rejoining *Life* magazine. He wrote the post-assassination interview with Mrs. Kennedy that established the "Camelot" mystique of JFK's presidency. White's book *The Making of the President, 1960* won a Pulitzer prize and set a standard for political reporting that is rarely met and never exceeded. His dozen books include: *Thunder Out of China* (with Annalee Jacoby); *The View from the Fortieth Floor; China: the Roots of Madness; The Making of the President, 1960* (with sequels in 1964, 1968, and 1972); *America in Search of Itself; In Search of History.*

William Allen White (1868-1944) made his fame as the small-town editor of the Emporia (Kansas) *Gazette.* His editorials attracted national attention, notably "What's the Matter with Kansas?" in 1896. White's roots were staunchly conservative, middle class America. After dropping out of the University of Kansas, he took a job with the El Dorado (Kansas) *Republican;* and later joined the rival *Journal* but left after an editorial dispute to join the Kansas City (Mo.) *Star.* In 1896 he purchased the *Gazette* and his liberal editorials attracted attention; he was active in politics and an ardent supporter of Theodore Roosevelt. In 1924 White unsuccessfully sought the Kansas governorship on an anti-Ku Klux Klan platform. He was an active political force with the Bull Moose Progressive movement, but later returned to the ranks of the Republican Party. White personified a way of life already disappearing with editorial homilies of virtue recalling America's golden age. White was awarded two Pulitzer prizes: in 1923 for editorial writing and in 1944 for his autobiography. His fame rests with his intangible influence on journalism. Books include: *A Certain Rich Man, Forty Years on Main Street, Puritan in Babylon, Defense for America, The Changing West, The Autobiography of William Allen White.*

Walter Winchell [Weinschel] (1897-1972) paved the way for today's keyhole journalism. He was the first columnist to exploit the public's insatiable appetite for salacious gossip and show business glamor. Winchell described himself to his public as "your newsboy" with a weekly radio program that reached millions dispensing rumor, innuendo, and intimate details of the private lives of celebrities. An indifferent student, Winchell, who began life in poverty, with two classmates managed to win a dancing appearance at a local theater. In 1910, he won a spot with the Gus Edwards Revue and began a career in vaudeville. Later, Winchell developed a dance act. He enlisted in the Navy in 1918 and saw limited sea duty before resuming his act after war's end. Winchell began submitting entries he called "Stage Whispers" to *Billboard,* a theatrical trade paper. He also had a number of his theater chit-chat published (at no fee) in the *Vaudeville News* in a column called "Broadway Hearsay." His entry into newspapering came with the New York *Evening Graphic* in 1924, with a column "Your Broadway and Mine." Winchell ferreted information and wrote in a slangy tone with made-up words such as "giggle-water" and "infanticapating." Winchell brought an air of intimacy and immediacy to the exciting world of show business and Broadway. His success attracted Hearst, always on the lookout for a circulation-builder. Winchell moved to the tabloid New York *Mirror* and a six-columns-a-week schedule. By 1930, Winchell had a CBS radio program with a national audience; he found time to star in a Vitaphone movie, "Bard of Broadway." In 1930, Winchell signed a five year contract with Hearst for $121,000 annually and a $1,000 weekly radio contract; shortly after Winchell signed a $35,000 contract to announce for the

"Lucky Strike Dance Hour." Winchell was America's best-known newspaperman and projected a fast-paced image of staccato reporting. His trademark, "Good Evening Mr. and Mrs. America and all the ships at sea" emerged in 1934. Insulated from the effects of the Depression, Winchell nevertheless became an ardent supporter of Franklin Roosevelt's New Deal. He never forgot, nor tried to hide, his Jewish origins, and was one of the first and most outspoken opponents of Hitler and the Nazis in Europe. The end began for Winchell when he lost his radio broadcast and he failed to make the transition to television. His lifeline newspaper connection failed when the *Mirror* folded and Hearst canceled his contract. Winchell faded from view. The motion picture, "Sweet Smell of Success" portrayed a Winchell-like Broadway columnist and a corrupt public relations toady. Winchell, for better or worse, shaped the role of modern journalism; television infotainment carries on the Winchell legacy. He was unable to have his autobiography published in his lifetime: *Winchell Exclusive: "Things that Happened to Me, And Me to Them."*

P(elham) G(reenville) Wodehouse (1881-1975), known more for his comic novels of Jeeves, the perfect gentleman's gentleman, had a sound grounding in journalism before he decided to pursue more-lucrative avenues. After school at Dulwich (U.K.), Wodehouse went into banking, but wrote for *Punch* and other magazines. That led to full-time employment writing a humor column, "By the Way," for the London *Globe*. He emigrated to the United States (and citizenship) when he discovered financial rewards were even greater with magazines such as *Cosmopolitan* and the *Saturday Evening Post*. He was drama critic for *Vanity Fair* (1915-18) before devoting full time to writing. Wodehouse was prolific; he wrote eighteen plays, thirty-five musical comedies, and ninety-six books. Wodehouse characters Psmith and Bertie Wooster reflect Psmith misadventures in journalism and the satire is sublime. The *New York Times* described Wodehouse as a "comic genius." Books include: *Psmith Journalist, Mike and Psmith, Leave it to Psmith, Carry on Jeeves, A Damsel in Distress, Cocktail Time, Bring on the Girls.*

Robert Woodward (1943-), with his *Washington Post* colleague Carl Bernstein, was the leading reporter who covered the Watergate scandal in the mid-1970s that led to resignation by President Richard M. Nixon. Woodward and Bernstein became household names because of the publicity and subsequent motion picture. No one should forget that it was the *New York Times* that led the way publishing the so-called Pentagon Papers, but the *Post's* subsequent follow-up and extensive coverage of the Watergate scandal won the paper a Pulitzer prize. Woodward and Bernstein inspired a generation of would-be "investigative" reporters to flood "communication" schools in the 1970s. Every good reporter is an investigative reporter as Ida Tarbell demonstrated. Woodward continues as an editor at the *Post* (he was accountable for Janet Cooke and her bogus story that resulted in the return of a Pulitzer prize). Books (with Bernstein) *All the President's Men, The Final Days.* Woodward's solo books include: *The Commanders; Veil: The Secret Wars of the CIA 1981-1987; Wired: The Short Life and Fast Times of John Belushi; Maestro: Greenspan, the Fed and the American Boom.*

Alexander Woollcott (1887-1943) dished out wit and satire to the knowing, treacle and platitudes to the mass public. During the years of the Great Depression, Woollcott at one time commanded the highest salary of any newspaperman in America. He joined the *New York Times* in 1909 and eventually became its drama critic. He enlisted in 1918 and became a staff member of *Stars and Stripes.* Upon his return, he rejoined the *Times,* shifting to the New York *Herald* in 1922, and to the New York *Sun* in 1924. He joined the New York *World* the following year and remained until 1928. Woollcott's *New Yorker* "Shouts and Murmurs" column was one of the highest-paid features and most-read in the magazine; Woollcott was one of its original staff members. He wrote also for *Collier's,* the *Smart Set* and other magazines with extensive free-lance writing. After 1929, Woollcott devoted his activities to free-lance writing and radio. Woollcott was the prototype for the Moss Hart-George S. Kaufman play "The Man Who Came to Dinner." A founding member of the Algonquin Round Table and author of many books, Woollcott reigned over New York literary and newspaper circles, dispensing vitriol and violets as his mood dictated. At the time of his death, he was one of the nation's most popular radio personalities with a twice-weekly program, "The Town Crier." His many books include *Shouts and Murmurs, Enchanted Aisles, Going to Pieces, The Woollcott Reader, The Portable Woollcott.*

Art (Arthur H.) Young (1866-1943), editorial cartoonist and editor, was a liberal crusader–for women's suffrage, racial equality, the abolition of child labor and other Socialist causes. He served as co-editor of the *Masses* (1911-15) and at the time of his death was a contributing editor for the *New Masses.* His early training focused on art; he was a student at the Academy of Design, Chicago (1884-86), the Art Students' League, New York (1888-89), Academie Julien, Paris (1889-90) and Cooper Union (1903-06). Young was a contributing cartoonist for the Chicago *Daily News,* and then the *Tribune.* He became editorial cartoonist for the *Inter-Ocean.* (and by management's direction, drew the Republican-slanted cartoons demanded). Young went to work for the Denver *Times,* as editorial cartoonist with a mission to build Denver's civic reputation. In 1900 he joined Arthur Brisbane on the New York *Journal* and used his art to elect more Republicans and mock the Populists. Not until 1901, when he met Eugene

Debs, did Young exhibit the ultra-liberal tendencies that marked his career. From that point on, he vowed to draw only cartoons he believed in. Piet Vlag recruited Young as a founding member of the *Masses* and he continued as an editor through 1915. He contributed to the *Coming Nation* in 1912 and became the Washington correspondent for *Metropolitan Magazine* for the next six years. From 1919-21, Young was editor and publisher of his own publication *Good Morning,* patterned after Charles Dickens' *All the Year Round,* Young was a prolific worker whose cartoons appeared regularly in *Leslie's Monthly, Cosmopolitan, Life, Puck, Judge, Collier's,* the *Saturday Evening Post,* and the *Nation.* Young was on assignment in Russia covering the revolution with John Reed for *Metropolitan Magazine* when Reed died. Earlier, Young was indicated with a group of *Masses* editors–including fellow cartoonist Boardman Robinson, writer John Reed, and editor Max Eastman–who were tried under the Sedition Act (all were acquitted) for opposition to World War I. With the suppression of the *Masses,* Young and Eastman were among the founders of a new liberal magazine, the *Liberator.* Young ran unsuccessfully for public office several times in New York on the Socialist ticket. His books include: *Trees at Night. On My Way, The Best of Art Young, Art Young's Inferno,* and *Art Young: His Life and Times.*

Notable Newspaper Comics and Their Creators

Newspaper comic strip artists, unlike editorial-page cartoonists, are not journalists. Nevertheless, ever since the emergence of so-called "yellow journalism" the comic strip or panel cartoon has earned a place as an integral part of most newspapers. The Wall Street Journal *and the* New York Times *are notable exceptions. Over the past century a number of cartoons have played a central role in American culture and their characters have often jumped from the comic pages to radio, television, motion pictures, and the Broadway stage. A number of comic strips have been around for a major portion of the twentieth century and become institutions in American life. These belong here and it is especially appropriate that their creators be acknowledged; a number of the most enduring are included here.*

Dick (Richard W.) Calkins (1895-1962) led America's comics into the space age in 1929 with "Buck Rogers in the Twenty-fifth Century." Calkins' interest in science fiction began when he was a schoolboy; he served as a flight instructor during World War I, thereafter signing all his work as Lt. Dick Calkins. After study at the Chicago Art Institute, he became a cartoonist for the Detroit *Free Press* and after his Army discharge, for the Chicago *Examiner.* He joined the Dille Syndicate and worked on two strips, "Sky Roads," and "Amateur Etiquette." Buck Rogers was created through three men: John Flint Dille, writer Phil Nowlan, and Calkins. Buck Rogers won wider fame as a radio serial and in motion pictures as a series of Saturday afternoon episodes, starring Buster Crabbe (who also played Flash Gordon). In later years Calkins collaborated with Rick Yager, who continued the strip after Calkins' death, until 1967. Books: (with Phil Nowlan) *Buck Rogers in the Dangerous Mission, Buck Rogers in the Twenty-fifth Century.*

Milton Caniff (1907-88) won popularity with the adventure-action comic strip, "Terry and the Pirates," where Terry Lee's exploits against the evil Dragon Lady were followed by millions of readers. Caniff later created, "Steve Canyon " that depicted the adventures of an Air Force colonel. His strip, "Male Call," drawn for *Stars and Stripes* during the war years for service members, was a bit more racy and featured a leggy pinup named Lace. Caniff was drawing cartoons by age thirteen for the Dayton (Ohio) *Journal-*

Herald Boy Scout page. He contributed cartoons to the Columbus *Dispatch* during his college years at Ohio State University. After he graduated in 1930, Caniff tried acting, but returned shortly to cartooning. He began his career drawing "Dickie Dare" and "The Gay Thirties" for the Associated Press. He began "Terry and the Pirates" in 1934 for Chicago Tribune-New York Daily News Syndicate; by 1946 the strip appeared in 300 newspapers and earned Caniff $75,000 annually. But Caniff wanted to own his own strip (and earn more money) and through Marshall Fields' Chicago Sun Syndicate, he created the "Steve Canyon" strip that earned him $2,000 weekly. (Artist George Wunder inherited "Terry" and continued the strip until 1973.) Caniff was a founder of the National Cartoonist Society and an honorary member of the Eighth Air Force Historical Society. "Terry and the Pirates" continues in national syndication by Tribune Media Services, drawn by Michael Uslan and the brothers Hildebrant. Books include: *Terry and the Pirates, Male Call: The Complete War Time Strip, 1942-1946.*

Al (Alfred Gerald) Capp (1909-79) made hillbillies respectable in his strip "Li'l Abner," and was responsible for "Sadie Hawkins Day" on college campuses in the 1940s and '50s. Through his strip, Capp brought the lovable Shmoos to a short-lived fame. In his later years, a sordid sex charge and Capp's right-wing satire lost him readers, however. No less an authority than John Steinbeck suggested Capp be awarded a Nobel Prize as America's best satirist. Capp had an excellent background with art training at the Chicago Academy of Fine Arts, the Designers Art School, the Philadelphia Museum, and the Boston Museum of Fine Arts. In 1912–as A.G. Caplin–he took over an existing strip, "Mr. Gilfather," distributed by the Associated Press. He became an assistant to Ham Fisher, creator of "Joe Palooka." In one episode Capp introduced some hillbilly characters that became the prototype for his Yokum family. United Features Syndicate introduced "Lil' Abner" in 1934 to wide acceptance. Capp used his strip to satirize Fisher and Chester Gould–"Fearless Fosdick," a parody of "Dick Tracy," became a regular sub-feature in the "Li'l Abner" strip. The strip became a successful motion picture and Broadway musical. Books: *The World of Little Abner, The Life and Times of the Shmoo, The Bald Iggle.*

Percy L. Crosby (1890-1964), created "Skippy," a comic strip favorite of millions of readers and the character that made Jackie Cooper a movie star when it appeared on the screen. Despite his comic art success, Crosby was a tragic figure; his strip was canceled in 1945 and alcoholism and mental illness kept him confined to a hospital the last years of his life. He studied art at New York's Pratt Institute and the Art Students' League. At 19 he landed a job as editorial cartoonist for the Socialist New York *Call.* That dollar-a-week job lasted ten weeks before he switched to the *Globe* and for a short time, the *World* with a strip called "The Clancy Kids." After service in the war as a first lieutenant, Crosby returned with a new strip, "The Rookie from the Thirteenth Squad" and a book of war cartoons. From 1921-25, he created several strips as a free-lance, one of which, "Always Belittlin'" became a prototype for "Skippy." Skippy was a nine-year-old kid from the city who came to life in a full-page feature in the old *Life* magazine. By 1925 his strip was a nation-wide favorite, syndicated by King Features. The Wall Street Crash of 1929 and the New Deal pushed Crosby to political dementia. He attacked FDR as a Communist and his comic strip, reflecting his political views, lost its whimsy and pathos and was canceled in 1945. Crosby, with a sinking fortune, alcoholism, and delusions of persecution–he asserted that Skippy peanut butter infringed his patent–was committed to the Kings Park Veterans Hospital as a paranoid schizophrenic in 1948. He died in 1964. Books include: *Between Shots, Skippy, Dear Sooky, Always Belittlin' A Cartoonist's Philosophy, The Red, Red and Red.*

Rudolph Dirks (1877-1968) originated "The Katzenjammer Kids" strip in 1887 for Hearst's New York *Journal* to compete with Joseph Pulitzer's New York *World* feature, "The Yellow Kid." Hence, "yellow journalism" became a force in American newspaperr culture. Dirks' German family was modeled from the long-running "Max und Moritz" strip, created by William Busch. Dirks' version featured a family–the Captain, Momma, Hans and Fritz and the school inspector. Dirks was entirely self-taught and after service in the Spanish-American War, he free-lanced work to *Judge* and *Life* before he joined the *Journal.* In 1912, when Dirks moved to the *World,* the *Journal* retained the title and the strip was drawn by Harold H. Knerr. During the year-long litigation over ownership, the strip disappeared from the comic pages. When Dirks joined the *World,* he renamed the strip "Hans und Fritz," but anti-German sentiment during World War I brought a new name, "The Captain and the Kids." American newspaper readers had two versions of the same strip, but Dirks' version was considered superior and it continued for sixty-one years. His son, John Dirks continued the strip when Dirks retired in 1958. More than a hundred years after its inception, "The Katzenjammer Kids," is drawn today by artist Hy Eisman, and the comic continues syndication through King Features. Books: *The Cruise of the Katzenjammer Kids, The Katzenjammer Kids: Early Strips in Full Color.*

Will (William Erwin) Eisner (1917-), an outstanding innovator in the field of graphic illustration, is creator of "The Spirit," a comic work of art. Eisner studied at the Art Students' League under George Bridgeman and joined the New York *American* as an advertising artist. He then went to work for *Wow,* a producer of original comic books. Following *Wow's* demise, Eisner joined with Jerry Iger in 1937 to become a comic book producer, and following that brief episode, Eisner joined Quality Comics. In 1940, Eisner produced his own comic book supplement for Sunday newspapers through the Des Moines Register & Tribune Syndicate. Wartime service from 1942-45 in the Pentagon enabled him to continue his art; "Joe Dope" was one feature for servicemen. Eisner continued contract work for the armed forces after his discharge. The sixteen-page supplement included three comics: "The Spirit," "Mr. Mystic," and "Lady Luck," but only "The Spirit" was notable for its motion picture-like graphics and crisp art."The Spirit" ended in 1952 and Eisner continued his illustration for a number of books. Books include: *The Dreamer, A Contract with God, The Spirit.*

Hal (Harold R.) Foster (1892-1982) established an extraordinary standard of art excellence in his classic strip "Prince Valiant." Before that strip began in 1937, Foster had already made a name as an outstanding artist with the work he did for the "Tarzan" comic beginning in 1929. Prince Valiant is the central character in the strip laid in the time of King Arthur and the Round Table era and for years it ran as a full-page illustration that was distributed by King Features Syndicate to more than 350 newspapers. With the comic page shrinkage, the strip has been reduced to half-page or one-third size. During his lifetime William Randolph Hearst dictated that every newspaper publish Foster's art in full-page format. The draftsmanship is excellent and its accuracy unimpeachable. After study at the Art Institute in Chicago, Foster turned to advertising illustration and was commissioned to illustrate a book, *Famous Books and Players.* He was invited to illustrate the Tarzan strip in 1931. Foster continued with the strip until he retired in 1971 and the strip continues under the fine work of John Cullen Murphy (creator of "Big Ben Bolt") and son Cullen Murphy. Books: *Prince Valiant in the Days of King Arthur, Prince Valiant Fights Atilla the Hun.*

Fontaine Fox Jr. (1884-1964) was inspired by the people in his home town to create "Toonerville Folks," a collection of people that America took to its heart. As the Toonerville trolley passed through town, readers observed the activities of the inhabitants–the Terrible Tempered Mr. Bang, Aunt Eppie Hogg, and Mickey 'Himself' McQuire.(the first motion picture role for Mickey Rooney). The trolley conductor and operator, The Skipper, observed all. After high school, Fox worked for the Louisville *Herald,* then attended Indiana University for two years, and returned to the *Herald.* Later he worked for the Louisville *Times* and the Chicago *Post,* where he drew boys' cartoons from 1910-15. He then joined the Wheeler Syndicate and launched "Toonerville Folks." The trolley made its last run from Toonerville to Funkville in 1955 and the strip disappeared from America's landscape. Ironically, at the time trolleys were giving way to busses all over America, just as "Toonerville" represented a by-gone era. Books include: *Fontaine Fox's Toonerville Trolley, Toonerville Folks and Other Cartoons.*

Theodore Suess Geisel (Dr. Suess) (1904-91) was an important influence on twentieth-century American childhood, exceeded perhaps only by Walt Disney. His many books include classics, such as *The Cat in the Hat* and *The Grinch Who Stole Christmas.* From 1941-43, however, Suess had a career as a newspaper editorial cartoonist for the New York *PM.* His work, leftist and liberal, reflected his newspaper's stand, with attacks on Nazism, Hitler, race relations, and anti-Semetism. His education was at Dartmouth College, where his pen-name emerged as an artist for the college humor magazine. A year at Oxford convinced Geisel that academic life held little interest. Before joining *PM,* Suess (his work was under that name) did advertising work and became well-known for his comic ads for Flit, a bug spray. Geisel served as an officer with Frank Capra's Signal Corps unit, during World War II producing propaganda films. After the war, Geisel turned to full-time writing. His children's books became a publishing phenomenon–his forty-six books have sold over twenty million copies and been translated into twenty languages. Books also include: *Dr. Suess Goes to War, Yertle the Turtle, The Butter Battle Book.*

Chester Gould (1900-85), originated one of America's best known comic strips, "Dick Tracy" that at its height of fame was syndicated to more than 1,000 American newspapers and to twenty-seven abroad. The strip appeared on the front page of the New York *Daily News* for forty-five years.. Rival cartoonist Al Capp, creator of the "Li'l Abner," regularly inserted a satiric character, Fearless Fosdick, into his own strip that readers readily recognized. as America's favorite crime fighter. Dick Tracy moved from the comic pages to movie houses with a feature motion picture, as well as Saturday afternoon serials. After study at Oklahoma A&M and Northwestern Universities, Gould joined King Features to draw "stinker" cartoons "Fillum Fables" and "Radio Cats." Seeking a cartoon of his own, Gould bombarded Joseph Medill Patterson, publisher of the New York *Daily News,* with ideas which were rejected. In 1929 Gould joined the Chicago *Daily News* and inspired by the Capone-era racketeering in Chicago, created a strip, "Plainclothes Tracy," which he submitted to Patterson, who changed the name, created a story line and made the strip a success. Gould's comic was violent, bloody, and gruesome and full of technological innovations. His villains entered the lexicon–B.O. Plenty, Gravel Gertie, Prune Face, and 88 Keys to mention a few. Gould retired in 1977 and died eight years later, but his strip continues. Tribune Media Services syndicates the modern version of "Dick Tracy," politically correct and up-to-date, drawn by Dick Locher and Mike Kilian. Books: *Dick Tracy and Dick Tracy Junior, and How They Captured 'Stooge' Viller, Dick Tracy and Dick Tracy Junior and How They Captured the Racketeers.*

Dave Graue (1926-2001) inherited the popular "Alley Oop" in 1950 from Vincent T. Hamlin, who originated the strip in 1933. Graue drew and wrote the strip until 2001, and was associated with "Alley Oop" longer than its creator. Vincent's creation was syndicated by NEA and is now distributed by United Media. Graue was hired by Hamlin as an inker in 1944. Graue's wartime service as an Army pilot allowed him time to contribute cartoons to the Pacific *Stars and Stripes.* After the war, he attended the Art Institute of Pittsburgh and worked for the Pittsburgh *Post-Gazette,* and returned to work for Hamlin in 1950. The strip recounts the adventures of caveman Alley, who travels with his pet dinosaur, Dinny (forget the fact that humans and dinosaurs are separated by 65 million years). A time-machine carried Oop and friends beyond the stone age to all areas that offered adventure. The fantasy held readers' interest for more than seven decades and continues; it is now written and drawn by Jack and Carole Bender. Jack Bender took over as the artist for daily and Sunday strips beginning in 1991, while Graue confined his activity to writing continuity until late 2001.

Harold Gray (1894-1968) drew his comic strip, "Little Orphan Annie" for adult readers and his message was right-wing, conservative Republican gospel. The orphan waif with the support of frequently absent benevolent Daddy Warbucks, a wealthy munitions manufacturer (war bucks), accompanied by her faithful dog Sandy, won the hearts of readers even if the real message of the strip was arcane to most. Annie and all the characters in the strip were invariably drawn with oval blank eyes; Sandy's contribution whatever the situation, was "Arf, Arf." Annie was another comic contribution by New York *Daily News* publisher Joseph Medill Patterson. With no art training, Gray became a newspaper artist after his strip was launched in 1924. The comic–often grim and violent–was syndicated at the time of his death to more than 400 newspapers. Annie found wider fame as a continuing radio serial (that made Ovaltine a household word), in motion pictures, and on Broadway. Tribune Media Services syndicates the modern version of "Annie," drawn by Leonard Starr, absent the conservative propaganda. Books: *Little Orphan Annie; My Folks, As Told by Little Orphan Annie.*

John Held Jr. (1889-1958) defined visually the Jazz Age for America as F. Scott Fitzgerald did with his writing. Held's identification of that era's "flapper" was known to millions of readers who never saw one in life. Held, with no formal training, began submitting his cartoons to the old *Life* in 1904; the next year he was hired by the Salt Lake City (Utah) *Tribune* as a sports cartoonist. In 1910, Held moved to New York and worked for the Collier's Agency. As Myrtle Held, he published cartoons in *Vanity Fair* from 1915-16. By 1918 his distinctive characters arose and he hit his stride with the *New Yorker* when that magazine emerged. He produced a series,

"Merely Margie," for King Features from 1931-36. The showcase for Held was the *New Yorker.* In later years, Held served as an artist-in-residence at Harvard College and the University of Georgia. Books include: *Frankie and Johnny, Outlines of Sport, Grim Youth, Women Are Necessary, A Bowl of Cherries, The Flesh is Weak.*

George Herriman III (1880-1944) created a unique art form with his surreal comic "Krazy Kat" and not everyone understood its characters or story line. Kat could be male or female; trees grew in pots; Herriman's sky could be purple or polka-dot; and the horizon became a wall the characters could climb over. Even the brick that Ignaz, the mouse, repeatedly hurled at Kat took on dimensions sometimes human. The strip must be seen to be explained and even then defies explanation. Herriman's strip, that disappeared with his death, remains an influence on newspaper illustrators. The dialogue reflected Herriman's background–his parents were Creole–and he employed language derived from black and Spanish-American vernacular. Herriman began as an office boy for the Los Angles *Herald,* but met no success with his early cartoons. He moved to New York and a succession of jobs before landing with the New York *World* and later the *Evening Journal.* He found some acceptance with a number of early comics: "The Dingbat Family," "Professor Otto and His Auto" and "Doc Archie and the Bean," before making a hit with "Krazy Kat" in 1913. King Features syndicated "Krazy Kat," and if few readers appreciated the art and genius of Herriman, publisher Hearst did with enthusiasm and directed his editors to run the strip. Herrriman also illustrated Don Marquis' Archy and Mehitabel, two other characters that delighted newspaper readers. Books: *Krazy Kat, Baron Bean, The Family Upstairs, The Komplete Kolor Krazy Kat.*

Bil Keane (1922-) created the popular cartoon, "The Family Circus" (not a panel, but confined within a circle format); its appeal has kept it in newspapers for more than forty years. Distributed by King Features to more than 1,500 newspapers, daily and Sunday (a panel). After high school in 1940, Keane worked for the Philadelphia *Bulletin* as a messenger; from 1942-45, he served in the Army drawing cartoons for *Yank* and *Stars and Stripes.* After his discharge, Keane returned to the *Bulletin* and created a Sunday cartoon, "Silly Philly." Another Keane cartoon feature is "Channel Chuckles, that ran for a half-dozen years, beginning in 1954. "The Family Circus" is one of America's long-running, popular comics Early syndication was by the Des Moines Register and Tribune and then the Cowles Syndicate. A number of the episodes, are highly laced with doses of fundamental Christian theology–Grandfather regularly descends from heaven to oversee events. In recent years the strip is signed by Bil Keane and his son, Jeff (in the cartoon he remains a child of seven). Book: *The Family Circus.*

Walt Kelly (1913-73) produced America's most notable political satire encountered in a comic strip, "Pogo." The little possum and his fellow swampland denizens created by Kelly had characteristics more human than animal. Kelly combined his humor with whimsy and pointed satire to produce art of excellent draftsmanship and sometimes savage commentary on the human condition. After high school, Kelly worked from 1928-35 on the staff of the Bridgeport (Conn.) *Post* and from 1935-41 he worked as an animator for the Disney Studios. After that he worked as a commercial artist in New York until 1948. He joined the New York *Star* as art director and served as the editorial cartoonist during the short life of that newspaper. It was one of the few in the nation backing Harry Truman and Kelly's satirical drawing of GOP candidate Thomas E. Dewey was a classic."Pogo" appeared as a comic feature in 1949, syndicated by Publishers-Hall. Its following soon took on the aspects of a cult. Despite efforts to continue the strip after his death, it was apparent that no one could match Kelly's genius. A number of books remain in print to remind us of the charm of this unique comic art. Books include: *Outrageously Pogo, Pluperfect Pogo, Everlovin' Pogo, Pogo: We Have met the Enemy and He Is Us, Pogo's Body Politic, The Best of Pogo.*

Hank (Henry) Ketcham (1920-2001) created the popular strip, "Dennis the Menace," that featured a freckle-faced, prekindergarten kid in a daily and Sunday strip that ran for nearly fifty years (after Ketcham's death the strip continued with other artists). The popular character was featured in books, a television series, a motion picture, and a Broadway musical. "Dennis" began in 1951 to immediate popularity and fifty years later was being syndicated by NAS (North American Syndicate) to 1,000 newspapers in forty-eight countries and nineteen languages. Ketcham ceased drawing the Sunday version in 1980 and in 1994 turned over production, which he supervised, to a team of artists. Ketcham dropped out of the University of Washington and worked as an animator for Walter Lantz and later Walt Disney productions. He served in the U.S. Navy during World war II and then turned to free-lance cartoon work. Books: *Dennis the Menace, More Dennis the Menace, The Merchant of Dennis the Menace.*

Frank O. King (1883-1959) seized on America's love affair with the automobile to create "Gasoline Alley," a strip that centered around backyard mechanics and recounted the family adventures of the Wallets. The foundling left at their door, Skeezix, was the inspiration of Joseph Medill Patterson, publisher of the New York *Daily News.* Innovations that King introduced into his strip was that the characters aged; Skeezix grew up, Uncle Walt aged into a grandfather; and "Gasoline Alley" was absent violence and adventure. King's career as a cartoonist began with the Minneapolis *Times* after study at Chicago's Academy of Fine Arts. King moved to the Chicago *Tribune* in 1909 and he drew cartoons overseas during World War I. His first strip was "Bobby Make-Believe" in 1915. The people and setting for "Gasoline Alley" were drawn from life and it began its successful run in 1919. King continued the strip until he retired in 1951 and it was drawn then by Dick Moores until 1986. The strip continues today under the direction of Jim Scancarelli. The day to day story of the Wallets' extended family continues to enchant readers. Books: *Skeezix and Uncle Walt. Skeezix and Pat, Gasoline Alley.*

Winsor McKay (1867-1934) was creator of one of the most beautifully drawn comic strips, "Little Nemo in Slumberland," ever to appear in American newspapers. McKay also developed in 1909 one of America's first animated cartoons, a feature depicting "Gertie the Dinosaur" a 10,000-panel saga drawn by hand that paved the way for a major motion picture industry. He also produced "Little Nemo," "The Sinking of the Lusitania," and many others. McKa, with no formal art training, began illustrating posters and worked briefly for two Cincinnati newspapers, the *Cumberland* and the *Enquirer,* where his illustrations accompanied his stories. In 1902, he joined the New York *Telegram* and developed the comics that made him famous: "Little Nemo in Slumberland," "Little Nemo and the Princess," "Tale of the Jungle Imps," and others. His fame led him to the vaudeville stage with a $1,000 weekly salary. He left the *Telegram* in 1911 for the *Herald* and later joined the New York *American.* The horrors of the first World War caused him to abandon comic art and his work took on a more serious tone with editorial cartoons. He revived Little Nemo briefly as "In the Land of Wonderful Dreams." Books: *Little Sammy Sneeze, Little Nemo in Slumberland, Dreams of the Rarebit Fiend.*

George McManus (1884-1954) found fame and a considerable fortune with the story of a working-class Irish family who rose in society. "Bringing Up Father," which began in 1912, deals with Jiggs, who longs for little more than Dinty Moore stew, and his shrewish wife Maggie and her aspirations to attend the opera and other upper-class activities. The strip began in an era when the Irish were not accepted in society, and an acceptable butt of humor. McManus failed to finish high school and went to work as a janitor for the St. Louis *Republic's* art department. When he reached the level of fashion art director, he began his first comic strip, "Alma and Oliver." He joined the New York *World,* where he originated a series of strips: "Panhandle Pete," "Let George Do It," "Snoozer," "Nibsy the Newsboy in Funny Fairyland," "Cheerful Charlie" and "The Newlyweds." When he joined King Features in 1912, he originated "Their Only Child" and "Bringing Up Father," freely adopted from a Broadway play. The strip was a success, itself inspiring a Broadway production, a radio serial, and several motion picture versions. King Features continued the strip after

McManus' death with Frank Fletcher as its artist; "Bringing Up Father" is carried on today by Frank Johnson. Books: *The Newlyweds. Bringing Up Father, Fun for All, Jiggs is Back.*

R.F. (Richard Felton) Outcault (1863-1928) was the father of the "The Yellow Kid," the comic that introduced "yellow journalism" to America. He was also creator of "Buster Brown." First introduced to newspapers in Pulitzer's New York *World,* the popular character was lured by William Randolph Hearst to the rival *Journal* for a much higher salary. Consequently, the *Journal* continued the Kid (real name Mickey Hogan), now drawn by George B. Luks in "Hogan's Alley" and Outcault continued his version of the Kid in a new locale, "McFadden's Flats"–both neighborhoods entered the American lexicon as a description of urban slums. By the beginning of the century, the Yellow Kid was appearing in the *Journal* and the *World* simultaneously. Both became known as the "Yellow Kid Papers." This evolved into "yellow journalism"–a misnomer for sensational journalism. Outcault's early art training was at the Cincinnati McMiken University and after graduation, he located in New York. He contributed work to *Judge, Life, Electric World,* and *Truth;* in this later publication, the Kid made his first appearance. The *World* began publishing Outcault's cartoon panel in 1894 and it was a comic aimed at adults, not children. The humor was grim and today would be labeled racist and anti-Irish. Outcault left the *Journal* in 1901 and created a now-forgotten strip "Poor Li'l Mose" before he created "Buster Brown" in 1902. If the Yellow Kid made him famous, Buster Brown made Outcault wealthy. Buster and his bulldog Tige were immensely popular and still are associated with a brand of footwear. Outcault returned to the *Journal* and remained there until 1920 when he discontinued the strip and concentrated on painting. Motion pictures and product endorsements, not to mention thousands of dogs named Tige, kept Buster Brown alive in American homes The Outcault Advertising Company of Chicago was a pioneer in creating advertisements for children's products and Buster Brown played a major role. Books: *Buster Brown and His Resolutions, Buster Brown and His Friends, Buster Brown Abroad.*

Alex (Alexander Gillespie) Raymond (1909-56) is known primarily for the action-adventure, space age comic "Flash Gordon" in the 1930s, but he also created "Rip Kirby" and, in cooperation with Dashiel Hammett, "Secret Agent X-9." Raymond's education at Iona Preparatory School was followed by art training at the Grand Central School of Art. In 1930 he joined King Features and worked on two comic strips–with Russ Westover's "Tillie the Toiler" and Lyman Young's "Tim Tyler's Luck." In 1934 "Flash Gordon" made its debut and was an instant success–for its fine art and futuristic space adventures. He also created another strip, "Jungle Jim" that accompanied "Flash Gordon" to fill a full-page. At about the same time, he teamed with Hammett to create "Secret Agent X-9." Success came with the "Flash Gordon" strip: a radio series, three motion picture serials, and books. In 1944 Raymond served in the Marine Corps in the South Pacific as a combat artist and public information officer aboard a Navy carrier. Upon his return, Raymond created "Rip Kirby" in 1946. It was the only strip he continued to draw until his death. King Features keeps "Flash Gordon" alive with the art of Jim Keefe. Books include: *Flash Gordon: Mongo, the Planet of Doom, Flash Gordon in the Caves of Mongo, Flash Gordon.*

Charles M. (Sparky) Schulz (1922-2001) created one of the most-beloved strips, "Peanuts," featuring Snoopy, a dog with qualities of imagination and insight. The ostensible star of the strip is "Good ol' Charlie Brown" surrounded by a cast of characters who reflect every facet of life. "Most of us are acquainted with losing. Very few of us ever win," Schulz observed. Charlie Brown is one of life's losers, beloved nonetheless. Schulz served as an enlisted man in Europe during World War II, as a squad leader of a machine gun unit. After the war, he trained as an artist with a correspondence school then became a staff member of the Art Instruction School. His first job was with *Timeless Topics,* lettering texts for finished cartoons. He hit the big time in 1948 with the *Saturday Evening Post;* his comic panel "Little Folks" was bought by the St. Paul (Minn.) *Pioneer Press.* United Features liked the idea and suggested a strip and remained it "Peanuts." Schulz's art was not the typical gag cartoon; readers laughed because of his harrowing sanity and hard truths about life's indifference to most of us. His characters include Lucy, the crabby know-it-all, Linus, with his cryptic observations, and especially Snoopy, with his a fertile imagination–atop his dog house he refights World War I in his Sopwith Camel and serves in the French Foreign Legion. Beyond the newspaper pages, Schulz reaped huge rewards from the strip. All sorts of commercial ties-ins are commercialized; television specials, beginning in 1965 with "Merry Christmas, Charlie Brown," appear annually; a Broadway production, "You're a Good Man, Charlie Brown," ran for 1,597 performances. Schulz's income surpassed six million dollars annually. Part of the success is that the "Peanuts" characters embody human qualities identifiable universally. Illness compelled Schulz to announce his strip's end, but he died before the final strip appeared; United Features continues the strip using drawings from the past. No other artist could be expected to continue his genius, but the syndicate holds a half-century inventory. Books include: *Charlie Brown, Snoopy and Me, Peanuts Jubilee: My Life and Art with Charlie Brown and Others, You Don't Look 35, Peanuts: A Golden Celebration.*

E.C. (Elzie Crisler) Seegar (1894-1938) introduced Popeye, a character in his King Features comic "Thimble Theatre," in 1929, and the sailor with muscles in his forearm eventually dominated the strip, now named "Popeye." After finishing high school, a series of odd jobs, and a correspondence course in cartooning, Seegar–with the assistance of R.F. Outcault–landed a job with the Chicago *Herald*. Seegar did a strip, "Charlie Chaplin's Comic Capers," then in 1918 he drew a strip for the Chicago *Evening American,* "Looping the Loop." The next year he moved to New York when King Features hired him to present "The Thimble Theatre." He also created another strip in 1920, "The Five Fifteen," renamed "Sappo" in 1926. "Thimble Theatre" was populated primarily by the Oye family–Olive, Castor and other assorted characters. Popeye, who held a particular liking for spinach, was hired to sail their ship in 1929. Popeye was an instant hit, but other characters captured America's imagination–Alice the Goon, the Sea Hag, Sweepea, and J. Wellington Wimpy, a cowardly moocher who craved hamburgers. The Jeep won permanent fame during its incarnation as the World War II rugged, four-wheeled Army vehicle. Popeye won fame on the radio, in the motion picture world and television. Credit for the motion picture animation must be given Max Fleischer (creator of Betty Boop, with a unique voice, who made her way into newspaper comic pages), who created the movie cartoons from 1933-42. After Seegar's death a number of people carried on the strip: Tom Sims, Bela Zaboly, Bud Sagendorf, Bobby London, and Hy Eisman, who is in charge today. Books include: *Thimble Theatre Starring Popeye, Popeye Among the White Savages, Popeye and the Pirates, Popeye Cartoon Book.*

Garry B. (Garretson Beekman) Trudeau (1948-) is one of the few comic strip artists to win a Pulitzer prize (in 1975) for newspaper editorial cartooning; his "Doonesbury" strip is banished from the comic page in many newspapers for its heavy political message. Trudeau attended St. Paul's Preparatory School, then Yale University. His central cartoon character was born in those schools' publications His Weenie Man creation at St. Paul's evolved into Mike Doonesbury and the strip, "Bull Tales," for the Yale *Daily News* and the *Record*. After graduation, the Universal Press Syndicate renamed the strip and syndicated it in 1970. Trudeau is hard on the president of the United States, whatever the party, and other incompetent or pompous public figures, including the media. His political slant is usually liberal, But a major thrust of Trudeau's satire is aimed with deadly accuracy at liberal Walden College, its hypocrisy toward a football program, a scholastic program where no one ever fails, with academic standards that are barely adequate. Trudeau's Pulitzer prize brought criticism–technically, he is not an editorial-page cartoonist. Berke Breathed's "Bloom County" won a similar honor in 1987, but the precedent was set in 1945 when Bill Mauldin's wartime "Up Front" received a Pulitzer. "Doonesbury" appears in some 900 newspapers and readers either love the cartoon or hate it, the messages leave little room for neutrality. Books: *Doonesbury, Still a Few Bugs in the System, But This War has Such Promise, The President is a Lot Smarter than You Think, The Doonesbury Chronicles.*

Mort Walker (1923-) is best known as the creator of "Beetle Bailey." Beetle, a drop-out college kid who ended up in the Army, is surrounded by a wacky group of similar misfits led by a befuddled General Amos Halftrack. Walker also created "Hi and Lois" (1954), "Boner's Ark" (1969), and "Sam and Silo" (1977). After wartime service in Italy, Walker graduated from the University of Missouri in 1948. He spent time designing greeting awards for Hallmark and free-lanced for magazines. "Beetle" was created in 1950 and for more than a half-century has seen service at Camp Swampy, constantly on KP, bedeviled by "Sarge," a complacent "lifer," without even earning a Pfc stripe (Beetle and his gang have somehow avoided all wartime engagements). Beetle, related to Lois from another Walker strip, muddles through life seeking only more sleep. This strip has earned Walker enmity from the politically correct who take umbrage at his portrayal of women. Walker, a recipient of numerous awards, is founder of the Museum of Cartoon Art. In addition to the dozens of paperback cartoon collections, his books include: *Most, Land of Lost Things, Backstage at the Strips, The Lexicon of Comicana, Mort Walker's Private Scrapbook.*

Chic (Murat Bernard) Young (1901-73) left a legacy that has endured; in 1930 he created "Blondie," a comic character known to millions of readers. A broad appeal to middle-class values with a suburban and office setting led to "Blondie's" appearance in more than 1,600 newspapers in sixty countries at the time of Young's death. His beginnings were modest: after high school, Young tried his luck in Chicago and with the help of a hastily prepared strip, "The Affairs of Jane," landed a position with NEA (Newspaper Enterprise Association). There he developed a successful strip, "Dumb Dora" (which he owned) and another, "Beautiful Babs." In 1923 he joined King Features and in 1930 introduced "Blondie" (to which he prudently retained full ownership). Its success led to an annual $300,000 income for Young. His supplemental strips "The Family Foursome" and "Colonel Potterby and the Duchess" were Sunday run-above strips for "Blondie." The strip evolved. Originally, Blondie was a flapper who was taken with Dagwood, a rail tycoon's son who was disinherited for marrying such a ditz. Eventually, children and a dog came along; Baby Dumpling became Alexander and sister Cookie aged, at least until they reached their late teens, but Daisy and the pups (who eventually disapeared) remained ageless. In recent years the strip has followed the times–Blondie runs a catering service, Dagwood no longer smokes a pipe and Mr. Dithers, his boss, has abandoned cigars. Readers continue to like the comic; it gave birth to a radio show, twenty-eight B-grade motion pictures, toys and games. Illness forced Young to turn over his strip to his son Dean and Jim Raymond. Later, cartoonist Stan Drake was a collaborator; today Dean Young and Denis Lebrun continue the strip.

Selected Bibliography

A selective list of books dealing with journalists or journalism and a number written by practicing journalists. These sources will provide a useful guide to additional facts and anecdotes for specific individuals and should be helpful for further investigation into more information pertaining to the work of people and events of twentieth-century journalism. Note: Only a representative group of published work is included for a number of authors; additional works are available beyond the sources identified.

Abbot, Wills J. *Watching the World Go By* (Boston: Little, Brown, 1933).

Adams, Franklin P. *By and Large* (Garden City: Doubleday, Page and Co., 1914).

_________, *The Conning Tower Book* (New York: Macy-Massius, 1926).

Adams, Samuel Hopkins *A. Woollcott: His Life and his World* ((New York: Reynal and Hitchcock, 1945).

Ade, George *The America of George Ade: 1866-1944* Jean Shepard, ed. (New York: G.B. Putnam, 1960).

_______, *The Permanent Ade: The Living Writings of George Ade* Fred C. Kelly, ed. (Indianapolis: Bobbs-Merrill, 1947).

Alsop, Joseph and Alsop, Stewart *The Reporter's Trade* (New York: Reynal & Co., 1958).

Alterman, Eric *Sound & Fury* (New York: Harper/Collins, 1992).

Altman, Billy *Laughter's Gentle Soul: The Life of Robert Benchley* (New York: W.W. Norton, 1997).

Anderson, Jack with James Boyd *Confessions of a Muckraker* (New York: Random House, 1979).

Anderson, Sherwood *Hello Towns!* (New York: Liveright, 1929).

Anthony, Edward *O Rare Don Marquis* (Garden City: Doubleday, 1962).

Ashley, Sally *F.P.A.: The Life and Times of Franklin Pierce Adams* (New York: Beufort, 1986).

Ayer, Eleanor H. *Margaret Bourke-White: Photographing the World* (New York: Dillon, 1992).

Baker, Russell *The Good Times* (New York: Wm. Morrow, 1989).

Baldasty, Gerald J. E.W. *Scripps and the Business of Newspapers* (Urbana: University of Illinois, 1999).

Baldwin, Hanson *Great Mistakes of the War* (New York: Harper, 1950).

Barnouw, Erik *The Golden Web: A History of Broadcasting in the United States: 1930-1953* (2 vols. (New York: Oxford University Press, 1970).

_______, *Tube of Plenty: The Evolution of American Television* (New York: Oxford University Press, 1979).

Barrett, James W. *The End of the World* (New York: Harper & Bros., 1931).

Beasley, Norman *Frank Knox, American* (New York: Doubleday, Doran, 1936).

Beebe, Lucius *The Lucius Beebe Reader* Charles Clegg and Duncan Enrich, eds. (Garden City: Doubleday, 1967).

Benchley, Nathaniel, *Robert Benchley: A Biography* (New York: McGraw-Hill, 1955).

Bennett, Michael J. *When Dreams Came True: The GI Bill and the Making of Modern America* (Washington: Brassey's, 1991).

Benson, Jackson J. *The True Adventures of John Steinbeck, Writer* (New York: Penguin, 1984).

Berger, Meyer *The Story of the New York Times* (New York: Simon and Schuster, 1951).

Bierce, Ambrose *The Collected Works of Ambrose Bierce* (New York: Citadel Press, 1989).

Bishop, Jim *The Mark Hellinger Story* (New York: Appleton-Century-Crofts, 1952).
Blackbeard, Bill *R.F. Outcault's the Yellow Kid* (Northampton: Kitchensink

Press, 1995).

Block, Herbert *A Cartoonist's Life* (New York: Macmillan, 1993).

Bloom, James D. *Left Letters: The Culture Wars of Mike Gold and Joseph Freeman* (New York: Columbia University Press, 1992).

Bok, Edward W. *The Americanization of Edward Bok: An Autobiography* (Philadelphia: The American Foundation, 1965).

Bourke-White, Margaret *Portrait of Myself* (New York: Simon and Schuster, 1963).

Bowles, Jerry *A Thousand Sundays: The Story of the Ed Sullivan Show* (New York: Putnam, 1980).

Bradlee, Ben *A Good Life: Newspapers and Other Adventures* (New York: Simon & Schuster/Touchstone, 1995).

Brady, Kathleen *Ida Tarbell: Portrait of a Muckraker* (New York: Seaview/ Putnam, 1984).

Brash, Walter *Forerunners of Revolution: Muckrakers and the American Social Conscience* (Lanham: University Press of America, 1990).

Breslin, Jimmy *Damon Runyon* (New York: Ticknor and Fields, 1991).

Brian, Denis *Pulitzer: A Life* (New York: John Wiley & Sons, 2001).

Brinkley, David *A Memoir* (New York; Ballantine, 1995).

Brisbane, Arthur *Today and the Future Day* (New York: Alberson Publishing, 1925).

Broder, David S. *Behind the Front Page: A Candid Look at How the News is Made* (New York: Simon & Schuster/Touchstone, 1987).

Broun, Heywood *Sitting on the World* (New York: Putnam, 1924).

Broun, Heywood Hale *Whose Little Boy Are You?* (New York: St. Martin's/ Marek, 1983).

Brown, Eve *Champaign Cholly* [Maury Paul] (New York: Dutton, 1947).

Buchwald, Art *Leaving Home: A Memoir* (New York: G.P. Putnam, 1993).

Busch, Noel *Briton Hadden* (New York: Ferrrar & Straus, 1949).

Cahan, Abraham *The Education of Abraham Cahan* 2 vols. (Philadelphia: Jewish Publication Society of America, 1969).

Caen, Herb *Only in San Francisco* (Garden City: Doubleday, 1960).

Canham, Erwin D. *Commitment to Freedom: The Story of the Christian Science Monitor* (Boston: Houghton Mifflin, 1958).

Cannon, Jimmy *Nobody Asked Me, But...The World of Jimmy Cannon* (New York: Holt, Rinehart and Winston, 1978).

Capa, Robert *Slightly Out of Focus* (New York: Henry Holt, 1947).

Carlson, Oliver *Brisbane–A Candid Biography* (New York: Stackpoole Sons, 1937).

Carney, Robert *What Happened at the Atlanta Times* (Atlanta: Business Press, 1969).

Carter, Hodding *Where Main Street Meets the River* (New York; Rinehart, 1953).

Cater, Douglass *The Fourth Branch of Government* (Boston: Houghton Mifflin, 1957).

Catledge, Turner *My Life and The Times* (New York: Harper & Row, 1971).

Chapman, Elisabeth Cobb *My Wayward Parent: A Book about Irvin S. Cobb* (Indianapolis: Bobbs-Merrill, 1945).

Chapman, John *Tell it to Sweeney: An Informal History of the New York Daily News* (New York: Doubleday and Co., 1961).

Childs, Marquis *I Write from Washington* (New York: Harper and Bros., 1942).

Christ-Joiner, Albert *Boardman Robinson* (Chicago: University of Chicago Press, 1946).

Churchill, Alan *Park Row* (New York: Rinehart, 1958).

Ciccone, F. Richard *Royko: A Life in Print* (New York: Public Affairs, 2001).

Clapper, Raymond *Watching the World* Olive Ewing Clapper, ed. (New York: Whittlesey House, 1944).

Clarke, Nick *Alistair Cooke: A Biography* (New York: Arcade, 1999).

Cloud, Stanley and Olson, Lynn *The Murrow Boys* (Boston: Houghton Mifflin, 1996).

Clurman, Richard *To the End of Time* (New York: Simon and Schuster, 1992).

Cochran, Negley D. *E.W. Scripps* (New York: Harcourt, Brace, 1933).

Commanger, Henry Steele *The American Mind: An Interpretation of American Thought and Character Since the 1800's* (New Haven: Yale University Press, 1954).

Conrad, Will et al *The Milwaukee Journal: The First Eighty Years* (Madison: University of Wisconsin Press, 1984).

Considine, Bob *It's All News to Me* (New York: Meredith, 1967).

Cook, Fred *The Muckrakers* (New York: Doubleday, 1972).

Cooke, Alistair *Memories of the Great & the Good* (New York: Arcade, 1999).

Cooper, Kent *Kent Cooper and the Associated Press* (New York: Random House, 1959).

Cort, David *The Sins of Henry R. Luce* (Secacus: Stuart, 1974).

Cottrell, Robert C. *Izzy: A Biography of I.F. Stone* (New Brunswick: Rutgers University Press, 1992).

Cowley, Malcolm *A Second Flowering* (New York: Viking/Compass, 1973).

Cox, James M. *Journey Through My Years* (New York: Simon and Schuster, 1946).

Craig, Douglas B. *Fireside Politics: Radio and Political Culture in the United States, 1920-1949* (Baltimore: Johns Hopkins University Press, 2001).

Creel, George *Rebel at Large: Recollections of Fifty Crowded Years* (New York: Ayer Co., 1927).

Croly, Herbert *The Promise of American Life* (New York: Macmillan,1919).

Cronkite, Walter *A Reporter's Life* (New York: Knopf, 1996).

Daniels, Josephus *Editor in Politics* (Chapel Hill: University of North Carolina Press, 1941).

Davis, Elmer *But We Were Born Free* (Garden City: Garden City Books, 1954).

Davis, Richard Harding *Notes of A War Correspondent* (New York: Scribner's & Sons, 1912).

Dennis, Charles H. *Eugene Field's Creative Years* (Garden City: Doubleday, Page and Co., 1924).

Diamond, Edwin *Behind the Times: Inside the New York Times* (Chicago: University of Chicago Press, 1995).

Dolmetsch, Carl, ed. *The Smart Set: A History and Anthology* (New York: Dial, 1966).

Donovan, Hedley *Right Places, Right Times* (New York: Henry Holt. 1989).

Downey, Fairfax *Richard Harding Davis* (New York: Scribner, 1933).

Dreiser, Theodore *Newspaper Days* (Philadelphia: University of Pennsylvania Press, 1991).

Driscoll, Charles B. *The Life of O.O. McIntyre* (New York: Greystone Press, 1938).

Dunne, Finley Peter *Mr. Dooley* Barbara Schaef, ed. (Springfield, Ill.: Lincoln Herndon Press, 1938).

Duranty, Walter *I Write as I Please* (New York: Simon and Schuster, 1935).

Earle, Neil *The Wonderful Wizard of Oz in American Culture* (Lewistown: Edwin Mellin Press, 1993).

Eastman, Max *Journalism versus Art* (New York: Knopf, 1915).

Edelman, Maurice *The Mirror: A Political History* (New York: Hamish Hamilton, 1966).

Elledge, Scott *E.B. White: A Biography* (New York: W.W. Norton, 1984).

Ellis, Elmer *Mr. Dooley's America* (New York: Knopf, 1941).

Emerson, Gloria *Winners & Losers* (New York: Random House, 1976).

Endres, Kathleen L. and Lueck, Theresa L., eds. *Women's Periodicals in the United States Consumer Magazines* (Westport: Greenwood Press, 1995).

Ernst, Robert *Weakness is a Crime: The Life of Bernarr MacFadden* (Syracuse: Syracuse University Press, 1991).

Fairfax, Beatrice [Marie Manning] *Ladies Now and Then* (New York: E.P. Dutton, 1944).

Fang, Irving E. *Those Radio Commentators* (Ames: Iowa State University Press, 1977).

Fanning, Charles *Peter Finley Dunne and Mr. Dooley: The Chicago Years* (Louisville: University Press of Kentucky, 1978).

Farber, Myron *Someone Is Lying* (New York: Doubleday, 1982).

Farr, Finis *Fair Enough: The Life of Westbrook Pegler* (New York: Arlington House, 1975).

Farson, Negley *The Way of a Transgressor* (New York: Zenith, 1983).

Faulk, Odie B. and Faulk, Laura E. *Frank Mayborn: A Man Who Made a Difference* (Baylor: University of Mary Hardin, 1989).

Febenthal, Carol *Power, Privilege and the Post* (New York: G.P. Putnam, 1993).

Ferber, Edna *A Peculiar Treasure* (New York: Literary Guild, 1939).

Fetherling, Doug *The Five Lives of Ben Hecht* (Toronto: Lester & Orpen, 1977).

Field, Eugene *Poems of Childhood* (New York: Simon and Schuster, 1966).

Fielding, Raymond *The American Newsreel: 1911-1967* (Norman: University of Oklahoma Press, 1972).

Filler, Louis *The Muckrakers: Crusaders for American Liberalism* (Chicago: Gateway/Regnery, 1968).

Fine, Barnett *A Giant of the Press* [Carr Van Anda] (New York: Editor & Publisher Library, 1933).

Fischer, Roger A. *Them Damned Pictures: Explorations in American Political Cartoon Art* (North Haven: Archon Press, 1996).

Fisher, Charles *The Columnists* (New York: Howell, Soskin, 1944).

Fitzpatrick, Daniel R. *As I Saw It* (New York: Simon and Schuster, 1953).

Ford, Cory *The Time of Laughter* (Boston: Little, Brown, 1967).

Forrest, Wilbur *Behind the Front Page* (New York: Appleton-Century, 1934).

Fountain, Charles *Sportswriter: The Life and Times of Grantland Rice* (New York: Oxford University Press, 1993).

Fowler, Gene *Skyline* (New York: Viking Press, 1961).

Frankel, Max *The Times of My Life* (New York: Random House, 1998).

Friendly, Fred W. *Due to Circumstances Beyond Our Control* (New York: Vintage, 1968).

Gabler, Neil *Winchell: Gossip, Power and the Culture of Celebrity* (New York: Viking, 1994).

Gardner, Mark and Nye, Russell B. *The Wizard of Oz and Who He Was* (East Lansing: University of Michigan Press, 1994).

Garis, Howard *Tom Swift and His Airship* [as Victor Appleton] (New York: Grosset and Dunlap, 1910).

________, *Uncle Wiggly Stories* (New York: Grosset and Dunlap, 1965).

Garis, Roger *My Father was Uncle Wiggly* (New York; McGraw-Hill, 1966).

Gates, Gary Paul *The Inside Story of CBS News* (New York: Harper & Row, 1978).

Gatewood, Wirth *Fifty Years in Pictures: The New York Daily News* (New York: Doubleday, 1979).

Gauvreau, Emile *My Last Million Readers* (New York: Dutton, 1941).

Germond, Jack *Fat Man in a Middle Seat* (New York: Random House, 2001).

______ and Witcover, Jules *Mad as Hell: Revolt at the Ballot Box, 1992* (New York: Warner Books, 1993).

Gibbons, Edward *Floyd Gibbons: Your Headline Hunter* (New York: Exposition, 1953).

Gies, Joseph *The Colonel of Chicago: A Biography of Robert R. McCormick* (New York: E.P. Dutton, 1980).

Gill, Brendan *Here at the New Yorker* (New York: Random House, 1975).

Gold, Mike *A Literary Anthology* Michael Folsom, ed. (New York: International Publishers, 1972).

Goldberg, Bernard *Bias: A CBS Insider Exposes How the Media Distorts the News* (Chicago: Regnary, 2001).

Golden, Harry *Harry Golden: An Autobiography* (New York: Putnam, 1949).

Goldstein, Tom *The News at Any Cost* (New York: Simon & Schuster, 1985).

Goulden, Joseph C. *Fit to Print: A.M. Rosenthal and His Times* (Secaucus: Stuart, 1988).

Graham, Katharine *Personal History* (New York: Knopf, 1997).

Grant, Jane *Ross, The New Yorker and Me* (New York: Reynal, 1968).

Grauer, Neil *Wits & Sages* (Baltimore: Johns Hopkins University Press, 1984).

Gunther, John *A Fragment of Autobiography* (New York: Harper & Row, 1964).

Halberstam, David *The Powers That Be* (New York: Knopf, 1979).

Hamill, Pete *Irrational Ravings* (New York: Putnam, 1971).

Hansen, Harry *Midwest Portraits: A Book of Memories and Friendships* (New York: Harcourt Brace, 1923).

Hapgood, Norman *The Changing Years* (New York: Ferrar and Rinehart, 1930).

Harris, Michael David *Always on Sunday, Ed Sullivan: An Inside View* (New York: Meredith, 1968).

Harris, Sydney *Strictly Personal* (Chicago: Regnary, 1953).

Harrison, S.L. *The Editorial Art of Edmund Duffy* (Cranbury: Fairleigh Dickinson University Press, 1998).

_______, *Mencken Revisited: Author, Editor & Newspaperman* (Lanham: University Press of America, 1999).

_______, *Twentieth-Century Journalists: America's Opinionmakers* (University Press of America, 2002).

Hecht, Ben *A Child of the Century* (New York: Simon & Schuster, 1954).

________, *Gaily, Gaily: The Memoirs of a Cub Reporter in Chicago* (Garden City: Doubleday and Co., 1963).

Hellinger, Mark *Moon Over Broadway* New York: W. Faro, 1931).

Hemingway, Ernest *By-Line: Ernest Hemingway* William White, ed. (New York: Touchstone/Simon and Schuster, 1998).

Herbst, Josephine *The Dark Blue Sky of Spain and Other Memoirs* (New York: HarperCollins, 1991).

Hertsgaard, Mark *On Bended Knee: The Press and the Reagan Presidency* (New York: Farrar, Straus Giroux, 1988).

Hess, Stephen and Northrop, Sandy *Drawn & Quartered: The History of American Political Cartoons* (Montgomery: Elliott and Clark, 1996).

Hewitt, Don *Tell Me a Story: 50 Years and 60 Minutes in Television* (New York: Public Affairs, 2001).

Hicks, Granville *John Reed: The Making of a Revolutionary* (New York:: Macmillan, 1936).

Higgins, Marguerite *War in Korea* (New York: Doubleday, 1951).

Hill, Edwin C. *The Human Side of the News* (New York: Black, 1934).

Hobson, Fred *Mencken: A Life* (New York: Random House, 1994).

Hohenberg, John *Foreign Correspondents: The Great Reporters and Their Times* 2nd ed. (Syracuse: Syracuse University Press, 1995).

Hoopes, Roy *Ralph Ingersoll* (New York: Atheneum, 1985).

Howe, E.W. *The Story of a Country Town* (New York: Signet, 1964).

Hoyt, Edwin Palmer *Alexander Woollcott: The Man Who Came to Dinner* (Radnor: Chilton Books, 1973).

Humes, Joy D. *Oswald Garrison Villard* (Syracuse: Syracuse University Press, 1960).

Huntley, Chet *Chet Huntley's News Analysis* (New York: Pocket Books, 1966).

Husk, Bill *Thunder in the Rockies: The Incredible Denver Post* (New York: Morrow, 1976).

Inabinett, Mark *Grantland Rice and His Heroes: The Sportswriter as Mythmaker* (Knoxville: University of Tennessee Press, 1994).

Ingersoll, Ralph *Point of Departure: An Adventure in Autobiography* (New York: Harcourt Brace & World, 1961).

Irwin, Will *The Making of a Reporter* (New York: Putnam's, 1942).

Israel, Lee *Kilgallen* (New York: Dial, 1980).

Jackson, Charles M. *The New Yorker: Yesterday and Beyond* (New York: Gill and Macmillan, 1995).

Johnson, Gerald L. *The Lines Are Drawn* (Philadelphia: J.B. Lippincott, 1958).

Johnson, Haynes *Sleepwalking Through History* (New York: Anchor, 1991).

Juergens, George *Joseph Pulitzer and the New York World* (Princeton: Princeton University Press, 1966).

Kahn, Jr., E.J. *The World of Swope* (New York: Press Publishing, 1965).

Kalb, Martin *One Scandalous Story: Clinton, Lewinsky & 13 Days That Tarnished American Journalism* (New York: Free Press/Simon & Schuster, 2001).

Von Kaltenborn, Hans *Kaltenborn Edits the War News* (New York: E.P. Dutton, 1942).

Kaplan, Justine *Lincoln Steffens* (New York: Simon & Schuster, 1974).

Keeler, Robert E. *Newsday: A Candid History of the Respectable Tabloid* (New York: Arbor House/Morrow, 1990).

Kelly, Fred *George Ade: Warmhearted Satirist* (Indianapolis: Bobbs-Merrill, 1947).

Kempton, Murray *Rebellions, Perversities, and Main Events* (New York: Times Books/Random House, 1994).

Kenny, Herbert A. *Newspaper Row* (Boston: Globe/Pequot Press, 1987).

Kent, Frank R. *The Great Game of Politics* (New York: Doubleday, Page, 1923).

Kilgallen, Dorothy *Girl Around the World* (Philadelphia: McKay, 1936).

Kilpatrick, James J. *The Writer's Art* (Kansas City: Andrews, McMeel, 1984).

Kinney, Harrison *James Thurber: His Life and Times* (New York: Henry Holt, 1997).

Kirby, Rollin *Highlights: A Cartoon History of the Nineteen Twenties* (New York: Payson, 1931).

Kluger, Richard *The Paper: The Life and Death of the New York Herald Tribune* (New York: Knopf, 1986).

Kluger, Steve *Yank, The Army Weekly* (New York: St. Martin's Press, 1991).

Knightly, Phillip *The First Casualty* (New York: Harcourt Brace Jovanovich, 1975).

Koppel, Ted *Off Camera: Private Thoughts Made Public* (New York: Vintage, 2001).

Kozel, Wendy *LIFE's America: Family and Nation in Post-War Photojournalism* (Philadelphia: Temple University Press, 1954).

Kramer, Dale *Heywood Broun: A Biographical Portrait* (New York: A.A. Wyn/Current, 1949).

Krock, Arthur *In the Nation: 1932-1966* (New York: McGraw-Hill, 1969).

Kroeger, Brooks *Nellie Bly: Daredevil, Reporter, Feminist* (New York: Times Books/Random House, 1994).

Kunkel, Thomas *Genius in Disguise: Harold Ross and the New Yorker* (New York: Random House, 1995).

Langer, Elinor *Josephine Herbst* (Boston: Little, Brown, 1984).

Lardner, Ring *Ring Around the Bases* (New York: Charles Scribner's Sons, 1963).

Lawrence, David *Diary of a Washington Correspondent* (New York: Kinsey, 1941).

Lee, Lynn *Don Marquis* (Boston: Twayne, 1981).

Lendt, David L. *Ding: The Life of Jay Norwood Darling* (Ames: Iowa State University Press, 1984).

Leonard, John *Private Lives in the Imperial City* (New York: Knopf, 1979).

Lerner, Max *Actions and Passions: Notes on the Multiple Revolution of Our Time* (New York: Simon and Schuster, 1949).

Lewis, Alfred Allen *Man of the World–Herbert Bayard Swope* (Indianapolis: Bobbs-Merrill, 1978).

Lewis, David Levering *W.E.B. DuBois: The Fight for Equality and the American Century, 1919-1963* (New York: Henry Holt, 2000).

Lewis, Tom *Empire of the Air: The Men Who Made Radio* (New York: Harper/ Perennial, 1993).

Lewinski, Jorge *The Camera at War* (New York: Simon & Schuster, 1978).

Liebling, A.J. *The Press* 2d ed. (New York: Ballantine, 1975).

_________, *The Wayward Pressman* (New York: Doubleday, 1947).

Lippmann, Walter *Interpretations: 1933-35* (New York: Macmillan, 1936).

________, *Public Opinion* (New York: The Free Press/Macmillan, 1963).

________, *The Phantom Public* (New York: Harcourt, Brace, 1925).

Loengars, John *Life Photogrphers: What They Saw* (Boston: Bullfinch.Little, Brown, 1998).

Long, E. Hudson *O. Henry: The Man and His Work* (Philadelphia: University of Pennsylvania Press, 1949).

Luce, Henry R. *The American Century* (New York: Farrar and Rinehart, 1941).

Lukas, J. Anthony *Big Trouble* (New York: Simon & Schuster, 1997).

Lyon, Peter *Success Story: The Life and Times of S.S. McClure* (De Land, Fla.: Edwards, 1967).

Lyons, Eugene *Assignment in Utopia* (New York: Harcourt, Brace, 1937).

MacAdama, William *Ben Hecht: The Man Behind the Legend* (New York: Charles Scribner's Sons, 1990).

MacCambridge, Michael *The Franchise: A History of Sports Illustrated Magazine* (New York: Hyperion, 1997).

McClure, Samuel S. *My Autobiography* (New York: Stokes, 1914).

McCorid, Richard *The Chain Gang: One Newspaper versus the Gannett Empire* (Columbia: University of Missouri Press, 2001).:

McCutcheon, John T. *Drawn from Memory* (Indianapolis: Bobbs-Merrill, 1950).

McFadden, Bernarr *The Truth About Tobacco* (New York: Physical Culture Publishing, 1921).

McGill, Ralph *Fleas Come with the Dog* (Nashville: Abingdon, 1954).

McIntyre, O.O. *The Big Town: New York Day by Day* (New York: Dodd Mead, 1935).

McKee, John DeWitt *William Allen White: Maverick on Main Street* (Westport: Greenwood Press, 1975).

McKelway, St. Clair *Gossip: The Life and Times of Walter Winchell* (New York: Viking Press, 1940).

McLemore, Henry *One of Us is Wrong* (New York: Holt, 1953).

McWilliams, Carey *Ambrose Bierce: A Biography* (New York: A. and C. Boni, 1921).

Maier, Thomas *Newhouse: All the Glitter, Power & Glory of America's Richest Media Empire and the Secretive Man Behind It* (Boulder: Johnson Books, 1997).

Manchester, William *The Glory and the Dream: A Narrative History of America, 1939-1972* 2 vols. (Boston: Little, Brown, 1972).

Marcosson, Isaac F. *David Graham Philips and His Times* (New York: Dodd, Mead, 1932).

Marquis, Don *The Best of Don Marquis* Christopher Morely, ed. (Garden City: Doubleday & Co, 1946).

Martin, Harold *Ralph McGill: Reporter* (Boston: Little, Brown, 1973).

Martin, Ralph *Cissy* (New York: Simon & Schuster, 1979).

Matthews, Herbert L. *The Education of a Correspondent* (New York: Harcourt, Brace, 1946).

Matusow, Barbara *The Evening Stars: The Making of the Network News Anchor* (Boston: Houghton Mifflin, 1983).

May, Antoinette *Witness to War: A Biography of Margueritte Higgins* (New York: Penguin Books, 1983).

Mayer, Jane and McManus, Doyle *Landslide: The Unmaking of the President, 1984-1988* (Boston: Houghton Mifflin Co., 1988).

Meade, Marion *Dorothy Parker: What Fresh Hell Is This?* (London: Heineman, 1988).

Mencken, H.L. *A Gang of Pecksniffs and other Comments on Newspaper Publishers, Editors and Reporters* Theo Lippman, ed. (New York: Arlington House, 1975).

_______, *My Life as Author and Editor* Jonathan Yardley, ed. (New York: Knopf, 1993).

_______, *Newspaper Days* (Baltimore: Johns Hopkins University Press, 1996).

Metz, Robert *CBS: Reflections in a Bloodshot Eye* (New York: Signet, 1973).

Meyer, Karl E. *Pundits, Poets, and Wits: An Omnibus of American Newspaper Columnists* (New York: Oxford University Press, 1990).

Miller, Leo *The Story of Ernie Pyle* New York: Viking, 1950).

Milton, Joyce *The Yellow Kids* (New York: Harper & Row, 1989).

Mitchell, Joseph *Up in the Old Hotel* (New York: Random House, 1993).

Montgomery, Ruth *Hail to the Chief: My Life and Times with Six Presidents* (New York: Coward-McCann, 1970).

Moore, William T. *Dateline Chicago* (New York: Taplinger Publishers, 1973).

Moorehouse, Ward *Just the other Day: From Yellow Pines to Broadway* (New York: McGraw-Hill, 1953).

Mullin, Linda *The Teddy Bear Man: Theodore Roosevelt and Clifford Berryman* (Cumberland: Hobby Horse Press, 1987).

Murrow, Edward R. *In Search of Light: The Broadcasts of Edward R. Murrow, 1938-1961* Edward Bliss, ed. (New York: Knopf, 1967).

Nasaw, David *The Chief: The Life and Times of William Randolph Hearst* (Boston: Houghton Mifflin, 2000).

Nathan, George Jean *The Entertainment of a Nation* (New York: Knopf, 1942).

Neuharth, Al *Confessions of an S.O.B.* (New York: Signet, 1992).

North, Robert *Robert Minor, Artist and Crusader: An Informal Biography* (New York: International Publishers, 1956).

O'Brien, Frank M. *The Story of the Sun* (New York: George H. Doran, 1918).

O'Connor, Richard *Ambrose Bierce: A Biography* (Boston: Little, Brown, 1967).

Older, Fremont *My Own Story* (New York: Macmillan, 1926).

Osgood, Charles *The Osgood Files* (New York: Fawcett, 1991).

O'Sullivan, Judith *The Great American Comic Strip: One Hundred Years of Cartoon Art* (Boston: Bullfinch Press/Little, Brown, 1990).

Patner, Andrew. *I.F. Stone: A Portrait* (New York: Pantheon, 1988).

Pearson, Drew *The Nine Old Men* (New York: Doubleday, Doran, 1937).

Pegler, Westbrook *Fair Enough: The Life of Westbrook Pegler* (New Rochelle: Arlington House, 1975).

Peplow, George *George S. Schuyler* (Boston: Twayne, 1980).

Persico, Joseph E. *Edward R. Murrow: An American Original* (New York: McGraw-Hill, 1988).

Phillips, Cabell *From the Crash to the Blitz, 1929-1939* (New York: Macmillan, 1969).

Pilat, Oliver *Drew Pearson: An Unauthorized Biography* (New York: Harper Magazine Press, 1973).

Povich, Shirley *All These Mornings* (Englewood Cliffs: Prentice-Hall, 1969).

Pyle, Ernie *Here Is Your War* (New York: Henry Holt, 1943).

Rascoe, Burton *We Were Interrupted* (Garden City: Doubleday, 1947).

Reasoner, Harry *Before the Colors Fade* (New York: Knopf, 1981).

Rechnitzer, F.E. *War Correspondent–The Story of Quentin Reynolds* (New York: Messner, 1943).

Reed, John *Ten Days That Shook the World* (New York: Boni and Liveright, 1919).

Reston, James *Deadline: A Memoir* (New York: Random House, 1991).

Reynolds, Quentin *Only the Stars Are Neutral* (New York: Random House, 1942).

Rice, Grantland *The Tumult and the Shouting: My Life in Sport* (New York: A.S. Barnes, 1954).

Rich, Everett *The Man From Emporia: William Allen White* (New York: Farrar and Rinehart, 1941).

Riis, Jacob A. *The Making of an American* (New York: Macmillan, 1929).

Roberts, Chalmers M. *The Washington Post: The First 100 Years* (Boston: Houghton Mifflin, 1977).

Rogers, Will *The Autobiography of Will Rogers,* Donald Day, ed. (Boston: Houghton Mifflin, 1949).

Rooney, Andrew A. *My War* (New York: Times/Random House, 1995).

Roosevelt, Eleanor *This I Remember* (New York: Harper, 1949).

Rosenstone, Robert A. *Romantic Revolutionary: A Biography of John Reed* (New York: Vintage, 1975).

Ross, Erika, ed. *Looking at Life Magazine* (Washington: Smithsonian Institution Press, 2001).

Rovere, Richard *Arrivals and Departures: A Journalist's Memoirs* (New York: Macmillan, 1976).

Royko, Mike *For the Love of Mike* (Chicago: University of Chicago Press, 2001).

Royster, Vermont *My Own, My Country's Time: A Journalist's Journey* (Chapel Hill: Algonquin, 1983).

Runyon, Damon *A Treasury of Damon Runyon* (New York: Modern Library, 1958).

Russell, Francis *The Shadow of Blooming Grove: Warren G. Harding and His Times* (New York: McGraw-Hill, 1968).

Safire, William *Safire's Washington* (New York: Times Books, 1980).

Salisbury, Harrison *Without Fear or Favor* (New York: Times Books, 1980).

Sanders, Marian K. *Dorothy Thompson: A Legend in Her Time* (Boston: Houghton Mifflin Co., 1973).

Schoenbrun, David *On and Off the Air: An Informal History of CBS News* (New York: E.P. Dutton, 1989).

Schorr, Daniel L. *Staying Tuned: A Life in Journalism* (New York: Pocket Books, 2001).

Schroth, Raymond A. *The American Journey of Eric Sevareid* (South Royalton, Vt.: Steerforth Press, 1995).

Schuyler, George S. *Black and Conservative: The Autobiography of George Schuyler* (New York: Arlington House, 1966).

Scripps, E. W. *Damned Old Crank: A Self-Portrait of E. W. Scripps* Charles R. McCabe, ed. (New York: Harper & Brothers, 1951).

Sedgwick, Ellery *The Happy Profession* (Boston: Little, Brown, 1946).

Seitz, Don C. *Artemus Ward: A Biography and Bibliography* (New York: Harper, 1919).

Seldes, George *Tell the Truth and Run* ((New York: Greenberg, 1953).

________, *Witness to a Century* (New York: Ballantine, 1987).

Seldes, Gilbert *The Seven Lively Arts* (New York: Harper and Bros., 1924).

Sevareid, Eric *Not So Wild a Dream* ((New York: Knopf, 1946).

Shivel, Gail *New Yorker Profiles: 1925-1992, A Bibliography* (Lanham: University Press of America, 2000),

Sinclair, Upton *American Outpost* (New York: Ferrar & Rinehart, 1936).

________, *The Brass Check* (New York: Boni, 1936).

Smith, Howard K. *Last Train from Berlin* (New York: Phoenix, 2000).

Smith, Merriman *Thank You, Mr. President: A White House Notebook* (New York: Harper and Bros, 1946).

Smith, Red [Walter] *To Absent Friends* (New York: Signet, 1986).

Smith, Richard Norton *The Colonel: The Life and Legend of Robert R. McCormick: 1880-1955* (Boston: Houghton Mifflin Co., 1997).

Sokolov, Raymond *Wayward Reporter* (New York: Harper & Row, 1988).

Squires, James D. *Read All About It! The Corporate Takeover of America's Newspapers* (New York: Times/Random House, 1993).

Steel, Ronald *Walter Lippmann and the American Century* (New York: Random House, 1980).

Steffens, Lincoln *The Autobiography of Lincoln Steffens* (New York: Harcourt, Brace, 1931).

Stevens, John D. *Sensationalism and the New York Press* (New York: Columbia University Press, 1991).

Stokes, Thomas Lunsford *Chip Off My Shoulder* (Princeton: Princeton University Press, 1940).

Stone, I.F. *The Haunted Fifties: 1953-1963* (Boston: Little, Brown, 1989).

Stone, Melville E. *Fifty Years a Journalist* (Garden City: Doubleday, Page and Co., 1921).

Sullivan, Mark *Our Times: 1900-1925*, 6 vols. (New York: Scribner's, 1936). [Reissued in one vol., Dan Rather, ed. (Scribner, 1996).]

_____, *The Education of an American* (New York: Doubleday, 1938).

Swanberg, W.A. *Citizen Hearst* (New York: Scribner's, 1964).

_______, *Luce and His Empire* (New York: Scribner's, 1972).

Swing, Raymond Gram *How War Came* (New York: W.W. Norton, 1939).

Swope, Herbert Bayard *Inside the German Empire* (New York: Press Publishing, 1917).

Talese, Guy *The Kingdom and the Power* (New York: Anchor Books, 1978).

Tarbell, Ida M. *All in the Day's Work* (New York: Macmillan, 1939).

Taylor, Bert Leston *The So-Called Human Race* (New York: Knopf, 1922).

Tebbell, John George *Horace Lorimer and the Saturday Evening Post* (New York: Doubleday, 1948).

Teichman, Howard *Smart Aleck: The Wit, World and Life of Alexander Woollcott* (New York: Morrow, 1976).

Thomas, Helen *Front Row at the White House: My Life and Times* (New York: Scribner, 2000).

Thompson, Dorothy *Let The Record Speak* Boston: Houghton Mifflin, 1939).

Thurber, James *The Thurber Carnival* (New York: Modern Library/Random House, 1957).

Tifft, Susan E. and Jones, Allen S. *The Patriarch: The Rise and Fall of the Bingham Dynasty* (New York: Summit, 1991).

Tobin, James *Ernie Pyle's War* (New York: The Free Press, 1997).

Wainwright, Loudon *The Great American Magazine: An Inside History of LIFE* (New York: Knopf, 1986).

Waldrop, Frank C. *McCormick of Chicago: An Unconventional Portrait of a Controversial Figure* (Englewood Cliffs: Prentice-Hall, 1966).

Walker, Stanley *City Editor* (New York: Frederick A. Sokes, 1934/Johns Hopkins University Press, 1998).

Wall, Joseph *Henry Watterson: Reconstructed Rebel* (New York: Oxford University Press, 1956).

Walsh, Justin E. *To Print the News and Raise Hell!: A Biography of Wilbur F. Storey* (Chapel Hill: University of North Carolina Press, 1968).

Watterson, Henry *"Marse Henry"–An Autobiography* (New York: Doran, 1919).

Weiner, Ed. *The Damon Runyon Story* (New York: Longman Green, 1948).

Wendt, Lloyd *Chicago Tribune: The Rise of a Great American Newspaper* (New York: Rand MacNally, 1979).

_____, *The Wall Street Journal* (New York: Rand MacNally, 1982).

White, Theodore H. *In Search of History: A Personal Adventure* (New York: Harper and Row, 1978).

White, William Allen *The Autobiography of William Allen White* (New York: Macmillan, 1946).

Wicker, Tom *On Press* (New York: Viking, 1978).

Wilds, John *Afternoon Story: The History of the New Orleans States-Item* (Baton Rouge: Louisiana State University Press, 1976).

Williams, Harold A. *The Baltimore Sun: 1837-1987* (Baltimore: Johns Hopkins University Press, 1987).

Wills, Gary *Lead Time: A Journalist's Education* (Garden City: Doubleday, 1983).

Wills, Kendall J., ed. *The Pulitzer Prizes* (New York: Simon & Schuster, 1988).

Winchell, Walter *Winchell Exclusive: "Things That Happened to Me–And Me to Them"* (Englewood Cliffs: Prentice-Hall, 1975).

Wodehouse, P.G. *Psmith Journalist* (New York: Penguin, 1970).

Woodward, Bob and Bernstein, Carl *All the President's Men* (New York: Simon and Schuster, 1976).

Woodward, Gary C. *Perspectives on American Political Media* (Boston: Allyn and Bacon, 1997).

Woollcott, Alexander *Shouts and Murmurs: Echoes of a Thousand and One First Nights* (New York: Century, 1922).

Yagoda, Ben *About Town: The New Yorker and the World It Made* (New York: Da Capo Press, 2000).

Yardley, Jonathan *Ring: A Biography of Ring Lardner* (New York: Random House, 1972).

Yoder, Edwin M. *Joe Alsop's Cold War: A Study in Journalism Influence and Intrigue* (Chapel Hill: University of North Carolina, 1995).

Young, Art *Art Young: His Life and Times* (New York: Sheridan House, 1939).

Zion, Sidney *Read All About It* (New York: Summit Books, 1982).

Zumwalt, Ken *The Stars and Stripes: World War II & the Early Years* (Austin: Eakin Press, 1989).

Index

"A Brighter Tomorrow" 36
ABC (American Broadcasting Co.) 8, 11, 23, 42, 70, 87
Abbott, Robert S. 1
Adams, Franklin P. (FPA) 1, 5, 45, 82
Adams, Samuel Hopkins 51
Ade, George 2, 52
Adventure Magazine 23
Acme Newsphotos 75
A.E.F. (American Expeditionary Force) 1, 6, 12, 32, 53, 71
A.G. Caplan (Al Capp) 96
Algonquin Round Table 2, 12-3, 93
All the Year Round 94
"All Things Considered" 87
Allen, Robert S. 2, 64
Alsop, Joseph and Stewart 2
Anderson, Jack 2
"America After Dark" 18
American Legion Monthly 43
American Scholar 7
American Labor Party 45
American Magazine 26, 43, 58, 75, 79, 84
American Mercury 2, 14, 39, 57, 74
American Spectator 59
Anthony Lenox (B. Bradlee) 10
AOL Time Warner 50
Argosy 57
Armed Forces Radio 77
Art Students' League 25, 93, 96-7
Arthur Loring Bruce (F. Crowninshield) 22
Ascoli, Max 90
Ashley Cooper (F. Gilbreth) 19
Astor Foundation 10
Associated Press 19, 24, 27, 41, 44, 48, 51, 59, 61, 67, 81, 96
Atlantic Monthly 75
Azrael, Louis 3

Baer, Arthur (Bugs) 3
"Bard of Broadway" 91
Baker, George 79
Baker, Newton D. 49
Baker, Ray Stannard 51
Baker, Russell 3
Baldwin, Hanson 4
Baum, L. Frank 4
BBC (British Broadcasting Corp.) 19, 82
Bell Syndicate 47
Bellows, James 27
Ben Lenox (B. Bradlee) 10
Benchley, Robert C. 5, 25, 48-9
Bender, Carole and Jack 100
Berger, Meyer 6
Berlin, Irving 5
Bernstein, Carl 92-3
Berryman, Clifford K. 6, 21
Berryman, James 6, 21
Bierce, Ambrose 6
Billboard 91
Block, Herbert L. 7, 25
Bohemian Magazine 58
Bok, Edward W. 8, 82
Bok Syndicate 8
Bookman 22
Bourke-White, Margaret 9
Bradlee, Ben 10, 32
Braley, Berton 11
Breslin, Jimmy 51
Bridgeman, George 97
Brinkley, David 11, 42

Brisbane, Arthur 11, 27, 93
Broder, David 12
Brookins, Gary 54
Brooklyn Magazine 8
Broun, Heywood 12, 20, 28, 35, 41, 45, 49, 56, 65, 82
Broun, Heywood Hale 13
Bulletin of Atomic Scientists 24
Burr McIntosh Monthly 58

Cahan, Abraham 13
Caen, Herb 13
Cain, James M. 14
Caldwell, Erskine 9
Calkins, Dick 95
Canby, Vincent 14
Caniff, Milton 95-6
Cannon, Jimmy 14
Capa, Robert 15
Capp, Al 96, 99
Capra, Frank 99
Carter, Pres. Jimmy (James E.) 77
Cassalt, Chris 54
Castro, Fidel 60
Cather, Willa 15, 51
Catholic University Review 51
Catledge, Turner 16, 67, 71
"CBS News" 67, 76, 90
CBS (Columbia Broadcasting System) 10, 13, 21, 23, 42, 46, 58-9, 67, 70, 76, 78, 81-3, 85, 87, 91
"CBS Reports" 58
Chancellor, John 16
Chandler, Harry 17
Chicago City News Bureau 72
Chicago Journal of Commerce 14
Chicago Tribune-New York Daily News Syndicate 96
Churchill, Winston 54
"Citizen Kane" 36
City Lights 44
Clapper, Raymond award 28
Cleveland, Pres. Grover 48
Clurman, Richard 17
CNN (Cable News Network) 12, 32
Cobb, Frank 18
Cobb, Irvin S. 18
Cohan, George M. 47
College Humor 65
Collier's Agency 100
Collier's Weekly (Collier's) 11, 18, 26, 33, 43, 47, 51, 68, 82, 90, 93-4
Columns
- A Conservative View (Kilpatrick) 46
- A Letter from Frank Sullivan (F. Sullivan) 82
- A Little About Everything (Taylor) 85
- A Line O' Type or Two (Taylor/ Little) 84-5
- About City Hall (Logan) 49
- Abroad (McCormick) 51
- Always in Good Humor (Adams) 1
- Assignment America (Robb) 69
- Baghdad-by-the-Bay (Caen) 13
- Bintel Brief (Cahan) 13
- Books and Other Things (Benchley) 5
- Books and Things (Broun) 12
- The Brighter Side (Runyon) 73
- Broadway Hearsay (Winchell) 91
- By the Way (Wodehouse) 92
- Capitol Stuff (Fleeson) 28
- The Conning Tower (Adams) 2

Covering the Courts
(Kilpatrick) 46
Day by Day (Azrael) 3
Doing the Charleston
(Cooper) 19
Dorothy Dix Talks (Dix) 24
Frank Sullivan's Private Mail
(F. Sullivan) 82
The Free Lance
(Mencken) 57, 85
Globe Sights (Howe) 41
The Great Game of Politics
(Kent) 46
In The Nation (Krock) 47
In the Wake of the News
(Lardner) 47
Inside Report
(Evans and Novak) 26
It Seems to Me (Broun) 12
The Lantern (Marquis) 56
Little Old New York
(E. Sullivan) 81
Matter of Fact (Alsop) 2
Monday Articles
(Mencken) 57
My Day (E. Roosevelt) 70
Notes and Comment
(E.B. White) 90
The Observer (Baker) 3
Of All Things (Benchley) 5
On the Line (Considine) 18
On the Record
(Thompson) 86
One Way of Putting It
(Cather) 15
One Word Led to Another
(Baer) 3
Our Times (M. Sullivan) 82
The Passing Show (Cather) 15
Personality Parade (Scott) 77
Saunterings (Mann) 55
Shafts and Darts (Schuyler) 74
Sharps and Flats (Field) 27
Shouts and Murmurs
(Woollcott) 93
The Sport Light (Rice) 68-9
Stage Whispers (Winchell) 91
Stories of the Streets and
of the Town (Ade) 2
The Sun Dial (Marquis) 11, 56
Sunday Salad (Dix) 24
Talk of the Town
(E.B. White) 90
Today (Brisbane) 11
Today and Tomorrow
(Lippmann) 49
Views and Reviews
(Schuyler) 73-4
Voice of Broadway
(Kilgallen/O'Brian) 61
Washington (Reston) 68
Washington Merry-Go-Round
(Pearson/Allen/
Anderson) 2, 3, 64
The Way of the World
(Taylor) 85
Wayward Press
(Fawkes/Liebling) 5
The Writer's Art
(Kilpatrick) 46
Your Broadway and Mine
(Winchell) 91
Cooke, Alistair 4, 19
Cooke, Janet 93
Coolidge, Pres. Calvin 20
Cooper, Jackie 96
Cooperative Commonwealth 38
Comic strips
The Affairs of Jane 107
Alley Oop 100

Alma and Oliver 103
Always Belittlin' 97
Amateur Etiquette 95
Beautiful Babs 107
Beetle Bailey 107
Betty Boop 106
Big Ben Bolt 98
Blondie 107-8
Bloom County 106
Bobby Make-Believe 103
Boner's Ark 107
Bringing Up Father 103
Buck Rogers in the 25th Century 95
Bull Tales 106
Buster Brown 104
The Captain and the Kids 97
Channel Chuckles 101
Charlie Chaplin's Comic Capers 106
Cheerful Charlie 103
The Clancy Kids 96
Colonel Potterby and the Duchess 107
Dennis the Menace 102
Dick Tracy 64, 96, 99
Dickie Dare 95
The Dingbat Family 101
Doc Archie and the Bean 101
Doonesbury 106-7
Dumb Dora 107
The Family Circus 101
The Family Foursome 107
The Five Fifteen (Sappo) 106
Flash Gordon 95, 104-5
Fearless Fosdick 96, 99
Fillum Fables 99
Gasoline Alley 64, 102
The Gay Thirties 95
Hans und Fritz 97
Hi and Lois 107
Hogan's Alley 104
In the Land of Wonderful Dreams 103
Joe Dope 98
Joe Palooka 96
Jungle Jim 104-5
The Katzenjammer Kids 97
Krazy Kat 101
Lady Luck 98
Let George Do It 103
Li'l Abner 96, 99
Little Folks 105
Little Nemo in Slumberland 103
Little Orphan Annie (Annie) 64
Looping the Loop 106
McFadden's Flats 104
Male Call 95
Max and Moritz 97
Merely Marge 100
Mr. Gilfather 96
Mr. Mystic 98
The Newlyweds 103
Nibsy the Newsboy in Funny Fairyland 103
Peanuts 105
Pogo 102
Poor Li'l Mose 104
Popeye 106
Prince Valiant 98
Professor Otto and His Auto 101
Radio Cats 99
Rip Kirby 104-5
The Rookie from the 13th Squad 97
Sad Sack 79
Sam and Silo 107

Secret Agent X-9 104-5
Shoe 54
Silly Philly 101
Skippy 96
Sky Roads 95
The Spirit 98
Steve Canyon 95-6
Snoozer 103
Tarzan 98
Terry and the Pirates 95-6
Their Only Child 103
Thimble Theatre 106
Tillie the Toiler 104
Tim Tyler's Luck 104
Toonerville Folks 98
Up Front (Willie and Joe) 106
The Yellow Kid 97, 104
Coming Nation 94
Commentary 17
Common Sense 72
Congressional Quarterly 12
Connally, Marc 45
Considine, Robert 18
Consolidated Press Assoc. 48
Cosmopolitan 6, 30, 92, 94
Cowles Syndicate 101
Cox Communication 20
Cox, James M. 20
Crabbe, Buster (Larry) 95
Creel, George 20
Crockett, Gib 21
Croly, Herbert 49
Cronkite, Walter 21, 67, 70, 76
Crosby, Percy 96
Crowninshield, Frank 22
Curtis, Cyrus H.K. 8
Curtis Publishing Co. 5
Custer, Gen. George A. 55

Daley, Arthur 22
Dana, Charles A. 88
Darling, J.N. (Ding) 22
Davis, Elmer 23, 82
Davis Rebecca Harding 23
Davis, Richard Harding 23
Day, Samuel H. 24
Debs, Eugene 93-4
Dempsey, Jack 29
Des Moines Register & Tribune Syndicate 98, 101
Dewey, Adm. George 52
Dewey, Thomas E. 44, 62, 102
Dickens, Charles 94
DiMaggio, Joe 3, 16
Dille, John Flint 95
Dille Syndicate 95
Dirks, John 97
Dirks, Rudolph 97
Disney, Walt 99, 102
Dorothy Dix (E. M. Gilmore) 24
Donovan, Carrie 25
Dr. Suess (T. Geisel) 99
Drake, Stan 108
DuBois, W.E.B. 25
Du Pont, Alfred I. award 29
Duffy, Edmund 7, 25, 63

E. W. Howe's Monthly 41
Eastman, Max 26, 94
Ebony 74
Economist 82
Editorial cartoonists 6,7, 21-2, 25, 28, 46, 52-3, 94, 99, 102-3, 106-7
"The Editors Speak" 74
"The Ed Sullivan Show" 81
"Edward R. Murrow and the News" 58
Edwards, Gus 91
Eisner, Will 97-8

Electric World 104
Eliot, T.S. 49
Emmy awards 11, 19, 70
Esquire 30
Evans, Rowland 26
"Evans and Novak" 26
Everybody's 60, 68, 79

Fanti, John 32
Ferber, Edna 45
Field, Eugene 27-8
Field, Marshall 16, 96
Fisher, Ham 96
Fitzgerald, F. Scott 100
Fitzpatrick, Daniel R. 28
Flair 19
Fleischer, Max 106
Fletcher, Frank 104
Fortune 9, 50
"48 Hours" 67
Fox, Fontaine Jr. 98
Fowler, Gene 29, 37
Franco, Francisco 75
Frankel, Max 16
Frank Leslie's Popular Monthly 75
Frederick, Pauline 29
Freeman, Douglas Southall 46
Friendly, Fred 59
Fritchey, Clayton W. 29, 30
"The Front Page" 29, 36
Fullerton, Hugh S. 30
Furlong, William B. 30

Gannett, Frank E. 31
Gannett Foundation 31-2
Gannett Newspapers 59
Garner, John Nance xi
Geisel, Theodore S. 99
George Foster Peabody awards 11, 19, 29, 42
Germond, Jack W. 31-2
Gilbreth, Frank Jr. 19
Gibbons, Floyd 32-3, 75
Gilmore, Elizabeth M. (Dorothy Dix) 24
Godfrey, Arthur 70
Gold, Mike 33, 60
Golden Argosy 57
Good Housekeeping 30
Good Morning 94
"Good Morning America" 8
Gould, Chester 96, 99
Governing 77
Graham, Katharine 19, 32
Graham, Philip L. 10, 32
Graham, Sheila 62
Graue, Dave 100
Gray, Harold 100
Greeley, Horace 88
Gunther, John 33
Guy Fawkes (R. Benchley) 5

Hadden, Briton 50
Hamlin, Vincent T. 100
Hammett, Dashiell 104-5
Hammond, Percy 34-5
Harper's Bazaar 25
Harper's Monthly 72
Harper's Weekly 24
Harding, Pres. Warren G. 20
Harris, Charles H. 35
Harris, Joel Chandler 35, 55
Hart, Moss 45, 93
Harvard Illustrated Review 49
Harvard *Crimson* 12
"Headline Hunter" 32
Hearst Headline Service 18
Hearst, Patricia 73

Hearst, William Randolph 36, 61-2, 65, 73, 75, 78, 91-2, 97-8, 101, 104
Heatter, Gabriel 36
Hecht, Ben 29, 36-38
Held, John Jr. 100-1
Hellinger, Mark 37, 39
Hemingway, Ernest 38-9
Hepburn, Katharine 86
Herbst, Josephine 39
Herblock (Herbert L. Block) 7, 25
Hermann, John 39
Herrimann, George 101
Hersey, John 39, 40, 86, 90
Herter, Christian 10
Hildebrant, the brothers 96
Higgins, Marguerite 40
Hitler, Adolf 78, 86, 99
Hodges, Eric 40
Holman, Richard 41
Home Monthly 15
Home Sector 71
Hoover, Pres. Herbert 23, 43
Hopper, Heda 61
Hovey, Walter 36
Howard, Roy W. 12, 41
Howe, E.W. 41
Hunter, Marjorie 42
Huntley, Chet 11, 42
"Huntley-Brinkley Report" 11, 42

Ickes, Harold L. 23, 63
In Fact 75
"Information, Please" 2
Ingersoll, Ralph 42
Ingersoll Publications 42
Inland Architect 60
"Inside Politics" 12
"Inside Washington" 31-2, 72
International News Service (INS) 2, 68-9, 73
Iger, Jerry 97
Irgun 86
Irwin, Will 43

James, Henry 49
James, Marquis 43
Jennings, Peter 69-70
Johnson, Earl 44
Johnson, Frank 104
Johnson, Pres. Lyndon B. 72
Johnston, Alva 44
Judge 65, 94, 97, 104

Kaltenborn, H. V. 44-5
Kaufman, George S. 37, 45, 93
Keane, Bil 101
Keane, Jeff 101
Keefe, Jim 105
Kelly, Walt 102
Kempton, Murray 45
Kennedy, Jacqueline 54, 90
Kennedy, Pres. John F. ix, 10, 26, 40, 54, 58, 67, 72, 90
Kent, Frank R. 46
Ketchum, Hank 102
Kilian, Mike 99
Kilpatrick, James J. 46
Kirby, Rollin 7, 46-7
King Features Syndicate 3, 5, 15, 18, 72-3, 97-8, 100, 103, 106-7
King, Frank O. 102-3
King, Martin Luther Jr. 74
Knerr, Harold H. 97
Krock, Arthur 14, 16, 47
Krupp, Alfried 3

Ladies' Home Journal 8, 82, 86
Lampoon (Harvard) 5

Lantz, Walter 102
Lardner, Ring 6, 38, 47
Lawrence, David 5, 48
Lebrun, Denis 108
Leopold, Nathan 73
Lewis, Sinclair 86
Liebling, A.J. 48
Leslie's Monthly 75, 94
Liberator 26, 32, 68, 94
Liberty 63
Lindsay, John 18
Life 5, 9, 15, 19, 39, 42, 44, 50, 90, 94, 97, 104
Lippmann, Walter 10, 14, 18, 47-9, 56, 79, 86
Literary Review 50
Locher, Dick 99
Loeb, Richard 73
Loeb, William 10
Logan, Andy (Isabel) 49-50
London, Bobby 106
Look 19, 38, 51, 54, 79
Louis, Joe 14
Luce, Henry R. 9, 39, 42, 50, 90
Luks, George B. 104
Lunn, George 49

Maas, Peter 51
MacArthur, Charles 37
MacArthur, Gen. Douglas 39
McCarthy, Joseph 23, 54
McCormick, Anne O'Hara 51-2
McCormick, Robert R. 52, 78
McCutcheon, John T. 2, 52
McClure, S.S. 43, 51, 79
McClure's Magazine 15, 43, 51, 60, 75, 79, 84
McClure's Syndicate 59
McCormick, Robert R. 36, 64
McFadden, Bernarr 53, 64
McGeehan, William O. 53
McGill, Ralph 53
McKay, Winsor 103
"McLaughlin Group" 31-2
McLean, Edward 65
McManus, George 103-4
MacNelly, Jeff 53-4
McWilliams, Carey 54
Magnum agency 15
Mahan, Adm. Alfred T. 4
Manchester, William 54
Mann, William d'Alton 55
"The Man Who Came to Dinner" 92
"The March of Time" 50
Mark Twain (S. Clemens) 4, 87-8
Marquis, Don 55-6, 101
Marshall, George 66
Marshall, Gen. George C. 30
Martin, Abe 56
Marx Brothers 65
"Masterpiece Theatre" 4, 19
Masses 20, 26, 32, 60, 68, 94
Masses and Mainstream 60
Maude Martin (E. Patterson) 63
"Meet the Press" 12, 31-2, 46
Metro-Goldwyn-Mayer 4
Metropolitan Magazine 68, 94
Mencken, H.L. ix, 3, 6, 11, 14, 23, 25, 34, 37, 41, 47, 54-5, 58-9, 65, 73, 85
Meyer, Eugene 32, 63
Mitchell, John 51
Moore, Gary 70
Moores, Dick 103
Motion Picture Herald 14
muckrakers 3, 51, 60, 64-5, 79, 82, 84
Mullin, Willard 21
Munsey, Frank A. 57-8

Munsey's Magazine 22, 57
Murphy, Cullen 98
Murphy, John Cullen 98
Murrow, Edward R. 58, 67, 76, 78
Museum of Cartoon Art 107
"Music Box Review" 5
Mussolini, Benito 51, 65, 79
Mutual Broadcasting Network 82

NAACP (National Association for the Advancement of Colored People) 25
NANA (North American Newspaper Alliance) 29, 33, 38, 43, 70, 74
NAS (North American Syndicate) 102
Nancy Randolph (I. Robb) 69
Nast, Conde 22
Nast, Thomas 89
Nathan, George Jean 11, 55, 58-9
Nation 12, 54, 72, 74, 80, 89, 94
National Cartoonist Society 96
National Institute of Arts and Letters 51
National Journal 32
National Press Club 42
National Review 26
NBC (National Broadcasting Co.) 11, 12, 16, 18-19, 29, 32-3, 42, 46, 48, 70, 82-3, 87
"NBC Nightly News" 16-7
"The Negro World" 74
Nelly Bly (Elizabeth C. Seaman) 7
New Deal 11, 31
New Masses 32, 38, 60, 72, 74
New Republic 39, 44-6, 49, 54, 90
New York 51
New York Review of Books 3, 80
New Yorker 67, 71-2, 81-2, 87, 89, 90, 93, 100-1
Newhouse, Samuel I. 71
Newman, M.W. 60
Newspaper Enterprise Association (NEA) 7, 75, 100, 107
Newspaper Guild, 12-3, 28, 32
Newspapers
- Atchinson (Kan.) *Daily Globe* 41
- Athens (Ga.) *Herald* 80
- Atlanta *Constitution* 35, 53, 80
- Atlanta *Georgian* 80
- Atlanta *Herald* 80
- Atlanta *Journal* 55
- Atlanta *News* 55
- *Auglaise* (Ohio) *Republican* 88
- Aurora (Ind.) *Bulletin* 23
- Baltimore *American* 14, 29
- Baltimore *Evening Herald* 56
- Baltimore *Evening Sun* 46, 54, 57
- Baltimore *News* 50
- Baltimore *News-Post* 3
- Baltimore *Post* 29
- Baltimore *Sun* 3, 4, 14, 16, 25, 32, 46, 52, 64, 88
- Baltimore *Sunpapers* 3, 46, 56
- *Beverly* (Mass.) *Evening Times* 10
- Bloomington (Ind.) *Pantograph* 12
- Boise (Ida.) *Evening Capitol* 69
- *Boston Common* 49
- Boston *Globe* 90
- Boston *Herald* 47
- Boston *Journal* 5
- Bradford (Penn.) *New Era* 4
- Bridgeport (Conn.) *Post* 102
- Brooklyn *Eagle* 11, 25, 45
- *Broun Nutmeg* 12
- Buenos Aires *Herald 19*, 33

Buffalo (N.Y.) *Courier-Express* 61
Buffalo (N.Y.) *Express* 48
Burlington (N.C.) *Times-News* 42
Chattanooga *Dispatch* 61
Chattanooga *Times* 61, 72
Chicago *American* 67, 106
Chicago *Daily News* 34, 37, 60, 63, 72, 81, 94, 99
Chicago *Daily Journal* 43
Chicago *Day Book* 75
Chicago *Defender* 1, 64, 74
Chicago *Evening Post* 34
Chicago *Examiner* 30, 47, 95
Chicago *Herald* 30, 62, 106
Chicago *Herald-Examiner* 37
Chicago *Inter-Ocean* 47, 81, 83, 94
Chicago *Journal* 37
Chicago *Morning News* 2, 52
Chicago *Post* 4, 25, 27, 98
Chicago *Record* 2, 30
Chicago *Republican* 81
Chicago *Sun* 16, 39
Chicago *Sun-Times* 17, 60
Chicago *Tribune* 2, 30, 32, 37, 43, 47, 52, 54, 57, 63-4 67, 72, 76, 78, 83, 87, 94, 103
Chicago *World* 32
Cincinnati *Cumberland* 103
Cincinnati *Enquirer* 20, 30, 103
Cincinnati *Post* 41
Cleveland *Evening Argus* 88
Cleveland *Herald* 88
Cleveland *Leader* 59
Cleveland *Plain Dealer* 16, 88
Cleveland *Press* 29, 75, 82
Columbus (Ga.) *Enquirer* 46
Columbus (Ohio) *Dispatch* 30, 96
Daily Worker 32, 60, 74
Dallas *Morning News* 89
Dayton (Ohio) *Evening News* 20
Dayton (Ohio) *Journal -Herald* 96-7
Denver *Post* 21, 29
Denver *Times* 94
Denver *Tribune* 27
Des Moines *Register and Tribune* 19, 22
Detroit *Evening News* 18
Detroit *Free Press* 18, 59, 95
El Dorado (Kan.) *Journal* 91
El Dorado (Kan.) *Republican* 91
Emporia (Kan.) *Gazette* 58, 91
Enid (Okla.) *Eagle* 43
Evanston (Ill.) *News-Index* 28
Florida Today 59
Georgia Countryman 35
Grand Rapids (S.D.) *Eagle* 18
Great Neck (L.I.) *News* 28
Christian Science Monitor 3
Hannibal (Mo.) *Journal* 88
Hartford (Conn.) *Post* 81
Honolulu *Commercial Appeal* 74
Houston *Chronicle* 16
Houston *Post* 21, 39
Houston *Press* 42
Idaho *International Observer* 24
Indianapolis *News* 41, 56
Indianapolis *Star* 23, 82
Ithaca ((N.Y.) *News* 31
International Herald Tribune 33
Jefferson City (La.) *Post-Tribune* 32
Jewish *Daily Forward* 13
Journal of Commerce 77
I.F. Stone Weekly 80
Kansas City *Independent* 21
Kansas City *Journal* 43-4

Kansas City *Post* 44, 91
Kansas City *Times* 27, 67
Kansas City *World* 21
Lafayette (Ind.) *Call* 2
Leavenworth (Kan.) *Times* 67
Lincoln (Neb.) *Courier* 15, 72
Lincoln (Neb.) *State-Observer* 15, 72
Lincoln-Belmont (Ill.) *Booster* 72
London *Daily Herald* 19
London *Globe* 92
London *News Chronicle* 82
London *Times* 19
Los Angeles *Herald* 73, 101
Los Angeles Times 17, 52, 62
Louisville (Kan.) *Herald* 98
Louisville (Ky.) *Evening Courier* 89
Louisville (Ky.) *Times* 98
Macon (Ga.) *Monroe Advertiser* 35
Macon (Ga.) *News* 80
Macon (Ga.) *Telegraph* 35
Manchester Guardian 19, 49, 90
Manchester (N.H.) *Union* 85
Manchester (N.H.) *Union-Leader* 74
Marion (Ohio) *Star* 20
Memphis *Commercial Appeal* 16
Memphis *Press* 16
Merrill (Wis.) *Advocate* 45
The Messenger 74
Miami (Fla.) *Herald* 59
Miami Beach *Sun* 36
Middleton (Ohio) *Weekly Signal* 20
Milwaukee (Wis.) *Sentinel* 78
Minneapolis (Minn.) *Daily News* 32
Minneapolis *Journal* 76
Minneapolis *Tribune* 32, 72
Minneapolis *Times* 102
Mobile (Ala.) *Register* 55
Monroe (Mich.) *Evening News* 32
Monterey (Cal.) *Beacon* 80
Montpelier (Vt.) *Argus and Patriot* 85
Nashville *Banner* 53
Nashoba (Miss.) *Democrat* 16
New Orleans *Crescent Monthly* 35
New Orleans *Picayune* 24
New Hampshire *Sunday Times* 10, 103
New York *Call* 32, 96
New York *Compass* 80
New York *City Advertiser* 79
New York *Daily News* 28, 30, 38, 63-4, 69, 99-100, 102
New York *Commercial Advertiser* 13
New York *Evening Graphic* 53, 81, 91
New York *Evening Mail* 2, 56, 81
New York *Evening Post* 2, 12, 13, 14, 48, 74, 82
New York *Evening Sun* 11, 23
New York *Globe* 96
New York *Herald* 58, 81-2, 85, 88-9, 103
New York *Herald Tribune* 2-4, 11, 27, 32, 34, 40, 43-4, 49, 51, 55, 71, 76, 78-9, 86, 89
New York *Journal* 7, 11, 23-4, 27, 36, 38, 94, 97, 101, 103
New York *Journal-American* 14, 18, 55, 61, 65

New York *Leader* 25
New York *Mail* 30, 45- 6, 57, 68
New York *Morning Herald* 6, 16, 22
New York *Morning Telegraph* 1, 25, 81, 83, 85
New York (L.I.) *Newsday* 17, 25, 30, 40, 45, 63
New York *New Era* 13
New York *PM* 9, 13-4, 37-8, 42, 54, 80, 82, 99
New York *Post* 45, 47, 67, 79, 80, 86, 89
New York (Saratoga) *Saratogian* 81
New York *Star* 13, 80, 102
New York *Sun* 11-2, 41, 43, 46, 55, 65, 88, 93
New York *Telegram* 12, 41, 62, 66
New York Times 3-4, 6-7, 14, 16, 22-3, 25, 30, 32, 38, 42, 44-5, 47-8, 51-2, 61-2, 68, 70-1, 77-8, 83, 88, 92-3, 95
New York *Tribune* 2, 5, 12, 22, 25, 43, 45, 53, 69, 81, 82-3, 88
New York *World* 1, 4, 5, 7, 11-2, 14, 18, 27, 36, 38, 41, 46-9, 65-8, 76, 81, 83, 93, 96-7, 101, 103-4
New York *World-Journal-Tribune* 18, 61, 78
New York *World-Telegram* 12, 14, 45-8, 65, 68, 80
New York *World-Telegram-Sun* 41
Newark (N.J.) *Evening News* 31
Northern Virginia Sun 30
Omaha (Neb.) *Bee* 67
Orville (Ohio) *Courier* 82
Philadelphia *Bulletin* 27, 101
Philadelphia *Enquirer* 78
Philadelphia *Ledger* 82
Philadelphia *North American* 59
Philadelphia *Press* 89
Philadelphia *Public Ledger* 3, 23, 74, 89
Philadelphia *Record* 23, 80
Pittsburgh (Kan.) *Sun* 28
Pittsburgh *Courier* 35, 73-4
Pittsburgh *Leader* 15, 76
Pittsburgh *Post* 7
Pittsburgh *Post-Gazette* 77, 100
Pittsburgh *Press* 75
Pueblo (Colo.) *Advertiser* 73
Raleigh (N.C.) *News and Observer* 42
Richmond (Va.) *News-Leader* 46, 54
Rochester (N.Y.) *Advertiser* 31
Rochester (N.Y.) *Times-Union* 31
Rocky Mountain News 21, 73
Sacramento (Cal.) *Bee* 13
Salt Lake City *Deseret News* 3
Salt Lake City *Tribune* 71, 100
San Francisco *Alta California* 88
San Francisco *Argonaut* 6
San Francisco *Bulletin* 62
San Francisco *Call* 53, 88
San Francisco *Call-Bulletin* 62
San Francisco *Chronicle* 13, 43, 60
San Francisco *Examiner* 6, 13, 73
San Francisco *News* 32, 75, 80
San Francisco *News Leader* 6
San Francisco *Post* 53, 73
San Francisco *Union* 88

San Francisco *Wasp* 6
San Francisco *Wave* 43, 60
St. Joseph (Mo.) *Gazette* 27
St. Louis *Evening Journal* 27
St. Louis *Post-Dispatch* 28, 41, 66
St. Louis *Republic* 103
St. Louis *Star* 78
St. Louis *Times-Journal* 27
St. Paul (Minn.) *Pioneer Press* 67, 105
St. Petersburg (Fla.) *Times* 77
Sacramento (Calif.) *Bee* 44, 88
Savannah (Ga.) *Morning News* 35
Seattle *Times* 89
Sioux City (Iowa) *Journal* 22
SoDak Sports (S.D.) 59
Southtown (Ill.) *Economist* 30
The Sporting News 47
Stars and Stripes 2-3, 14, 21, 70-1, 93, 100-1
Toronto *Star* 38
Trenton (N.J.) *Times* 61
USA Today 59
United States Daily News 29, 48, 64
Virginia City (Nev.) *Territorial Enterprise* 4, 88
Wall Street Journal 82, 95
Wall Street Transcript 41
Washington *Daily News* 67
Washington *Evening Star* 6, 10, 12, 21, 24, 28-9, 32, 40, 77
Washington *Herald* 18, 63
Washington *Mail* 81
Washington Post 2, 6-7, 10, 12, 25, 30, 32, 49, 61, 63, 65-6, 74, 92
Washington *Times* 45
Washington *Times-Herald* 63-4
Wilmington (N.C.) *Star-News* 11
Winfield (Kan.) *Courier* 44
Winston-Salem *Journal* 42
Wooster (Mass.) *Gazette* 75
Yank 77, 101
Newsweek 10, 30, 32, 49
Nixon, Pres. Richard M. 21, 92
Norris, Frank 43, 60
North American Review 70
North, Robert 60
Novak, Robert 26, 27
Nowlan, Phil 95

Office of War Information (OWI) 19, 23, 34, 39
O. Henry (W.S. Porter) 38, 88
Older, Fremont 62
"Omnibus" 19
"Outlook" 42
"Our Government" 48
Outcault, R.F. 104, 106
Overseas News Agency 90
Overseas Press Club 21
Owen Hatteras (Mencken/Nathan) 59

Paley, William 58
Palmer, Kyle D.
Parade 3
Paramount Pictures 5
Parsons, Louella 62
Partisan Review 44
Patterson, Alicia 63
Patterson, Eleanor 63
Patterson, Joseph Medill 63-4, 99, 102
Patton, Gen. George S. 2, 59
"Pauline Frederick Reports" 29

Payne, Ethel 64
PBS (Public Broadcast Service) 12
Pearson, Drew 3, 62-4
Pegler, Westbrook 9, 41
Pentagon Papers 92
People 50
People's World 32
Perelman, S.J. 65
Pershing, John J. 32, 52
Peterson, Gordon 69
Phillips, David Graham 65
Physical Culture 53
Plain Talk 74
Playboy 37
Porter, William S. (O. Henry) 39
Povich, Shirley 65-6
"Profiles," *New Yorker* 6, 44, 48, 67
Progressive 24
Puck 85, 94
Pulitzer, Joseph 7, 11-3, 18, 22, 25, 28, 36, 61, 66, 75, 83, 88, 104
Pulitzer prize 3, 4, 6, 7, 8, 12-3, 15, 22, 25, 28, 32-3, 38, 40, 43-4, 46-8, 51-3, 63, 65, 67-8, 71-2, 78, 80, 83, 89, 90-2, 99, 106-7
- recipients:
- Anderson 3
- Baker (two) 3
- Baldwin 4
- Berryman, C. 6
- Berryman, J. 6
- Bigart (two) 7
- Bok 8
- Breathed 106
- Broder 12
- Caen 13
- Cather 15
- Daley 22
- Darling (two) 22-3
- Duffy (three) 25
- Fitzpatrick (two) 28
- Geisel 99
- Graham 33
- Hemingway 38
- Herblock (three) 7
- Hersey 40
- Higgins 40
- James (two) 43
- Johnston 44
- Kaufman (two) 45
- Kempton 45
- Kirby (three) 46
- Krock (two) 47
- Lippmann (two) 48
- McCormick, A. 51
- McCutcheon 52
- McGill 53
- MacNelly (three) 53
- Mauldin (two)106-7
- Pegler 65
- Pyle 67
- Reston (two) 68
- Rosenthal 71
- Royko 72
- Smith 78
- Steinbeck 80
- Stokes 80
- Swope 83
- Trudeau 106-7
- Watterson 89
- White, T. 90
- White, W.A. (two) 91

Parade 77
"The Price of Peace" 67
Punch 92
Puritan 57
Putnam, George 22
Pyle, Ernie 66, 67

Quality Comics 97
Quick 19

"Radio of the Air" 58
Ramsaye, Terry 67
Rand, Ayn 11
Rather, Dan 67
Raymond, Alex 104-5
Raymond, Jim 108
Reader's Digest 26, 34, 40, 79
Reagan, Nancy 70
Reasoner, Harry 70
Red Cross Magazine 84
Redbook 40
Reed, John 68, 79, 94
Reid, Helen 40
Reporter 90
Research Institute of America 77
Reston, James 3, 32, 68
Reuther, Walter 5
Reynolds, Frank 70
Reynolds, Quentin 65, 68
Rice, Grantland 68
Rickard, Tex (George C.) 53
Riis, Jacob 69
Robb, Inez 69
Robeson, Paul 74
Robinson, Boardman 25, 94
Robinson, Max 69, 70
Rockefeller, Nelson 32
Rogers, Will 2
Rooney, Andy 70
Roosevelt, Eleanor 42, 70
Roosevelt, Pres. Franklin D. (FDR) 20, 22-3, 28, 31, 52, 63, 70, 80, 86-9, 90, 92, 97
Roosevelt, Pres. Theodore 3, 6, 35, 52, 69, 79, 91
Rosenthal, A.M. 70-1
Ross, Harold W. 2, 48, 71, 90
Rovere, Richard 72
Rowan, Carl 72
"Royko at Large" 72
Royko, Mike 72
Runyon, Damon 68, 73

Sagendorf, Bud 106
St. Johns, Adele Rogers, 73
Sandburg, Carl 75
Santayana, George 49
Saturday Evening Post 15, 18, 26, 30, 43, 47, 51, 79, 92, 94, 105
Scancarelli, Jim 103
Schulz, Charles M. 105
Schuyler, George S. 73-5
Scribner's Magazine 39
Scripps, E.W. 41, 75
Scripps-Howard Newspaper Alliance 41, 64, 67, 69, 74, 80
Scripps-McRae League 41
Sedgwick, Ellery 74
"See It Now" 58
Seegar, E.C. 106
Seldes, George 75
Serpico, Frank 51
Sevareid, Eric 67, 76-7
Shanahan, Eileen 77
Shawn, William 71
Shearer, Lloyd 77
Sherwood, Robert 22
Shirer, William L. 78
Sight and Sound 44
Sims, Tom 106
"60 Minutes" 46, 67
Sloan, John 25
Smart Set 11, 14, 34, 37, 39, 55, 57-8, 92
Smith, Red (Walter) 78-9
Spectator 72
Sports Illustrated 35, 50

Stalin, Josef 79
Standard News Association 6
Starr, Leonard 100
Steffens, Lincoln 51
Steinbeck, John 80, 96
Stewart, William 88
Stokes, Thomas 80
Stone, I.F. 80
Stone, Melville E. 81
Stratemeyer Syndicate 31
Strunk, William 46, 90
Sullivan, Ed 81
Sullivan, Frank 81-2
Sullivan, Mark 26
Sulzberger, Arthur Hays 16
Sulzberger, Punch (Arthur Ochs) 16, 68
Sunday, Billy 76
Swing, Raymond Gram 82-3
Swope, Herbert Bayard 2, 49, 81, 83
Szulc, Ted 83, 84

Tales from Town Topics 55
Tarbell, Ida 51, 84, 92
Tarkington, Booth 23
Taylor, Bert Leston (BLT) 84-5
Technical Review 40
Teddy Bear 6
Terkel, Studs 8
Thayer, John Adam 55
"This Week with David Brinkley" 11
Thomas, Lowell 85
Thompson, Dorothy 86-7
Thompson, Hunter 51, 87
Thurber, James 71, 78
Time 17, 40, 42, 50, 90
Time Inc. 40, 42, 50
Time-Life News Service 17
Time-Warner 50
Timeless Topics 105
"Toast of the Town" 81
"Today" 16, 32
Tom Watson's Journal 55
Topaz 74
"The Town Crier" 92
Town Topics 55
Transatlantic Tales 55
T.R.B. (F. Kent) 46
Tribune Media Services 54, 96, 99, 100
Trotsky, Leon 26
Trout, Robert 87
Trudeau, Garry 106-7
Truman, Pres. Harry S 6, 21, 28, 30, 45, 62, 64, 102
Truth 104

Uncle Remus' Magazine 35, 55
United Features Syndicate 3, 69, 75, 80, 105
United Mine Workers 21
United Nations 9, 30, 72, 83
United Press 2, 41, 43-4, 64, 75-7, 80, 90
United Press International 2, 44, 83
United States Information Agency (USIA) 58, 72
Universal News Service 78
Universal Press Syndicate 8, 79, 107
U.S. News & World Report 29, 48
Uslan, Michael 96

Vallachi, Joe 51
Van Anda, Carr V. 52, 61, 88
Van Horn, Abigail 27
Vanity Fair 5, 22, 49, 92, 100
Venture 19
Victor Appleton (H. Garis) 31

Villa, Pancho 6
Villard, Oswald 89
Vitaphone 92
Vlag, Piet 94
Vogue 25
Voice of America 17, 83
Volante 59
Vreeland, Diana 25

Walker, Mort 107
Walker, Stanley 89
Walter Scott (L. Shearer) 77
Warner Communications 50
Warren, Earl 62
Washington Monthly 72
"Washington Week in Review" 12
Watterson, Henry 89
"We, the People" 36
The Weekly 71
Weekly Review 70
Welles, Orson 36
Wesleyan University Press 54
Westover, Russ 104
Wheeler 51
Wheeler Syndicate 98
White, E.B. 46, 50, 71, 87, 89, 90
White, Theodore 90
White, William Allen 58, 91
"Who Said That?" 87
Winchell, Walter 53, 61, 63, 81, 91-2
Witcover, Jules 32
Wilkie, Wendell 16
Wilson, Pres. Woodrow 20, 48-9, 89
Wodehouse, P.G. 92
Wolfe, Tom 51
Woman's Home Companion 28
Women's Democratic Review 70
Woodward, Bob 92-3
Woollcott, Alexander 35, 45, 93
World Report 48
Wow 97
Wright, Wilbur and Orville 20
Wunder, George 96

Yager, Rick 95
Young, Art 93-4
Young, Chic 107-8
Young, Dean 108
Young, Lyman 104
Youth's Companion 40, 75

Zabody, Bela 106
Ziegfeld, Florenz 22
"Ziegfeld Follies" 47
Zit's Weekly 37